THE REPUBLIC

The Republic

P L A T O

Translated and with an Introduction by R. E. Allen

Yale University Press   New Haven and London

Designed by Sonia L. Shannon
Set in Adobe Garamond type by
The Composing Room of Michigan, Inc.
Printed in the United States of America.

The Library of Congress has cataloged the hardcover
edition as follows:
Plato.
[Republic. English]
The republic / Plato ; translated by R. E. Allen.
p.   cm.
Includes bibliographical references and index.
ISBN-13: 978-0-300-11451-5 (cloth : alk. paper)
ISBN-10: 0-300-11451-6 (cloth : alk. paper)
1. Political science—Early works to 1800.   2. Political
ethics—Early works to 1800.   I. Allen, Reginald E.,
1931–   . II. Title.
JC71.P3513   2006
321′.07—dc22
2006000550

ISBN 978-0-300-13637-1 (pbk. : alk. paper)

A catalogue record for this book is available
from the British Library.

The paper in this book meets the guidelines for
permanence and durability of the Committee on
Production Guidelines for Book Longevity of the
Council on Library Resources.

10 9 8 7 6 5 4 3

Contents

Preface

Plato of Athens was born in 428 B.C. and died at eighty in 348 B.C., while writing the *Laws*. The *Republic* ranks with the *Symposium* and *Phaedo* as a primary work of his middle period, perhaps first published in the late 370s, after his foundation of the Academy, the first university in Europe.

This version of the *Republic* is published with limited notes. A chart representing the Divided Line follows Book VI. A more fully annotated edition will follow.

The Greek text I have used is the 1903 edition by John Burnet; I have on occasion departed from it, often silently. The translation owes much to James Adam, *The Republic of Plato* (Cambridge, 1902; 2nd ed., ed. D. A. Rees, Cambridge, 1965). Paul Shorey, *Plato: The Republic* (Cambridge, Mass., 1935), has been a valuable guide in construing the Greek. So, too, G. M. A. Grube, *Plato's Republic* (Indianapolis, 1974). My greatest debt is to F. M. Cornford, *The Republic of Plato* (Oxford, 1941). Despite omissions and truncated dialogue, this is of great excellence as a translation, especially in its style and nuanced choice of words, and though very free, often true to Plato's sense where others are not. To the best of my knowledge, there is not now in English a translation which matches Cornford in style and accuracy of understanding; it is the standard against which a new translation may be judged.

I have preserved the division of the *Republic* into books, as it has come down to us, along with numbers and letters established in the 1578 Stephanus edition; Cornford departs from this with chapter headings of his own, but this is useful in locating passages and helps preserve a valuable sense of distance. I have also tried to preserve something of distance in manner and style of speech. This conversation did not take place between the folks next door.

In the rendering of moral and political terms, I have in general followed the settled habits of centuries: *arete* is virtue or excellence, not "morality"; *sophrosune* is temperance, and more than "self-control"; *psyche,* soul, includes but is broader than "mind." The one notable departure is in the translation of *politeia:* not "republic," *res publica,* but "constitution."

Quotations from Homer are taken from the translation of Richmond Lattimore. I must thank David Ambuel, Alan Bowen, Edward Halper, Richard Halverson, Deborah Nails, and David White. In a book of this length there must still remain errors, and I solicit the criticisms of readers, whose comments may best be addressed to me through the publisher.

This translation is dedicated to the memory of Walter Pattison, philosopher, philologist, and naturalist, in whose North Woods cabin, near the St. Croix, the Namakogan, the Totagatic, and the Brule, it was begun; and who taught how the love of wisdom may comport with the pursuit of brook trout and smallmouth bass and the dancing of sandhill cranes.

Introduction

And first, of Thrasymachus.

He is crude and boisterous, and rude even when he means to be polite. Socrates shuts his mouth in argument, and perhaps begins to convert him (V 450a–b). But if a philosopher can be identified by the acuteness of his questions, as distinct from the coherence of his answers, Thrasymachus is a quite considerable philosopher. He has two accounts of justice and injustice in Book I of Plato's *Republic,* and they raise two main questions: whether faction, *stasis,* does not enter into the very definition of government; and whether justice is a good for the just man. If these questions are important to the political theory and moral philosophy of the *Republic,* they remain important still. The most important American exponent of legal positivism, Justice Oliver Wendell Holmes, was beyond question a Thrasymachean, and his legacy endures.[1] Holmes had read the *Republic* and took from it, as so often happens, a message other than Plato intended.

---

1. See further, Albert W. Alschuler, *Law Without Values: The Life, Work, and Legacy of Justice Holmes* (Chicago, 2000), chs. 1 and 2.

The Political Problem

The *Republic* is many things: metaphysics and epistemology, social theory and moral psychology and ethics, educational theory and aesthetics, poetry and eschatology, soaring prose and intellectual drama and brilliant imagery and tight argument. But the threshold question is political. *Politeia,* the word which we translate "republic," is consistently used to mean "constitution," and we may legitimately read the *Republic* as an essay in constitutional law. The point is driven home by prosopography. Plato's original readers would have known that it was no accident, in a dialogue on justice and the constitution, that Plato should have chosen the family of Cephalus by way of introduction, for after Cephalus's death, that family was smashed and shattered by the Thirty Tyrants, the savage oligarchy which came to power in Athens at the end of the Peloponnesian War. We know something of the fate of Cephalus's sons, present at the conversation. Lysias was arrested but escaped; Polemarchus was executed, or murdered, by hemlock; the fate of Euthydemus is unknown. Their friend Niceratus son of Nicias was also executed, as Socrates himself would have been had the Thirty not fallen. Socrates, whom Plato elsewhere described as the best and most just and righteous man of his time, lived to be executed by the restored democracy on a charge of impiety. In a time of troubles, these were fated men.

They were victims of faction, which the *Republic* diagnoses as political injustice and the chief disease of a constitution. The argument of the *Republic* proceeds on the realistic assumption that government is not always benign, and politics can get you killed.

Justice as the Interest of the Stronger

Thrasymachus makes faction an element in the very definition of government: justice is the interest of the stronger. Law defines what is just and unjust for those subject to it; it issues from the party in power, which is the stronger, and which governs in its own interest. Law is essentially commands backed by punishment, or in H. L. A. Hart's excellent phrase, "orders backed by threats." Tyrannies make tyrannical laws, democracies democratic laws, aristocracies aristocratic laws; each makes laws in its own interest and punishes those who transgress as wrongdoers. So justice, because it is defined by law, is the interest or advantage of the stronger. Thrasymachus's account of justice is a variant of legal positivism: he assumes that law may have any content, as commands may have any content. But Thrasymachus also assumes that law is purposive, in that it aims at the interest of the stronger. This is the chink in his position.

The *Laws* (714c–715a) suggests that the interest of the stronger may indeed be the primary purpose of law in given cities—when they are ruled by a faction. But even if Thrasymachus were descriptively right, and every actual government is in the interest of a faction, it would not follow that it must be so as a matter of definition.[2] Borrowing from the *Euthyphro*, Thrasymachus's definition does not state essence but accident; it is at best an extensional equivalence. His definition suggests a universality and necessity which in no way follow from his premises.

The Argument from Mistake

Socrates in his reply to Thrasymachus puts an argument from mistake, a variant of which he had already used with Polemarchus in determining who is friend and enemy: the stronger, in laying down laws, can misapprehend their own advantage. The content of law then becomes inconsistent with the purpose of law, and if it is just to obey the law, justice will sometimes consist in doing what is not in the interest of the stronger. Thrasymachus's proposed definition fails. To save it, he suggests that the ruler *as* ruler must possess the art of ruling, which, as art, is infallible.

Socrates replies that every art aims not at the advantage of the artist but at the advantage of that to which it is ordered or directed. Medicine, for example, aims at the cure of sick people, not wages for the doctor. So Thrasymachus's definition of justice as the interest of the stronger fails again: reasoning from his own analogy, an art of ruling would be directed to the interest not of the ruler but of the ruled. His attempted definition has been stood on its head.

2. Compare Hans Kelsen, *General Theory of Law and State,* trans. Anders Wedberg (Cambridge, Mass., 1945).

To this Socrates opposes, in his own account of an art of ruling, the claim that government exists for the benefit of the governed. In Book IV this will enter into the definition of political wisdom: the state will be wise if, and only if, it is governed by a part of itself which is wise, and which looks to the good of the whole. The contrast with government by faction could hardly be more starkly drawn. But the attainment of wise government presents a political and therefore a constitutional problem, an account of concrete circumstances in the distribution of power which could make such government possible.

The *Republic's* solution is well known. There needs to be a governing class, the Guardians, who will identify their own good with the good of the city. Whereas for Thrasymachus the governing class seeks its own good at the expense of other classes, for Socrates the governing class in seeking its own good seeks the common good. To this end members of that class give up all private property, holding even women and children in common, directing their loyalty solely to the common good. This is at the heart of Plato's state, the foundation of his constitution. Faction, political injustice, is contrasted to political justice, which involves political unity defined in extreme terms. The various classes in the state, and in particular the political class, are united by familial bonds, the extreme of civil friendship, organically bound to each other as the finger is bound to the body. The just state depends for its existence on proper education, on the cultivation not only of appropriate habits but of wisdom, and ultimately knowledge of the Good; neither cities nor individuals will attain to a surcease of evils unless they come to be governed by a philosopher-king. Here then are constitutional devices which will produce and sustain unity and remove the causes of faction.

Federalist 10

The statement of the political problem in terms of faction, if not its Platonic solution, had a direct influence on the development of American constitutional law. Between October 1787 and April 1788 a series of articles by "Publius" appeared in New York newspapers, urging ratification of the

Constitution. Publius was Alexander Hamilton, John Jay, and James Madison, and their work was afterward published as *The Federalist*.

Madison's first contribution to the series was *Federalist* 10, in which he defends the Union because of its tendency to break and control the violence of faction: "By a faction, I understand a number of citizens, whether amounting to a majority or minority of the whole, who are united and actuated by some common impulse of passion, or of interest, adverse to the rights of other citizens, or to the permanent and aggregate interests of the community." This matches with precision the *Republic*'s concept of *stasis*.

There are two methods of controlling the mischiefs of faction: by removing its causes or by controlling its effects. Its causes can be removed either by destroying liberty, or "by giving to every citizen the same opinions, the same passions, and the same interests." The first remedy is worse than the disease; the second, which Plato recommends in the *Republic* at least for the rulers, is impracticable and unwise:

> As long as the reason of man continues fallible, and he is at liberty to exercise it, different opinions will be formed. As long as the connection subsists between his reason and his self-love, his opinions and his passions will have a reciprocal influence on each other: and the former will be objects to which the latter will attach themselves. The diversity in the faculties of men, from which the rights of property originate, is not less an insuperable obstacle to a uniformity of interests. The protection of these faculties is the first object of government. From the protection of different and unequal faculties of acquiring property, the possession of different degrees and kinds of property immediately results; and from the influence of these on the sentiments and views of the respective proprietors ensues a division of the society into different interests and parties. The latent causes of faction are thus sown in the nature of man.

This accepts the Platonic analysis and rejects the Platonic solution, the destruction of property interests for the governing class. As Madison remarks in *Federalist* 49, "A reverence for the laws would be sufficiently inculcated by the voice of an enlightened reason. But a nation of philosophers is as little to be expected as the philosophical race of kings wished for by Plato." Madison deals with human nature in politics not as it might be, but as it is:

> The most common and durable source of factions has been the various and unequal distribution of property. Those who hold and those who are without property have ever formed distinct interests in society. Those who are creditors, and those who are debtors, fall under a like discrimination. A landed interest, a manufacturing interest, a mercantile interest, a moneyed interest, with many lesser interests, grow up of necessity in civilized nations, and divide themselves into different classes, actuated by different sentiments and views. The regulation of these various and interfering interests forms the principal task of modern legislation, and involves the spirit of party and faction in the necessary and ordinary operations of government.

If the causes of faction cannot be removed, how then control its effects? Direct democracy can admit of no cure for the mischiefs of faction: it is shaken by every passion, and ends in tyranny. "A republic, by which I mean a government in which the scheme of representation takes place, opens a different prospect, and promises the cure for which we are seeking." In order to diminish and control faction, it is necessary to adopt representative government and enlarge the pool of conflicting interests; political friendship is fostered by the fact that your opponent today may be your ally tomorrow: "In the extent and proper structure of the Union, therefore, we behold a republican remedy for the diseases most incident to republican government." Madison accepts the Platonic analysis of the political problem but does not undertake to remove its causes. Rather, he undertakes to mitigate its effects by constitutional devices meant to contain the excesses of Thrasymachean man and the Thrasymachean state, and to sustain political friendship not by pursuit of a common good but by exchange and self-interest, resting on a firm acceptance of the institution of private property. Political friendship does not rest on virtue or respect for good character; it is a business relation founded on exchange.

In its emphasis on political unity, the *Republic* at times seems extreme, so extreme that it may well seem, on occasion, a variety of well-reasoned myth. But the problem with which it seeks to deal is both simple and fundamental: how to direct the powers of government, legislative, executive, judicial, to the good of all citizens, and prevent those powers from being twisted to the support of a faction. Scholars have long shown a mildly salacious interest in the marriage regulations of Book V; it would be helpful to reconsider them as addressing the main constitutional problem addressed by Madison's exposition of Federalism—namely, unity and faction.

Thrasymachus Changes Ground

Thrasymachus has begun by arguing that justice is the advantage of the stronger. His attempt to defend that thesis by invoking an art of rule to prevent the stronger from mistaking his own advantage has failed. He now argues in effect that political power is institutionalized injustice on a grand scale, and that it is better to do injustice than to suffer it. This is a reversal of his previous definition: it is now injustice, not justice, which is claimed to be the interest of the stronger.

In the *Gorgias* (466d–468e), when Polus praised the tyrant for his unlimited power, Socrates replied that the tyrant does what seems best to him, but since he mistakes his own interest, he does not do what he wishes and is therefore least of all men free. He acts in ignorance, unwillingly rather than willingly, even though he does what he desires (cf. 339e, and *Laws* IX 860d–e). Here, in the difference between real good and apparent good, is the root of the distinction between desire and rational wish, *boulesis,* between what we want and what we really need. Thrasymachus avoided this objection by claiming that there is an art of ruling which is, as such, infallible in calcu-

lating the interest of the ruler. His defense of that claim has collapsed, but
in his defeat, Thrasymachus states the main issue of the *Republic,* whether
justice is a good for the just man. The issue, restated by Glaucon in Book II,
is pursued through Book IV to the end of Book IX. Book I was not written
as an independent dialogue to which the rest of the *Republic* was adventitiously tacked. It was intended from the outset to introduce the *Republic* as
a whole.[3]

The Greek word *arete,* virtue, is an abstract noun corresponding to the
adjective *agathos,* good, as *kakia,* vice, corresponds to the adjective *kakos,*
evil or bad. Thrasymachus, having claimed that injustice is superior to justice and therefore better than justice, now holds that injustice is a virtue, a
human excellence, and justice a kind of noble simplemindedness or stupid-
ity, *gennaion euetheian.* The foundation of his argument is that injustice is a
source of strength, justice of weakness.

That foundation will hardly be moved by claiming that Thrasymachus
has mistaken the grammar of his own language, that it is somehow contradictory or meaningless to deny that justice is a virtue or human excellence.
It is not contradictory, though it is uncomfortable, to claim that justice is
not a virtue, and if Thrasymachus is right, we ought to change our grammar
on grounds of consistency and speak otherwise: if justice is not a good for
the just man, it is inconsistent to describe it as a virtue or human excellence.
It may be urged that in the claim that justice is not a virtue, Thrasymachus
has mistaken the "logic" of his own language: the rules of use or criteria of
application of the word "just" imply that justice is a virtue and injustice is
not a virtue. Socrates remarks that the claim is contrary to what is ordinar-
ily believed, but accepts that it is meaningful (348e–349a). And rightly: to
deny meaning to the claim that justice is not a virtue is intuitionism in the
guise of linguistic analysis. Thrasymachus means to shock our intuitions. If
he is right in supposing that injustice is more profitable than justice, this is
a reason to choose injustice rather than justice, as providing a better life.

---

3. Auguste Diès offers a fine discussion of this issue in his introduction to Emile Chambry's edition of the *Republic* in the Budé *Platon* (Paris, 1965), 6: xviii–xxii.

The issue, after all, is how to live well. If justice is not good for you, it can scarcely contribute to your human excellence, or constitute your virtue.

It may be replied that the very question confuses self-interest or expediency, what is good for the individual agent, with moral goodness: it abandons "the moral point of view." It suggests that there is some nonmoral answer to the question "Why should I be moral?" when the only possible answer is that I ought to do what I ought to do because I ought to do it. This pattern of reasoning, however, passes from moral intuition to tautology bounded by a definitional stop, and prevents the question Thrasymachus has raised from so much as being asked. If injustice is more profitable than justice, why is it not unreasonable to be just? This is not a question about the way words (more or less inconsistently) are used, but about the way the world is. If Thrasymachus is right, we sometimes use words wrong.

Thrasymachus denies that justice is a good for the just man. Indeed, he makes an even stronger claim on the basis of an appeal to perceived fact: justice is bad for the just man. Since justice minimally requires that one sometimes attend to the interests of others at the apparent expense of one's own—Socrates, it will be recalled, went to his death because it was just to do so, and unjust to harm the Laws of Athens by escape—the claim that justice is sometimes bad for the just man appears to have a plentiful foundation. But if justice is on occasion bad for the just man, it appears unwise on those occasions to be just; so justice is not a virtue if unwisdom or folly is not a virtue.

Thrasymachus's question makes sense and deserves an answer, which Socrates undertakes to provide: it is not true that injustice is more profitable than justice. On the contrary, it is always in one's own interest to act justly. Thrasymachus's claim that injustice is a virtue implies that it is better to do injustice than to suffer it. Socrates' claim implies that it is better to suffer injustice than to do it. Socrates in the *Crito* went to his death on the basis of that claim, which he recognized as a paradox, and defended against Polus in the *Gorgias* (474b–475e). It is the fundamental, and genuine, Socratic paradox, and a main moral theme of the *Republic*.

Civic Virtue

Perhaps the *Republic* has a broken back: it begins with justice as it applies to conduct, keeping promises, telling the truth, rendering to each what is due him, not overreaching; it ends with justice as it applies to character, a functional order of parts of the soul analogous to health and equivalent to happiness. This suggests equivocation. Keeping promises, for example, generally inures to the benefit of the promisee, but often to the detriment of the promisor: so keeping promises may be good for the soul but bad for the pocketbook. Perhaps the argument of the *Republic* is an extended *ignoratio elenchi,* involving a fallacy of four terms. It trades on an ambiguity in justice as applied to action and justice as applied to soul.

In fact, the equivocation is systematic, and involves equivocity by reference, primary and derivative uses of the predicate "just." In a primary sense, justice is not concerned with one's own outward action but with inward action as it concerns one's self and what is truly one's own. Actions are called just if and only if they produce or preserve justice of soul (IV 443d–e). So souls are just in a primary sense, and actions are just in a derivative sense, defined in terms of the primary sense. Aristotle in *Metaphysics* IV 1 supplies a similar account of "healthy," which, as it happens, is here a relevant term, as analogically applied to the health of the soul. Just men tend to perform just actions and not perform unjust actions, for they are wise and aim at the health of their own souls. Justice in this sense may be described as civic (VI 500c) or political (IV 430c), as based on right opinion. As a disposition to perform just actions, psychical virtue is later compared to bodily habit.

Justice in us is not other than what it appeared to be in the city. A just man will not differ from a just city in respect to the form of justice itself, but will be like it (IV 435a), for the same kinds, equal in number, are present in the city and the soul of each individual (IV 441c). This is confirmed by commonplace or ordinary tests (IV 442d). Judges in the city will render judgment desiring that no one should have what belongs to another, or be deprived of what is his own (IV 433e). So similarly for the man who in nature and upbringing is like the just city. The just man does what is his own. He abstains from overreaching, and plays his appropriate role in the social order to which he belongs—"Know thyself," "nothing too much," or as F. H. Bradley put it, "my station and its duties." In defining those duties, the just man will in general acknowledge the ordinary moral rules of the social order to which he belongs—*nomos* not only as law but as custom, *mos maiorum,* use and wont. No doubt the content of moral rules will differ from city to city; adultery meant something different under the laws of Athens than it does in the ideal state. And moral rules admit exceptions; as the discussion with Cephalus in Book I shows, one does not always tell the truth to a madman, or return what one has promised. Indeed, the Guardians sometimes engage in what might be described as principled lying.

Psychical virtue issues in civic morality. Civic morality is not popular morality, if by that we understand the positive morality of ancient Athens—or our own. Popular morality assumes it is better to do injustice than to suffer it, and accepts a concept of justice founded on reciprocity, benefiting friends and harming enemies. In the *Phaedo* (68c–69b) popular morality is made to rest on a disguised hedonism, exchanging pleasures for pains and pains for pleasures; in the hedonism of the *Protagoras,* that justice is a virtue is silently ignored, and temperance shown to be impossible. Socrates provoked a revolution in moral theory, a movement from outer to inner, and rejected such claims and the accompanying hedonism, substituting for the opinions of the multitude the dialectical test of self-consistency.

Is self-consistency an adequate test? Why is psychical justice not compatible with, say, theft? Why may we not imagine a psychically healthy and happy thief, rejoicing in his skill, whose strength is as the strength of ten because his heart is just—and not only just but attuned and well-integrated? But however pleased he may be in his craft, whistling while he works and delighting in the fruits of his crime, he is not happy, for happiness is not a state of feeling which differs from pleasure only in being more serene and prolonged, but a state of being. Since justice of action contributes to or sustains justice of soul, and justice of soul implies wisdom and concern for the common good, theft is unjust, and by so much destructive of the common good. If there is reason to define the justice of actions in terms of the justice of souls, there is also reason to define the justice of souls in terms of the justice of actions. This instability is mirrored by Aristotle in *Metaphysics* VII, in his discussion of form and substrate as candidates for substance in the primary sense; not until *Metaphysics* XII do we learn that substance in the primary sense is God. Here we are meant to realize that justice in the primary sense is a Form, the essence or nature of Justice. The theory of Forms discussed in the central books of the *Republic* is not adventitiously tacked on to the moral theory of Book IV: it is its foundation and completion.

Does Moral Philosophy Rest on a Mistake?

Benjamin Franklin once said that honesty is the best policy. The dictum infuriates people who deny that the right is somehow to be justified in terms of the good. *Fiat justitia et ruant coeli:* Let justice be done even though the heavens fall. It is also said, however, that the wicked flourish like the green bay tree—and the sky remains suspended all the while.

H. A. Prichard argued that the moral philosophy of the *Republic* rests on a mistake because it justifies morality by its profitableness:

> To show that Plato really justifies morality by its profitableness, it is only necessary to point out (1) that the very formulation of the thesis to be met, viz., that justice is another's good, implies that any refutation must consist in showing that justice is one's own good, i.e. really, as the context shows, one's own advantage, and (2) that the term "to profit" supplies the keynote not only to the problem but also its solution.

But, Prichard suggests, this justification of morality fails, because it fails to account for moral obligation:

> Suppose, when wondering whether we really ought to act in the ways usually called moral, we are told as a means of resolving our doubt that those acts are right which produce happiness. We at once ask "Whose happiness?" If

we are told "Our own happiness," then, though we shall
lose our hesitation to act in these ways, we shall not recover our sense that we ought to do so.[4]

So the history of moral philosophy has consisted in asking and trying to answer the wrong question. The *Republic* argues that there is no real conflict
between duty and advantage, for if asked why you should do your duty, the
answer is in terms of your advantage. But in fact, it is a mistake to ask why
you should do your duty—why you should refuse to lie or break promises,
why you should pay your debts, or act justly as between two parties. It is
simply self-evident that you should, even though "the balance of resulting
good may be, and often is, not on the side of justice." One may compare
Kant's rejection of utilitarianism: you cannot determine what is right from
a knowledge of what is good, because the rightness is determined not by
consequences but by sheer rationality, by the universalization implied by
the Categorical Imperative. Prichard's acceptance of self-evident rules in
place of the Categorical Imperative perhaps implies a criticism: that the
Categorical Imperative itself represents a tacit appeal to self-evidence, apparent in the choice of the maxim or rule to be universalized. As to the value
of founding knowledge of what is just on the apprehension of self-evident
rules, we may perhaps reflect on the conversation with Cephalus, or recall
Aristotle's account of equity as required to correct that wherein law is deficient by reason of its generality.

Prichard construes justice in terms of action, not as a condition of soul,
and by so much agrees with Thrasymachus. Both Prichard and Thrasymachus agree that justice is sometimes not profitable. But if it makes sense
to say that justice is sometimes not profitable, it surely also makes sense to
say that it is always profitable, and one cannot dismiss this as a mistake
without engaging the whole argument of the *Republic*. Moral philosophy
not only may but must involve the assertion of mistaken propositions, for
Prichard and Thrasymachus contradict Socrates. If either proposition is a

4. "Does Moral Philosophy Rest on a Mistake?" *Mind*, n.s. 21 (1912), rpt. in Prichard's *Moral
Obligation* (Oxford, 1949).

claim in moral philosophy, so is the other, and if one or the other is true, moral philosophy does not rest on a mistake.

The Right and the Good

Prichard's point, of course, is more fundamental than this. He is a deontologist. He believes that the Right is prior to the Good, in that the Right sets boundary conditions within which issues of goodness arise, and specifically, goodness as it pertains to the consequences of actions. There is a threshold question involved in any discussion of the good, and that question involves moral obligation: whether it is right to do this is a question prior to whether it is good to do this, as for example leading to the greatest good for the greatest number. Prichard's notion of mistake may be compared to G. E. Moore's notion of fallacy: Moore held that no list of natural attributes can define the unique, nonnatural nature of goodness. Prichard holds that no list of goods, in particular goods which benefit the agent, can define the unique nature of rightness or moral obligation. Prichard's essay, published in 1912, is meant in part to respond to Moore's *Principia Ethica,* published in 1903. Honesty may or may not be the best policy, and you may hire a herald to proclaim that justice implies happiness; but this is irrelevant to the claim of honesty and justice on conduct. If justice implies happiness, or the greatest good for the greatest number, the implication is extensional and accidental: it does not follow intensionally, from the nature of justice itself.

And yet Socrates, if he believes that justice is good in itself, must suppose that it is, as Kant supposed the good will to be, a supreme principle of morality, of primary value apart from any consequences. This reflects historical fact, for the primacy of justice, in the *Crito,* is the basis on which Socrates went to his death. Kant thought that nothing is good in itself except a good will. Socrates thinks that a good will is a will that wills the good. In the *Republic,* the right is not prior to the good because justice is in our own interest. The *Crito* refers to the soul or self as "that in us which is benefited by justice and harmed by injustice."

The Social Contract

Deontology is sometimes connected with the notion of a social or political contract, an agreement which establishes principles of justice within which goodness may be pursued. Contract implies a promise, promise an obligation, obligation a duty, duty an ought; so contract, it is inferred, is the foundation of the principles of justice. The agreement should not be conceived as historical: as Blackstone says, our forebears did not meet together on a large plain and elect the tallest man present king. The social contract is hypothetical—which, with an eye toward history, must at least mean contrary to fact.

Contract is not a satisfactory foundation for justice. Contract establishes rights *in personam,* between the parties, not good against all the world, so that if justice derives from contract, strangers to the contract have no claim to justice, and those bound by contract have no duties to strangers. This is surely an abomination.

Holmes said, in *The Path of the Law,* "The duty to keep a contract at common law means a prediction that you must pay damages if you do not keep it—and nothing else." Perhaps this is a mere reflex of Holmes's legal positivism: certainly it neglects the moral obligation involved in a promise. Yet Holmes's astringency can be justified. The law does not make the obligation of a promise, as distinct from an offer and an acceptance, a matter of primary concern: social contracts are unenforceable, as are penalty clauses; there is a duty to mitigate damages, and the measure of damages is not what one lost from the breach, but what one would have had if there had been no breach. Offer, acceptance, consideration: the law seems to reduce the promissory element to the terms of a deal. If we take the legal analogy seriously, the moral obligation of a promise is not a foundation for justice, since justice is a condition of moral obligation.

Certainly this is the Platonic view. The first clear statement of social contract theory is in *Republic* II by Glaucon, who offers it in support of Thrasymachus: justice is not good in itself but only in its consequences. The theory is conjoined with the wonderful story of the Ring of Gyges, which suggests that the most fundamental of all moral emotions is fear, and makes justice merely instrumental. But this involves a circle which is in more than one way vicious. The contract premise in the *Crito* requires that agreements are to be abided by, given that it is just to do so. The exchange with Cephalus shows that the performance of some promises is unjust: it is false that a promise implies an obligation, for the fact of agreement does not guarantee the rightness of what is agreed. Promises may be made for illegal or immoral purposes, and the social contract can produce states which are robber bands writ large. Justice is a condition, not a consequence, of the obligation of a promise.

Utilitarianism

There is a class of ethical theories which define the right in terms of the good. This was true of Jeremy Bentham and John Stuart Mill, and utilitarians generally, and many students besides Prichard have assimilated Plato's theory of justice to this tradition. It is characteristic, though not essential, that it should define justice in terms of a tendency or disposition to produce the greatest good for the greatest number, and further characteristic, though not essential, that it should define goodness in terms of pleasure. Utilitarianism often, though not always, is implicated with hedonism.

Plato, in a wonderfully economical and powerful account of hedonism in the *Protagoras,* shows why hedonism, even apart from the fact that there are bad pleasures, cannot provide a foundation for moral virtue: it is powerless to explain self-control or temperance, and justice, which has regard for other people's good, is not so much as even mentioned. The hedonism of the *Protagoras* is psychological hedonism, which is a theory of human nature: we are so constituted that we naturally pursue our own pleasure, proximate or remote. But utilitarianism requires other-regarding action. Bentham, in the *Principles of Morals and Legislation,* undertook to reconcile utilitarianism and psychological hedonism by the introduction of legal sanctions; but since the legislators themselves will be psychological hedonists, this makes faction essential to government—a Thrasymachean foundation for modern liberalism. Mill in *Utilitarianism* abandons psychological hedonism, and makes justice an instrumental good, valuable for its utility.

Glaucon, it will be recalled, contrasted Socrates and Thrasymachus on the ground that Thrasymachus thought justice good only for its consequences, like work or exercise or medical treatment, whereas Socrates thought it good both for its consequences and for its own sake, like knowledge and sight and health. Justice is good in itself. For the utilitarian, justice is not good in itself but good because of its utility. The utilitarian's conception of goodness is flat: a utile here, a utile there, it all adds up. The additive element in utilitarianism leads to a search for a commutative predicate, a character of goodness conceived as univocal. The *Republic*'s conception of goodness, on the contrary, is complexly textured, systematically equivocal over a broad range of primary and derivative uses.

Teleological Ethics

The utilitarian principle, that one ought so to act as to produce the greatest good for the greatest number, has been taken to be a nearly self-evident moral truth. But it is not found in ancient ethical systems, and in particular, those descended from Socrates; its self-evidence is merely psychological, and rests on long repetition. It is a version of the second commandment in the order of the Mass, that thou shalt love thy neighbor as thyself. Utilitarianism is a Christian heresy.

Bentham and Mill are frequently regarded as "teleologists." Right action is directed to the greatest good for the greatest number; so the right is defined in terms of the good; goodness is defined in terms of pleasure; so right action has an end or aim, a *telos,* namely pleasure. Now the ethical theory of the *Republic* is also teleological. So the *Republic, mutatis mutandis,* must be understood in terms of Bentham and Mill, and defines the right in terms of the good. So Prichard.

This account is merely verbal. It is worth seeing why.

If pleasure is the goal of action, then that goal is extrinsic to the action, in a way analogous to the way in which a house is extrinsic to house building, as a product distinct from the action which produces it. It is in this sense that Bentham and Mill are teleologists.

But there are also activities which have their end or goal within themselves. For example, living is an activity. So are thinking and seeing and being healthy. There is here no product or aim independent of the activity: the activity contains the aim which defines it. Aristotle went so far as to coin a special vocabulary for this: *energeia,* what has its function or work within itself; *entelecheia,* what has its end or purpose within itself. This answers to a nice point of grammar: it is a different thing to build and to have built; it is the same thing to see and to have seen, to live and to have lived. When the aim of an activity is complete within the activity itself, present and perfect aspects coincide.

This distinction may seem of minor importance: aims are aims. In fact, it is of very great importance, not only for metaphysics but for ethics. To see that this is so, take a point made by Freud in *Civilization and Its Discontents.* People, he says, keep asking him about the meaning of life; they must mean the purpose of life; but there is no purpose to life; so life has no meaning. Assuming extrinsic purpose, this is unanswerable. But the *Republic* suggests something different. The purpose of life is to live; the purpose is internal to the activity. But if to live, then to live well; if to live well, then to live courageously and wisely and temperately and justly; so the meaning of life is to live virtuously. And since the virtues are not one but coimplicatory, justice is not separate from virtue, nor a means to virtue as an end, but constitutive of virtue. The right is not extrinsic to the good, in the way that either utilitarians or deontologists claim. For it is not merely instrumental to the good nor prior to the good if it is constitutive of the good; so the *Republic* is neither utilitarian nor deontological. Perhaps, indeed, the claim that justice is constitutive of goodness has the additional merit of being true.

Justice and Goodness

The *Republic,* in its concern for justice, operates at various levels. It is a political document, and in its treatment of faction goes to the very heart of politics. But political justice is founded on a more fundamental concern for justice as a principle of moral psychology, and more fundamentally still, opens out into "a longer way," wherein the question of how the Form of Justice is related to just souls and just actions is at issue, and the question of its relation to the Form of Goodness is asked—and never answered. The *Republic,* directed to the question What is Justice? remains Socratic still, transcendent in its aim, modest and tentative in its estimate of attainment, clarity illuminating the verges of mystery. It is in these modest and tentative terms that we are to read the great essay on moral psychology in *Republic* IV.

That essay involves a failed theory by its own standard of success. For Justice is (presumably) a species of virtue, and therefore of Goodness, and Goodness—not a good, but the Good, *summum bonum*—is left undefined and without an account. The great likenesses of the Sun, Line, and Cave, which dominate the central books of the *Republic* and gratify our human love of images, are offered because they tell us what the Good is like; but they do not say what the Good is, and they offer no maps. Precisely because they are images, they confess failure. There is something ironic in the many scholarly attempts to treat them as transparent allegory without first coming to grips with the philosophical issues they are meant to illumine. If to understand Justice is to understand Goodness, and if Goodness is the ontological foundation of all that is and the first and unhypothetical principle of explanation, then the search for Justice is a search for principles which are the foundation of all knowledge. That principle presents itself to the mind as truth, to desire as beauty: *mysterium tremendum,* but also *mysterium fascinans.* The Good, which sets the stars in their courses and sustains the Sun and its light, is also the first principle of human love and striving.

The *Republic* is as Socratic as earlier Socratic dialogues such as the *Euthyphro* or the *Crito* or the *Meno,* and for the same reasons. It does not define Justice, or say what Justice is. It does, however, offer a subtle and complex argument—or shall we say a very highly educated guess?—that Justice is essentially connected with Goodness: contrary to Thrasymachus, Justice is therefore profitable. No doubt we can never be quite clear about essential connection without knowledge of essence; Socrates explicitly makes that point at the very end of Book I, as he did in the *Meno* concerning the connection of virtue and being teachable. But we are not, as rational beings, left with the bare and exclusive disjunction of knowledge or ignorance. Inquiry takes its rise in Recollection, and Recollection is latent or implicit knowledge, whose test is purposive self-consistency.

The *Republic* ends with the words *eu prattomen,* and learned commentators tell us that the phrase means both "Let us do well" and "Let us fare well." But translation, after all, is always a somewhat doubtful enterprise, and when we reflect that the *Republic* celebrates life as an intrinsic good, and claims that both thought and desire are essentially directed to Goodness itself, we may perhaps turn for translation from the hortatory subjunctive to an imperative: "Lift up your hearts."

R. E. Allen

THE REPUBLIC

Book I

INTRODUCTION (327A–328B)

I went down to the Piraeus yesterday with Glaucon son of Ariston, intend- $\quad$ 327a
ing to pray to the goddess and at the same time wishing to see how they
conduct her festival, because they are doing it now for the first time. Well, I
thought our own procession was beautiful, though the one the Thracians
sent appeared no less fine.

After we offered prayers and saw the spectacle, we left for the City. As we $\quad$ b
were heading home, Polemarchus son of Cephalus caught sight of us at a
distance, and told his slave to run and ask us to wait for him. The boy
caught my cloak from behind and said, Polemarchus asks you to wait. I
turned and asked where his master might be.

There he is, he said. Coming up from behind. Please wait.

Why, of course we will, Glaucon replied.

And a moment later Polemarchus arrived, along with Adeimantus, $\quad$ c
Glaucon's brother, and Niceratus son of Nicias and some others, as if from
the procession.

Polemarchus said, Socrates, it looks as if you're leaving and heading for
the City.

Not a bad guess, I replied.

Well, he said, you see how many we are?

Of course.

Then either you are stronger than we are, he said, or you're staying here.

Isn't one thing still left? I replied. Namely, to persuade you to let us go?

Can you persuade us if we won't listen? he said.

No, said Glaucon.

Count on it, then. We won't listen.

328a   And Adeimantus said, Don't you know there's going to be a torch-race
on horseback toward evening in honor of the Goddess?

On horseback? I replied. That's new. Will the riders compete in relays,
carrying the torches and passing them on?

Yes, said Polemarchus. And besides, they're holding an all-night festival
which will be well worth seeing. We'll go out after dinner and watch it, and
b   meet plenty of young people there and have a discussion. Please do stay.

It seems we must, Glaucon said.

Why, if it seems good, I replied, let us do so.

CEPHALUS: JUSTICE AS TELLING THE TRUTH AND
PAYING ONE'S DEBTS (328B–331D)

So we went to Polemarchus's house and found there Lysias and Euthydemus, the brothers of Polemarchus, as well as Thrasymachus of Chalcedon,
and Charmantides of Paeania and Cleitophon son of Aristonymus. Cephalus, the father of Polemarchus, was also at home.

I thought he had aged a good deal, for it was quite some time since I'd
c   seen him. He was seated on a cushioned chair and crowned with a wreath:
he had just sacrificed in the courtyard. So we sat down beside him, for there
were some chairs there arranged in a circle.

As soon as he saw me, Cephalus welcomed me and said, You don't often
come down to the Piraeus to visit us, Socrates. But you should. If I still had
strength to travel easily to the City, there would be no need for you to come
d   here—we'd come to you. But as it is, you must come here more often. Be

assured that for my own part, as the other pleasures of the body fade, the desires and pleasures of discourse increase. Please come then and be a companion to these lads, but visit us too as among friends and even family.

Why really, Cephalus, I replied, I delight in conversing with the very old. They have gone before us on a road we too perhaps must take, and I think we should inquire of them what sort of road it is, rugged and difficult, or smooth and easily traveled. I'd be especially glad to learn how it appears to you, since you are now at an age when your foot is on the threshold, as the poets say. Is it a difficult part of life, or what is your report of it?

I will certainly tell you how it appears to me, he said. For some of us of about the same age meet from time to time, confirming the old proverb. Well, many of us when we come together feel sorry for ourselves and long for the pleasures of youth, remembering sex and drinking and feasting and what went with them; and they are distressed, thinking they have lost things of great importance, and that they lived well then but now do not live at all. Some of them also complain of being treated badly by their families because of their age, and keep harping on old age as responsible for all their troubles. But Socrates, it seems to me they're not blaming the real cause. For if this were the cause, I would feel the same way because of my age too, and everyone else who has reached this time of life. But as it is, I have met others of whom this was not true, and especially the poet Sophocles. I was present when somebody asked him, "How about sex, Sophocles? Can you still enjoy a woman?" And he replied, "Hush, man. I've most gladly escaped from it as from a savage, brutal master." Well, I thought it well said then, and no less so now. For certainly in such matters old age brings great peace and freedom. When the desires cease their straining and relax their hold, there certainly comes, as Sophocles said, release from a great multitude of masters, and mad ones at that. Actually, there is only one cause of these complaints, and those about families too, Socrates, and it is not old age but a person's character. If one is well-ordered and content, even old age is but a moderate burden; if not, Socrates, then age and youth for such a person are both in consequence difficult.

I was delighted at his saying this and wished him to continue, so I drew

e

329a

b

c

d

e

him out and said, I expect most people do not accept this, Cephalus. They think you bear old age easily, not because of your character, but because of your great estate. The rich, they say, have many consolations.

You're right, he said. They do not accept it. And there is something in what they say, though not as much as they think. The story about Themistocles is in point. When somebody from Seriphus taunted him and said his fame was due to his city instead of himself, he replied that he would never have been famous if he had been a Seriphian, nor the other fellow if he had been an Athenian. The same holds for old age being difficult without money; a good man would not easily bear old age in company with poverty, nor a bad man ever be content with himself even if rich.

330a

Did you inherit most of what you have, Cephalus, I replied, or acquire it yourself?

b

Acquire it, Socrates? he said. As a businessman, I am somewhere between my father and my grandfather. The grandfather for whom I am named inherited slightly less than the estate I now have and made it many times as great; my father Lysanias made it less than it is now. I will be glad if I leave my sons here not less, but at least a little more than I inherited.

I asked because you do not seem overly fond of money, I replied. That is generally true of those who didn't make it themselves; those who did are twice as fond of it as other people. Even as poets love their own poems and fathers their children, so businessmen care about money as a work of their own, and of course for its usefulness, as others do too. They are hard to associate with, because they refuse to praise anything but wealth.

c

That is so, he said.

d

Yes, I replied, but tell me still: what is the greatest good you think you enjoy from a large estate?

I may not persuade many people in saying it, he replied. But rest assured, Socrates, that when someone begins to face the thought that he is going to die, there comes upon him a troubled fear about things that never used to worry him before. The stories told about the place of the dead, and how those who did injustice here must suffer justice there, were once ridiculous; but now they torture his soul for fear they may be true. And he himself—

e

either from the weakness of old age, or perhaps because he is as it were closer now to the things beyond and sees them somewhat more clearly— however it may be, he is filled with fearful second thoughts, and begins to cast up accounts and consider whether he has ever done any injustice to anyone. Well, if he finds numerous injustices in his own life, he wakes often even from sound sleep in fear as children do, and lives with foreboding; but 331a in him whose conscience finds nothing unjust, hope is ever present to cheer him, a kindly nurse to old age, even as Pindar says. He put it gracefully, Socrates. For those who pass their lives in justice and holiness,

> Sweet is the hope which delights the heart,
> Nurse to old age:
> Hope, which chiefly rules the much-changing
> Judgment of mortals.

Well said, admirably so. It is in this that I assume the greatest value of having money consists, not perhaps for everyone, but for those who are decent b and well-ordered. Not to have cheated or misled anyone even unintentionally, nor again to owe sacrifice to a god or money to a man and then depart to that other world in fear—the possession of money in large part makes this possible. It has many other uses too; but still, taking one thing with another, Socrates, I would assume that, for a man of sense, this is not the least important use of wealth.

Excellently put, Cephalus, I replied. But speaking of this very thing, jus- c tice, shall we say simply and without qualification that it is truthfulness and returning what one has received from someone? Or is it in fact sometimes just to do these things, but sometimes unjust? I mean, for example: everyone would surely say that if one received weapons from a friend in his right mind who then went mad and demanded them back, one ought not return such things. The man who returned them would not be just, nor again should one be willing to tell the whole truth to a person in that condition.

You're right, he said. d

So this is not a defining mark of justice, to tell the truth and return what one received.

Of course it is, Socrates, Polemarchus broke in, at least if we are to believe Simonides.

Indeed, I bequeath the argument to you, said Cephalus; for I must at this point attend to the ceremonies.

Then your part falls to me as heir? said Polemarchus.

Of course, he said with a smile, and with that he left for the ceremonies.

POLEMARCHUS: JUSTICE IS HELPING FRIENDS AND HARMING ENEMIES (331E–336A)

e   Tell me then, as heir to the argument, I said, what you claim Simonides says, and says rightly, about justice?

That rendering to each what is due is just, he replied. I think this excellently put.

Why, it is certainly not easy to doubt Simonides, I replied; he was a wise and divine man. But as to what it means, Polemarchus, you perhaps know, but I do not. For clearly it does not mean what we mentioned just now, returning something on deposit to anyone who demands it back even if he is

332a   unsound of mind. And yet, what was deposited is in some sense due, is it not?

Yes.

But not to be returned whenever someone unsound of mind demands it?

True, he replied.

So Simonides meant something else, it seems, by it being just to render what is due.

Certainly he did, he said. He thinks friends owe it to friends to do something good and nothing evil.

I see, I replied. Someone who returns gold on deposit to someone else

b   does not render what is due, if the return and acceptance are harmful and the two of them are friends. Is that what you claim Simonides means?

Yes.

But then, one must also render to enemies whatever happens to be due?

Yes indeed, he said, what is really due them. But what is due, I think, is what is appropriate from enemy to enemy, namely, some evil.

So Simonides spoke in riddles it seems, as a poet will, I replied, about   c
what justice would be. For it appears he meant it would be just to render to each what is fitting, but he called this what is due.

Of course, he said.

Suppose then, I replied, someone asked him, "Simonides, what does the art called medicine render as due and fitting, and to what?" How do you think he would answer us?

Clearly drugs and food and drink, to the body, he said.

And the art called cooking? What does it render as due and fitting, and to what?

Seasonings, to foods.   d

Very well then, what would the art called justice render, and to what?

If we keep to what was said before, Socrates, it renders benefits and harms to friends and enemies.

So Simonides means justice is treating friends well and enemies badly?

I think so.

Then who is most able to treat friends well and enemies badly relative to disease and health?

A doctor.

And in sailing, relative to danger at sea?   e

A pilot.

What about the just man? In what action and relative to what work is he most able to benefit friends and harm enemies?

In warfare and in alliances, I think.

Very well. But surely, my dear Polemarchus, a doctor is useless except to the sick.

True.

And a pilot except to those sailing.

Yes.

Is the just man also useless to those not at war?

I certainly do not think that.

So justice is also useful in time of peace?

333a It is.

As is farming?

Yes.

Relative to having crops?

Yes.

And again, shoemaking?

Yes.

Relative to having shoes, I suppose you would say.

Of course.

Very well then. Relative to what need or possession would you say justice is useful in time of peace?

Business contracts, Socrates.

By business contracts you mean partnerships and so on?

Partnerships especially.

b Now, is the just man a good and useful partner in respect to positioning the pieces, or an expert in backgammon?

The latter.

But the just man is a better and more useful partner than a builder in respect to positioning bricks and stones?

Not at all.

In respect to what sort of partnership, then, would the just man be a better partner than the harp player, in the way that the harp player is a better partner than the just man in respect to notes and melodies?

In money matters, I think.

Except perhaps in putting money to use, Polemarchus, when buying or
c selling a horse in common. Then, I suppose, it is the horseman.

It appears so.

And surely when a boat, the shipwright or the pilot.

So it seems.

When then is the just man more useful than others in putting silver and gold to use in common?

When it is deposited and saved, Socrates.

You mean, when it is not to be put to use but lies idle?

Yes.

So when money is useless, justice is useful for it?

Perhaps.   d

And when a pruning knife needs to be guarded, justice is useful both in common and individually; but when put to use, the vintner's art?

It appears so.

You will also say that justice is useful when a shield or a lyre needs to be guarded and not used, but when put to use, the arts of the soldier and the musician?

Necessarily.

In general then, justice is useless in the use of each thing, but useful in its uselessness?

Perhaps.

Justice would scarcely be a thing of much importance, my friend, if it is   e
useful only relative to what is useless. But let us consider: in battle or boxing or anywhere else, is the person most skilled at striking a blow also most able to ward it off?

Of course.

And whoever is skilled at warding off disease is also most skilled at secretly causing it?

I think so.

Moreover, it is the same good guardian of an army camp who also steals   334a
the plans of the enemy and their other dispositions?

Of course.

So a skilled guardian of something is also a skilled thief of it?

It seems so.

Then if the just man is skilled at guarding money, he is also skilled at stealing it?

So at any rate the argument signifies, he said.

Then the just man, it seems, turns out to be a kind of thief. Very likely you learned that from Homer. Actually, he is very fond of Autolycus, the   b
grandfather of Odysseus on his mother's side, and says he surpassed all

mankind in perjury and theft. So according to you and Homer and Simonides, it seems, justice is an art of stealing—for the benefit of friends, however, but to the harm of enemies. Is that what you meant?

Good god, no, he said, I no longer know what I meant. However, it still seems to me that justice benefits friends and harms enemies.

c   By friends do you mean those who seem good to each man, or those who are really good even if they do not seem so? And enemies similarly?

Very likely one is a friend to those whom he believes good, he said, and hates those he believes bad.

Now do people make mistakes about this, with the result that many seem good who are not, and many the opposite?

Yes, they do make mistakes.

So to them, the good are enemies, the bad friends?

Of course.

d   Nevertheless, it is just for them then to benefit the bad but harm the good?

It appears so.

Moreover, the good are just and not of a sort to do injustice?

True.

By your account, then, it is just to do ill to those who have done no wrong.

No, no, Socrates, he said; the argument seems bad.

So it is just to harm the unjust, I replied, but to benefit the just?

This looks better.

e   So for many people who have mistaken their man, Polemarchus, it will follow that it is often just to harm their friends because they have bad ones, but to benefit their enemies because they are good. And thus we will say the exact opposite of what we said Simonides meant.

Yes, that follows, he said. But let us change positions. Very likely our position about friend and enemy was incorrect.

In what respect, Polemarchus?

That the friend is he who seems good.

What change should we make now? I replied.

That he who both seems and is good is the friend, he replied; he who
seems good but is not good seems to be but is not a friend. And the same for   335a
the enemy.

Then by this account, it seems, the good man will be a friend, the bad
man an enemy.

Yes.

Then you bid us add to what we were saying about justice, namely, that
it is just to treat friends well and enemies badly: we are now to add the following, that it is just to do good to our friend if he is good, evil to our enemy if he is bad?

Exactly, he said. I think that is excellently put.   b

But does it pertain to a just man, I replied, to do harm to anyone at all?

Yes, of course it does, he said. He ought to do harm to bad men and enemies.

If horses are harmed, do they become better or worse?

Worse.

In respect to the excellence or virtue of dogs, or of horses?

Of horses.

Now, if dogs also are harmed, they become worse in respect to the excellence or virtue of dogs, but not in respect to the virtue of horses?

Necessarily.

May we not say the same thing about men, my friend? That if harmed,   c
they become worse in respect to their human excellence or virtue?

Of course.

But is not justice a human excellence or virtue?

That too is necessary.

And so people who are harmed, my friend, necessarily become more unjust.

It seems so.

Now, can musicians make people unmusical by the art of music?

Impossible.

Or riding teachers bad riders by the art of horsemanship?

They cannot.

d   But do the just then make people unjust by justice? Or in general, do the good make people bad by excellence or virtue?

Why, it is impossible.

Because it is not, I suppose, a work of heat to chill, but the opposite.

Yes.

Nor of dryness to moisten, but the opposite.

Of course.

Nor of the good to do harm, but the opposite.

It appears so.

But surely the just man is good?

Of course.

So it is not a work of the just man to do harm, Polemarchus, either to friend or anyone else, but the work of his opposite, the unjust.

I think what you're saying is completely true, Socrates, he replied.

e   So if someone claims it is just to render to each his due, but means by this that harm is due from the just man to enemies and benefit to friends, it was not a wise man who said this, because it is not true. For it has not appeared just ever to harm anyone at all.

I agree, he replied.

So we shall make common cause, you and I, if anyone claims that Simonides or Bias or Pittacus or any other wise and blessed man ever said this, I replied.

Yes, he said, I am ready to join the fray.

336a   But as for claiming it is just to benefit friends and harm enemies, I replied, do you know whose statement I think it is?

Whose? he said.

I think it comes from Periander or Perdicas or Xerxes or Ismenias the Theban, or some other rich man who supposed himself to have great power.[1]

You are quite right, he said.

---

1. Supposed, but falsely supposed. Cf. *Gorgias* 467a ff., IX 577d. Bad men do what seems good to them, what they desire, but they do not do what they wish and are therefore least of all men free.

Very well, I replied. But since it appears that this is not at all what justice is, or the just, what else should one say it is?

THRASYMACHUS INTERVENES (336B–338A)

Even as we were speaking, Thrasymachus several times tried to interrupt in the midst of the conversation, though he was restrained by those sitting near him who wished to hear the argument through. But when we paused after I said this, he could keep still no longer; he coiled himself up like a wild beast crouching, and came at us as if to tear us to pieces. Polemarchus and I were both panic-stricken.

b

What is this stale old nonsense you are babbling, Socrates? he roared out in the midst of the company. And why do you keep politely deferring to each other like simpleminded fools? If you truly wish to know what the just is, do not merely ask questions or refute out of emulousness when someone suggests an answer because you know it is easier to ask than to answer. Answer for yourself, and say what you claim the just to be. And see to it that you do not tell me it is the obligatory or the useful or the beneficial or the profitable or the advantageous, but state clearly and precisely what you mean, because I will not accept it if you talk stuff like that.

c

d

I listened with astonishment and looked at him in fear. I think if I had not seen him before he saw me, I would have been struck dumb.[2] But as it was, I had glanced at him before the argument began to make him savage, so I was able to answer him. I trembled and said, Please do not be hard on us, Thrasymachus. If my friend here and I have made mistakes in our examination of arguments, rest assured that we err against our will. If we were looking for a piece of gold, we would never willingly defer to each other in our search and spoil our chance of finding it. You surely do not believe, then, that in looking for justice, a thing far more precious than gold, we would thus foolishly defer to each other and not do our best to bring it to light. Believe me, my friend. I think it is our lack of ability. Clever folk like you might more reasonably pity us than be angry.

e

2. The superstition was that if a wolf sees you first, you are struck dumb.

337a   He listened with a biting grin and a laugh. Heracles! he said. Here, is that accustomed irony of Socrates. I knew it! I told these people in advance you would refuse to answer, that you would play the sly fox and do anything rather than answer if someone asked you something.

Because you are wise, Thrasymachus, I replied. You are well aware that if you asked somebody how many twelve is, but told him in advance, "See to

b   it, fellow, that you do not tell me twelve is twice six, or three times four, or six times two, or four times three, because I will not accept such nonsense from you"—it is clear to you, I take it, that no one could answer a question put like that? But suppose he said to you, "How do you mean, Thrasymachus? Am I forbidden any of these answers? Even if the truth happens to be among them, my friend, am I to say something other than the truth? Is that what you mean?" How would you reply?

c   Oh, sure, he said. As if this is like that!

Nothing prevents it, I replied. Still, suppose they are actually not alike but appear so to the person being questioned. Do you think he would any the less answer what appears to himself, whether we forbid it or not?

That is what you're going to do too, is it not? he said. Offer one of the answers I forbid?

I should not be surprised, I replied, if on reflection it seems true to me.

d   Well, he said, what if I indicate a different answer about justice besides all these, and better than they are? he said. What penalty would you pay?

What else, I replied, except what it befits an ignorant man to pay? Surely, to learn from one who knows. So I propose to pay that.

You're sweet, he said. But besides learning, you also have to pay money.

When I get some, I replied.

You have it, Glaucon said. Speak for the money, Thrasymachus: we will all contribute for Socrates.

e   Oh yes, he replied. So that Socrates can go on in his usual way. He will not answer questions himself, but he takes an account from someone else and refutes it.

Yes, because how can anyone answer, my distinguished friend, I said, if in the first place he does not know or claim to know, and then if he does actually suppose something, he is forbidden, and this by no ordinary man, to say what he believes about it? No, it is more reasonable for you to speak, for you claim you know and can tell. So please gratify me by answering, and don't begrudge teaching Glaucon here and the others.

338a

THRASYMACHUS: JUSTICE IS THE INTEREST
OF THE STRONGER (338A–340C)

After I said this, Glaucon and the others begged him to go on. Thrasymachus obviously wanted to speak in order to distinguish himself, because he believed he had a quite wonderful answer, but he pretended to insist that I should be the respondent. Finally he gave way, and said:

So this is the wisdom of Socrates! He refuses to teach, but goes around learning from others and offers no thanks in return.

b

It is true that I learn from others, Thrasymachus, I replied, but you are wrong to claim I do not pay thanks. I pay what I can, but I can only pay in praise, because I do not have money. This I do eagerly, if I think someone speaks well, as you will very soon learn when you answer; for I am sure you will speak well.

Listen then, he replied. I say the just is nothing other than the advantage of the stronger. Well, where is your praise? You won't give it!

c

Yes, if I first understand what you mean, I said, for as it is, I do not yet know. You say the advantage of the stronger is just. Exactly what do you mean, Thrasymachus? You are not saying, surely, that if Polydamus the pancratiast is stronger than we are and it is to his advantage to eat beef for his body, this food is also advantageous and right for those of us weaker than he.

d

You are disgusting, Socrates, he said. You understand me in the way you can best hurt the argument.

Not at all, dear friend, I replied. But do please say more clearly what you mean.

You don't know that among cities, he said, some are governed by tyrannies, some by democracies, some by aristocracies?

Of course.

Now what rules is in each city the strongest?

Certainly.

e   Yes, but each kind of rule makes laws to its own advantage. A democracy makes democratic laws, a tyranny tyrannical laws, and so for the rest. By making laws, they declare this to be just for those ruled, namely, what is to their own advantage, and they punish whoever transgresses as a lawbreaker

339a   and wrongdoer. So this is what I mean, dear friend: in every city the same thing is just, namely, the advantage of the established government. But this is surely the strongest. So it follows by the correct account that the same thing is everywhere just, namely, the advantage of the stronger.

Now I see what you mean, I replied. I will try to learn whether or not it's true. You also answer that the advantageous is just, Thrasymachus—and yet, you would not let me give this answer—but then, "of the stronger" is added here.

b   A small addition, perhaps! he said.

It's not yet clear whether it matters, but it is clear that we must inquire whether it is true. For I also agree that the just is something of advantage— but when you also add "of the stronger," I do not know. So we must inquire.

Do so, he said.

I will, I replied. Tell me: do you also claim it is just to obey those who rule?

I do.

c   But are the rulers in the various cities infallible, or can they also make mistakes?

Of course they can make mistakes, he said.

Then in undertaking to legislate, they make some laws correctly, others incorrectly?

I suppose so.

Correctly if made to their own advantage, incorrectly if not to their advantage? Is that what you mean?

Yes.

But those ruled are to do what they legislate, and this is just?

Of course.

So by your account, it is just not only to do what is to the advantage of   d
the stronger, but also to do the opposite, what is not to their advantage.

What's that you're saying!

What you are, I think. But let us see. Wasn't it agreed that the rulers, in
commanding those ruled to do certain things, sometimes mistake what is
best for themselves, but that it is just for those ruled to do what the rulers
command? Wasn't this agreed?

I suppose so, he said.

Then also suppose, I replied, that you agree it is just to do what is not to   e
the advantage of those who rule and are stronger, when the rulers unwit-
tingly command evils for themselves, but you claim it is just for the others
to do what they command. Does it not then necessarily follow, my most
wise Thrasymachus, that it is just in that case to do the opposite of what you
say? For the weaker, surely, are commanded to do what is not to the advantage of the stronger.

Good god, Socrates, it could hardly be more clear, said Polemarchus.   340a

Yes, if you are going to testify in his behalf, said Cleitophon, breaking in.

Who needs a witness? he replied. Thrasymachus himself agrees that
rulers sometimes command evils for themselves, but that it is just for those
ruled to do these things.

That, Polemarchus, is because Thrasymachus held that what the rulers
order is just.

In fact, he also held that the advantage of the stronger is just, Cleitophon. Having assumed both those things, he also agreed that the stronger   b
sometimes order the weaker whom they rule to do what is not to their own
advantage. But from these agreements, the advantage of the stronger would
no more be just than what is not to their advantage.

But he meant by the advantage of the stronger what the stronger believes
is to his own advantage, said Cleitophon. That is what is to be done by the
weaker, and that is what he assumed is the just.

But that is not what he said, Polemarchus replied.

It makes no difference, Polemarchus, I replied. If Thrasymachus says so   c now, we will so accept it from him. Tell me, Thrasymachus, was this what you meant to say the just is: what seems to the stronger to be to the advantage of the stronger, whether or not it is so? May we say that's what you meant?

Hardly, he said. Do you suppose I call someone who is mistaken stronger when he is making a mistake?

Yes, I did suppose you meant that, I said, when you agreed that rulers are not infallible but in fact mistaken in some things.

d   Because you are a false accuser in argument, Socrates. Do you call someone a doctor at the very moment he is making a mistake about the sick, and in respect to the very thing in which he is mistaken? Or a calculator who errs in calculation, precisely when he errs and in respect to his error? Oh, I suppose we do talk that way: we say the doctor makes mistakes, the calculator makes mistakes, and the grammarian. But none of them ever errs, I think, in

e   so far as he is what we call him. So in the strict sense, since you are such a stickler for precision, no craftsman makes mistakes: for he who makes a mistake does so from defect of knowledge, in which respect he is not a craftsman. So no craftsman or wise man or ruler ever makes mistakes when he is a ruler, even though everyone would say that the doctor made a mistake and the ruler made a mistake. Understand, then, that the answer I gave just now was also of this sort. In the strictest sense, the ruler in so far as he rules does

341a   not make mistakes, and since he does not make mistakes, he enacts what is best for himself, and this is to be done by him who is ruled. So as I said to begin with, I say doing what is to the advantage of the stronger is just.

Well, well, Thrasymachus, I replied. You think I am a false accuser?

Very much so, he said.

Because you think I questioned you maliciously, so as to hurt your argument?

I well know it, he said. But it won't get you anywhere. You can neither

b   hurt me by guile, nor compel me openly by argument.

I wouldn't even try, dear friend, I replied. But in order that this sort of thing may not happen to us again, please distinguish whether you mean the ruler and stronger in the ordinary way of speaking, or in that strict sense you just now mentioned, for whose advantage as stronger it will be just for the weaker to act.

I mean the ruler in the strictest sense, he said. Hurt this and accuse it falsely if you can—I ask no quarter from you. But you cannot.

Do you think I'm mad enough to try to shave a lion, I said, or falsely ac-   c
cuse a Thrasymachus?[3]

You just tried, he said, but you're not up to it.

Enough of this stuff, I replied. Tell me: is the doctor, in the strict sense you were just now using, a money maker, or a servant of the sick? Who is the real doctor?

A servant of the sick, he said.

What about a ship's pilot? Is he properly a sailor, or a ruler of sailors?

A ruler of sailors.   d

I suppose it is to be ignored that he sails in the ship; he still should not be called a sailor. He is called a pilot, not because of sailing, but because of his art and his governance of the crew.

True, he said.

Now, there is something of advantage to each of these people?

Of course.

And art, I replied, is directed to seeking and providing that advantage?

Yes, he said.

Now, is anything of advantage to each art except to be as complete and perfect as possible?

Why do you ask this?   e

Suppose you were to ask me whether it is enough for body to be body, I said, or whether it needs something in addition. I would reply, Of course it needs something in addition. That is why the art of medicine has been in-vented, because body is defective and not self-sufficient; so the art was de-vised for this purpose, to provide what is of advantage. Do you think I would be right in saying that? I said.

---

3. Socrates plays on the name: Thrasymachus = bold in battle.

Yes, he said.

342a   Then is the art of medicine itself defective? Is there any other art which needs some virtue or excellence in addition, as eyes need sight and ears hearing and for that reason require an art which will consider and provide for their advantage in respect to these things? Is there some defect in the art itself? For each art, must there be another art which will consider its advantage, that art again requiring another of the same sort, and so without limit?

b   Or will each art consider its own advantage? Or does it need in addition neither itself nor any other art to consider its advantage in respect to its own defect because there is neither defect nor error present in any art, nor does art seek the advantage of anything except that of which it is the art? It is without flaw or blemish, since it is correct as long as each art is strictly and wholly what it is. Consider this in that strict sense of yours. Is it so, or otherwise?

It appears so, he said.

So the art of medicine considers, not what is to the advantage of the art

c   of medicine, I replied, but what is to the advantage of a body.

Yes, he said.

And horsemanship not of horsemanship, but of horses. And no other art of itself—for it needs nothing in addition—but of that of which it is an art.

It appears so, he said.

Furthermore, Thrasymachus, the arts rule and govern that of which they are arts.

He here conceded it, just barely.

So no art or knowledge considers or commands the advantage of the

d   stronger, but of what is weaker and ruled by itself.

He finally agreed to this too, though he undertook to fight it. When he agreed, I replied, Then no doctor, in so far as he is a doctor, considers or commands the advantage of the doctor, but the advantage of the patient? For it was agreed, was it not, that the doctor in the strict sense is a ruler of bodies, not a money maker?

He concurred.

Then too, the pilot in the strict sense is a ruler of sailors, not a sailor?

He agreed.

So this sort of pilot and ruler will consider and command not what is of   e
advantage to the pilot, but the advantage of the sailor who is ruled.

He assented, barely.

Then no one else in authority, Thrasymachus, I rejoined, in so far as he
is a ruler, considers or commands what is of advantage to himself, but the
advantage of the ruled, for which he himself acts as craftsman. He looks to
that and to what is of advantage and suited to that, in all that he says and
does.

THRASYMACHUS CHANGES GROUND (343A–345E)

Well, when we came to this point in the argument, and it was clear to every-   343a
one that his account of justice had been turned upside down, Thrasymachus, instead of answering, said, Tell me, Socrates, do you have a nanny?

What? I replied. Shouldn't you answer, instead of asking a thing like
that?

Because she lets you go around sniveling and doesn't wipe your nose
when you need it. You can't even tell sheep from shepherds.

What exactly do you mean? I replied.

You think shepherds or cowherds consider what is good for the cows and   b
the sheep, and fatten them up and take care of them with a view to something other than their masters' good and their own. Specifically, you believe
that those who rule in our cities—those who truly rule—differ at all in
their thoughts toward those they rule, except as one might be disposed toward sheep, and consider anything else, day and night, but how to derive
profit from them. You are so far off about justice and the just, and injustice   c
and the unjust, that you do not even know that justice and the just are really "another's good," an advantage of the stronger who rules but his own
peculiar harm to him who obeys and serves. Injustice is the opposite, and
rules those who are in truth simpleminded and just: those ruled do what is
to the advantage of the stronger and make him happy by serving him, but
not themselves in any way at all. You must consider it this way, my most   d

simpleminded Socrates: a just man everywhere gets a lesser share than an unjust man. First, in business dealings when the one is in partnership with the other, you would nowhere at the dissolution of the partnership find that the just man gets more than the unjust, but less. Again, when in civic affairs some special tax is levied, the just man contributes more from an equal portion and the unjust less, but when it is a question of receiving, the one gets nothing and the other profits greatly. In fact, when each of the two hold an office, the just man, even if there is no other penalty, is more badly off through neglect of his own affairs; he derives no benefit at all from public funds because he is just, and in addition he is hated by his family and friends and acquaintances when he refuses to serve them contrary to what is just. For the unjust man, quite the opposite obtains. I mean the fellow I was just mentioning, who can overreach on a grand scale. Look then to him, if you wish to judge how much more advantageous it is to be unjust in one's own affairs rather than just. You will learn it most easily of all if you go to that complete and perfect injustice which makes the doer of injustice most happy and those who suffer injustice and refuse to do injustice most miserable. This is tyranny, which both by stealth and open force takes what is another's, sacred or profane, public or private, not little by little but in wholesale lots. When someone does injustice piecemeal and gets caught, he is punished and treated with utmost opprobrium—in fact, they are called temple robbers and kidnappers, housebreakers and thieves, perpetrators of those kinds of crimes. But when someone in addition to taking the property of citizens also kidnaps them and reduces them to slavery, then, instead of shameful names, he is called happy and blessed not only by the citizens themselves but also by others who have learned that his doing of injustice extends to the whole of it. For when people denounce injustice, it is not because they fear doing unjust things, but because they fear suffering them. So injustice, Socrates, become sufficient, is stronger and more free and more masterful than justice, and as I said to begin with, what is just happens to be the advantage of the stronger, but what is unjust is profitable and advantageous to oneself.

Having said this like a bath-man drenching our ears with a sudden flood of words, Thrasymachus meant to depart. But the bystanders would not let him. Instead, they made him stay to provide an account of what he had said. I myself begged him especially hard and said, Do you really intend to leave after pouring out a speech like that, my dear Thrasymachus, before sufficiently teaching or learning whether it is so or otherwise? Or do you think it a small thing you are undertaking to determine, and not the whole conduct of a life, by which each of us would live most profitably if we followed it?

e

Do you think I deny that? said Thrasymachus.

You seem to, I replied—or else you do not care at all about the rest of us, or think it matters whether we shall live better or worse for being ignorant of what you claim to know. Please, good friend, take the trouble to show us—it will hardly be a bad investment for you to be a benefactor of such a company as this. For my part, I tell you I am not convinced. I do not think injustice is more profitable than justice, even if one allows it and does not prevent it from doing what it will. On the contrary, dear friend. Let there be an unjust man, and let him be able to do injustice either by escaping detection or by violence. Nevertheless, it still does not persuade me that injustice is more profitable than justice. Perhaps I am not alone, and there is someone else among us similarly affected. Sufficiently persuade us then, my fortunate friend, that we are wrong to count justice preferable to injustice.

345a

b

And how am I to persuade you? he said. If you are not convinced by what I just now said, what more can I do for you? Take the argument and stick it in your soul?

Good god, don't do that, I replied. But first, stand by what you said, or if you change ground, do it openly and do not mislead us. You see now, Thrasymachus—let us go back again to your earlier argument—that though you at first marked off the true physician, you no longer thought it necessary afterward to guard so strictly the true shepherd. No, you thought that in so far as he is a shepherd, he tends his sheep not with a view to what is best for them, but with a view to a meal, like a glutton about to dine, or again, toward selling them, like a merchant instead of a shepherd. The shepherd's art is surely not concerned for anything except to provide what is

c

d

best for that to which it is directed, the sheep—since what belongs to itself has surely been sufficiently provided so that it is best, in so far as it does not fall short of being the shepherd's art. That is why I thought we had to agree now that all rule, in so far as it is rule, considers nothing, in public and private, except what is best for what is ruled and served.

e

THE WAGES OF RULING (345E–347E)

(Socrates continues) But do you think the rulers in our cities, the true rulers, rule willingly?

I don't just think it, he said, I know it.

Really, Thrasymachus? I replied. Do you not realize that in other kinds of rule, no one rules willingly but demands pay, thinking it is not they but those ruled who benefit from their ruling? Though tell me this: do we not usually claim that one art differs from another in having a different power? Please do not answer contrary to your real opinion, my friend, so that we may actually settle something.

346a

Yes, he said, they differ in this.

Then too, each of them provides a benefit not common, but proper and peculiar to itself. For example, medicine provides health, the pilot's art safety in sailing, and so on?

Of course.

b

Again, the art of wage earning provides wages? For this is its power. Or do you call medicine and piloting the same? Or, if you wish to draw distinctions with the strictness you proposed, if a pilot becomes healthy through the benefit of a sea voyage, would you for this reason any the more call his art medicine?

Of course not, he said.

Nor wage earning medicine, I suppose, if someone becomes healthy while earning wages.

Of course not.

Is medicine then wage earning, if someone practicing medicine receives a fee?

No, he said

c

Now, we agreed that the benefit obtained from each art is proper and peculiar to it?

Let it be so, he said.

So whatever benefit all craftsmen gain in common clearly derives from
some same thing they further use in common, and they benefit from that.

It seems so, he said.

Yes, but we say that the benefit of earning wages accrues to craftsmen
from their use in addition of the art of wage earning.

He assented, barely.

So this benefit, the receipt of wages, does not accrue to each craftsman

d

from his own art. If considered strictly, medicine produces health, but wage
earning wages; house building produces a house, but wage earning attends
on it with wages; and so for all other arts. Each does its own work and benefits that to which it has been ordered. But if pay is not present to it in addition, does the craftsman derive any benefit whatever from his art?

It appears not, he said.

Does he provide no benefit when he works for free?

e

I suppose he does.

Well then, Thrasymachus, at this point it is clear that no art or rule provides what is of advantage to itself, but as we said a while back, it provides
and orders the advantage of those ruled, and considers the advantage of the
weaker, not the stronger. That's why I claimed just now, my dear Thrasymachus, that no one volunteers to rule and take in hand the ills of others to
straighten them out, but instead demands pay, because anyone who intends
to practice his art properly never does or commands what is best for himself

347a

but for the subject ruled, when issuing orders according to his art. Which is
why, it seems, wages must be provided to those willing to rule—either
money or honor, or a penalty for not ruling.

What do you mean by that, Socrates? said Glaucon. I recognize the two
kinds of wages, but I do not understand what sort of penalty you mean, and
why you have called it part of wages.

Then you do not understand the wages of the best sort of men, I said, by

b

reason of which men of the most decent sort rule, when they are willing to rule. Do you not know that ambition and avarice are said to be, and are, a matter of reproach?

I do, he said.

That is why good men refuse to rule for the sake of money or honor, I replied. For they wish to be called neither mercenary by openly taking pay for ruling, nor thieves for receiving it secretly from their rule; nor again for honor, because they are not ambitious. So one must impose on them a necessity and a penalty, if they are going to be willing to rule—which is why it is considered shameful to seek office voluntarily and not await the necessity. The greatest penalty for refusing to rule is to be ruled by an inferior. It is fear of that, I think, that causes good men to rule, when they do, and they enter an office not because they think they are going to something good or a thing to be enjoyed, but because they think it a necessity, and they have no one as good or better than themselves to turn it over to. It is likely that if there were ever a city consisting of good men, they would compete to avoid office as people now compete to gain it, and it would there be evident that a genuine ruler really looks not to his own advantage but to that of those he rules. All who know and understand would choose to be benefited by another rather than put to the trouble of benefiting another. So I do not at all agree with Thrasymachus that justice is the advantage of the stronger. But this we will examine later. I think what Thrasymachus is saying now is much more important: he claims that the unjust life is stronger and superior to the just life.

THRASYMACHUS: INJUSTICE IS A VIRTUE (347E–349B)

(Socrates continues) Well, which do you choose, Glaucon? I said. Which do you think more truly said?

That the just life is more profitable.

You heard how many good things Thrasymachus assigned to the unjust life? I replied.

I did, he said, but I am not convinced.

Then would you have us convince him that he is wrong, if we can find a way?

Of course, he replied.

Then we might contend against him speech for speech, I said, listing how many goods derive from being just, and he will reply, and we will go again. We will have to count up the goods and measure how many each of the two of us lists in each of the two speeches, and at that point we will need judges and jurymen to decide between us. But if we examine the matter by coming to terms with one another as we did just now, we will ourselves be at once advocates and judges.

b

Certainly, he said.

Which do you prefer? I replied.

The latter, he said.

Come then, Thrasymachus, I replied. Answer us from the beginning. You claim that perfect and complete injustice is more profitable than perfect and complete justice?

I most certainly do, he replied, and I've said why.

c

Come then, what do you say about this: you no doubt call one of the two an excellence and virtue, the other a vice?

Of course.

Then justice is a virtue, injustice a vice?

Likely enough, my sweet fellow, he said, since I also say injustice is profitable, but justice is not.

But what, then?

The opposite, he replied.

Justice is a vice?

No, but a quite generous good nature.[4]

Then you call injustice bad character?

d

4. Good character, simplicity of heart, but also simplemindedness, gullibility, silliness. Compare "silly" and *selig*.

No, rather good counsel, he said.

Then the unjust also seem to you to be wise and good, Thrasymachus?

Yes, if they can be perfectly unjust, able to make themselves masters of cities and whole tribes of men. Maybe you thought I meant cutpurses. Well, there's profit even in that sort of thing, he replied, if you escape detection. But it's not worth mentioning, compared with what I was just now talking about.

e   I'm not unaware that this is what you meant to say, I said. But I was surprised at your putting injustice as part of virtue and wisdom, justice among their opposites.

I certainly do put it so.

This is a much more stubborn position, my friend, I replied, and it is no longer easy to know what to say. If you had put injustice as profitable, but agreed that it is either a vice or shameful, as certain others do,[5] we might perhaps have something to say according to what is customarily acknowledged. But as it is, you will clearly say it is noble and strong, and add to it all

349a   the other things we used to add to justice, since you venture to put it in virtue and wisdom.

An accurate prophecy, he said.

Still, I replied, we must not shirk following out the argument and examining it, so long as I understand you to be saying what you think. For I don't think you're joking at all now, Thrasymachus, but saying what you think about the truth.

What difference does it make to you whether I think it or not? he said. Why don't you refute the argument?

b   No difference, I replied.

EXCESS IS NEITHER WISE NOR GOOD (349B–350C)

(Socrates continues) But try to tell me this still in addition. Do you think one just person would be willing to overreach and outdo another just person?[6]

---

5. For example, Polus in the *Gorgias,* 474a ff., 482d–e, 483c.
6. Thrasymachus claims that injustice is superior to justice and commends injustice as a human

Not at all, he said, for then he wouldn't be civilized and simpleminded, as he now is.

Or overreach and outdo the just action?

No, he said.

Would he see fit to overreach and outdo the unjust person, and believe it just? Or would he not believe it just?

He'd believe it just and see fit to do it, he replied, but he couldn't.

But that's not what I asked, I replied. I asked whether the just person would not see fit to overreach and outdo another just person nor wish it, but overreach and outdo the unjust person.   c

Why, that's so, he replied.

Then what about the unjust person? Would he see fit to overreach and outdo the just person and the just action?

Of course, he said. He'd see fit to overreach in everything.

So the unjust person will also overreach and outdo an unjust person and action, and will strive to take the most of everything?

That's so.

Then let's put it this way, I said. The just person does not overreach and outdo one who is like but unlike, while the unjust person overreaches both   d like and unlike.

You've put it very well, he replied.

Yes, I said, but the unjust person is wise and good, the just person neither.

That's well put too, he said.

So the unjust person in fact resembles a wise and good person, I replied, but the just person does not?

Of course, he said. He who is of that sort will also resemble those of that sort; the other won't.

Fine. So each of the two of them is of the same sort as what he resembles.

What else? he said.

---

excellence or virtue allied to wisdom. He also describes it as excess, overreaching—having or getting or taking more in the sense of mere difference in measure, but often with the further sense of getting or taking more than one's share—taking advantage or unfairness.

e   Very well, Thrasymachus. You say that one person is musical, another not?

I do.

Which of them is wise, and which unwise?

The musical person is doubtless wise, the unmusical person unwise.

Then also good where he is wise, bad where he is unwise?

Yes.

So too the physician?

Yes.

Do you think then, dear friend, that a musician tuning a lyre would be willing to overreach and outdo another musician in tightening and loosening the strings, or see fit to take more?

No, I don't.

But overreach and outdo someone not musical?

Necessarily, he said.

350a   What about a doctor? In prescribing food or drink, will he overreach and outdo another medical man or procedure?

Of course not.

But overreach and outdo a layman?

Yes.

Concerning every kind of knowledge and ignorance, consider whether you think anyone who knows would choose, in what he says or does, to overreach and outdo and have more than anyone else who knows, but not choose the same things in respect to the same action as someone like himself.

Well, perhaps that must be so, he said.

What about someone who is ignorant? Wouldn't he alike overreach and
b   outdo and have more than someone who has knowledge and someone who hasn't?

Perhaps.

But he who has knowledge is wise?

Yes.

The wise man is good?

Yes.

So he who is good and wise will not overreach and outdo and have more than someone like himself, but someone unlike and opposite.

So it seems, he said.

But the bad and ignorant will overreach and outdo both someone like himself and the opposite.

It appears so.

Now, Thrasymachus, I replied, our unjust person overreaches both his like and his unlike? Didn't you say that?

I did, he said.

Yes, but the just person will overreach and outdo not his like, but his un- c like?

Yes.

So the just person, I replied, resembles the wise and good, the unjust man the ignorant and bad.

Perhaps.

Moreover, we agreed that each of the two would be of the same sort as what each is like.

Yes.

So the just person has been revealed to us as good and wise, the unjust as ignorant and bad.

INTERLUDE: THRASYMACHUS EMBARRASSED (350C-E)

Thrasymachus agreed to all this, not as easily as I now describe it, but with considerable difficulty, as if it were being dragged out of him—and with an d astonishing amount of sweating, because of course it was summer. And then I saw what I'd never seen before, Thrasymachus blushing.

Well, when once we'd agreed that justice is virtue and wisdom, injustice vice and ignorance, I said, Very well, let's take this as settled. But we were also saying that injustice is strong. Don't you recall, Thrasymachus?

I do, he said. But I don't like what you're saying now at all and I can give a speech about it. Though if I do, I know you'll say that I'm being rhetori- e cal. Well, either let me speak as much as I wish, or if you wish to ask ques-tions, do so, and I'll say to you, "Well, well," and nod and shake my head, as I would to old women telling their tales.

No, not contrary to your own opinion, I replied.

To please you, he said, since you won't let me speak. And yet, what else do you wish?

Not a thing, I replied. But if indeed you will do this, please do it: I'll ask the questions.

Ask away.

INJUSTICE CAUSES DIVISION AND ENMITY (350E–352D)

I ask then as before, so that we may also examine the argument in sequen-tial order, what sort of thing justice happens to be relative to injustice. It was said no doubt that injustice is more powerful and stronger than justice. But as it is, I said, if justice is wisdom and virtue, I think it will easily be shown that it is also stronger than injustice, since injustice is ignorance—no one could still be ignorant of that. Still, I don't want to take it quite so simply, Thrasymachus, but to inquire in some such way as this: would you say that it is unjust for a city to try to enslave other cities unjustly, and hav-ing so reduced them, to hold many cities in subjection?

Of course, he said. And that's exactly what the best city will especially do, the most perfectly unjust.

I understand that was your argument, I said. But consider this about it: will the city which becomes stronger than another city have this power without justice, or does it necessarily have it with justice?

With justice, he said, if justice is wisdom, as you were now claiming. With injustice, if as I claimed.

I'm quite delighted, Thrasymachus, I replied. You don't merely nod and shake your head, but answer very nicely.

To please you, he said.

Thank you. But please me still further by telling me this: do you think a city or an army camp, a gang of robbers or a band of thieves or any other tribe of people, in so far as they unjustly go after something in common, could accomplish anything if they constantly did injustice to each other.

Of course not, he replied.

They will accomplish more if they don't?

Certainly.

Because injustice would surely produce faction and hatred and warfare among them, Thrasymachus, but justice produces unanimity and friendship. Not so?

Let it be so, he replied, in order that I may not differ with you.

Thank you again, my friend. But tell me this: if it is the work of injustice to introduce hatred wherever it is present, will it not, when it comes to be present among people, whether free men or slaves, cause hatred and faction among them, and render them incapable of acting in common with each other?

Of course.

If it should come to be present in two people, won't it set them at odds? They'll be enemies and hate both each other and those who are just.

Yes, he said.

What if it comes to be present in only a single person, my friend? Will injustice lose its own power, or have it nonetheless?

The latter, he said.

Then it appears that the power it has is such that, wherever it may come to be present, in city or family, in army camp or anywhere else, it first makes concerted action impossible by reason of faction and disagreement, and again, it is everywhere an enemy both to itself and to its opposite, the just. Not so?

Yes.

And I suppose then that if present in a single individual, it will do all that it naturally effects. First, it will make him incapable of action, as self-divided by faction and in disagreement with himself, and next, he will be an enemy to himself and to the just. Not so?

Yes.

But the gods are just, dear friend?

b   Let it be so, he said.

So the unjust person will be an enemy to the gods, Thrasymachus, but the just person a friend.

Feast on the argument in confidence, he said. I won't contradict you, in order not to offend the company.

Come then, I replied, and complete the remainder of my feast by continuing to answer as you now do. For the just appear, so far, wiser and better and more powerful in action, the unjust incapable of acting in company

c   with each other. No doubt we do sometimes say that people act vigorously and in concert even though they are unjust, but that's not completely true. For if they were completely unjust, they wouldn't be able to keep their hands off each other: rather, it is clear that there was a certain justice in them through which they did what they did, and which caused them at least not to wrong each other and those they attacked at the same time. They were impelled toward things unjust only half-corrupted by injustice, since if they were completely vicious and perfectly unjust, they'd also be

d   perfectly incapable of acting. This then I understand to be so, but not what you at first assumed.

VIRTUE AND FUNCTION (352D–354A)

(Socrates continues) But the question we afterward put for consideration must be faced: whether the just also live better than the unjust and are more happy. Well, it appears so even now, I think, from what we've said. Nevertheless, we must consider it even more carefully. For the argument is not about something adventitious, but about the way one ought to live.

Go on, he said.

I will, I replied. Tell me: do you think there is some work or function of a horse?

Yes.

e   Then would you assume that the work or function of a horse, or anything else, would either be what one can alone do with it, or best do with it?

I don't understand, he said.

Look at it this way: can you see with anything except eyes?

Of course not.

Or hear with anything except ears?

Not at all.

Then we could justly say these are their functions?

Of course.

Again, you could cut the shoots of a vine with a sword or a chisel, and 353a
many other tools?

Certainly.

But with nothing so well, I take it, as a pruning knife made for the purpose.

True.

Then won't we put this as its work or function?

Yes.

Then at this point you might better understand what I was asking just
now, when I inquired whether the function of a thing is the work which it
alone can do, or do better than anything else.

Why, I do understand, he said, and I think this is the function of each b
thing.

Very well, I replied. Then do you think that there is also an excellence or
virtue for each thing to which a function has been appointed? Let us go
back again to the same examples. We say there is a function for eyes?

Yes.

Then there is also a virtue of eyes?

Yes.

Again, ears have a function?

Yes.

Then also a virtue?

Yes.

And so in all other cases?

Yes.

Hold it right there. Would eyes perform their own work well, if they did not have their own peculiar excellence and virtue, but a vice instead of the virtue?

How could they? he said. No doubt you mean blindness instead of sight.

Whatever their virtue is, I replied—for I haven't asked that yet, but whether things which perform a function will perform their own work well by their own peculiar virtue, badly by their vice.

That's true, he said.

Then ears deprived of their own virtue will perform their own work badly?

Of course.

We can put the same account for everything else?

I think so.

Come then, next consider this: is there some function of soul which you could not perform with anything else among things which are? For example: exercising care and concern, and ruling and deliberating and all that sort of thing. Is there anything other than soul to which we could justly assign them, and claim them as its peculiar work?

Nothing.

Again, what about living? Shall we not say it is a function of soul?

Yes, most especially, he said.

Now, we also claim there is a certain excellence or virtue of soul?

Yes.

Then will a soul ever perform its own work well, Thrasymachus, if deprived of its peculiar virtue, or is it impossible?

Impossible.

So a bad soul necessarily rules and exercises care and concern badly, a good soul does all this well.

Necessarily.

Now, we agreed that justice is an excellence or virtue of soul, injustice a vice?

Yes.

So the just soul and the just man will live well, but the unjust badly?

It appears so, he said, by your account.

Again, he who lives well is blessed and happy, he who does not is the op-   354a
posite?

Of course.

So the just man is happy, the unjust wretched?

Let it be so, he said.

Furthermore, it is unprofitable to be wretched, profitable to be happy?

Of course.

And so, my blessed Thrasymachus, injustice is never more profitable
than justice.

Let this be your feast at the Festival of Bendis, Socrates, he said.

CONCLUSION (354A–C)

It is you who has provided the feast, Thrasymachus, I replied, ever since you
became gentle with me and stopped being angry. I haven't dined well, however, though it's my own fault, not yours. Gluttons keep grabbing at each   b
new dish that's passed, and taste it before they've properly enjoyed the previous course. I think I am that way too. Before we found out the first issue
under consideration, what justice is, I dropped that and hurried on to inquire whether it is vice and ignorance or wisdom and virtue. Later on, when
an argument was thrown in that injustice is more profitable than justice, I
could not refrain from going from this to that. So the result of the discussion to this point is that I know nothing. For when I do not know what jus-   c
tice is, I will scarcely know whether it happens to be a virtue or not, and
whether he who has it is unhappy or happy.

Book II

THE PROBLEM STATED (357A–358E)

357a Well, in saying this I thought the argument was done, but it seemed it was after all only a prelude: Glaucon, ever most courageous in everything, specifically refused at that point to accept Thrasymachus's giving up. Socrates, he said, do you wish merely to seem to have persuaded us that it is in every way better to be just than unjust, or to persuade us in very truth?

b If it were up to me, I said, I would choose to persuade you in very truth.

Then you are not doing what you wish, he said. For tell me: do you think there is a kind of good we would accept having, not because we desire what follows from it, but as welcome for its own sake? For example, enjoyment, and all harmless pleasures through which nothing else arises in after time except having the enjoyment while they last.

Yes, I replied, I think there is a good of that sort.

c What about a good which we welcome both for its own sake and for the consequences which arise from it? For example again, thinking and seeing and being healthy? We surely welcome such things for both reasons.

Yes, I said.

Do you discern a third, he said, a form of good which contains athletic

38

training and being treated when sick, and medical practice and money-making generally? For we would say that these are burdensome but benefit us; we would not accept having them for their own sake, but for the rewards and other benefits that derive from them.

Yes, I said, there is also this third. What about it?   d

In which of these do you put justice? he said.

I suppose in the most excellent, I replied, to be welcomed both for itself   358a
and for the things that arise from it, by those who intend to be happy.

Well, most people do not agree, he said. They think it belongs to the burdensome form, to be practiced for the sake of rewards and a good reputation, but to be avoided in and of itself, because they suppose it is difficult.

I know they think so, I replied, and Thrasymachus condemned justice awhile ago because he thought it was that way and praised injustice. But I am a slow learner, it seems.

Come then, he said. Hear me out, and see if it still seems the same to   b
you. Thrasymachus appeared to me to give up too easily, before he had to, as though you had charmed him like a snake. But to my mind, demonstration has yet to take place about either justice or injustice: for I want to hear what each of the two are, and what power justice has alone by itself when present in the soul, dismissing the rewards and other things which arise from it. So if you agree, here is what I will do: I will renew the argument of Thrasymachus, and first I will say what sort of thing people claim justice is   c
and whence it has arisen. Second, that all who practice it do so unwillingly, as necessary but not as good. Third, that in this they act reasonably: for the life of the unjust man is much better than that of the just man, so they claim, though for myself, Socrates, it does not at all seem that way. However, I am perplexed. My ears have almost been talked deaf by listening to Thrasymachus and countless others, but I have never yet heard the case for   d
justice as better than injustice stated by anyone as I wish. I wish to hear it praised in and of itself. I suppose I might especially inquire of you; therefore, I will speak strenuously in praise of the unjust life, but I do so to show you how I wish to hear you condemn injustice and praise justice. Does this suit you?

e   Most certainly, I replied. For of what would a sensible man more enjoy speaking and hearing?

GLAUCON'S DEFENSE OF INJUSTICE (358E–362C)

Excellent, he said. Hear then what I said I would speak of first: what justice is, and whence it has arisen.

People say that it is by nature good to do injustice but bad to suffer it, and the evil of suffering it far exceeds the good of doing it, so that when 359a they do injustice to each other and suffer it and get a taste of both, those who lack power to avoid the one and choose the other think it profitable to contract with each other neither to do injustice nor suffer it. From this then began the making of laws and contracts among them, and what the law prescribes they name lawful and just. This is the origin and essential nature of justice: it is intermediate between what is really best, which is to do injustice and not be punished for it, and what is worst, to suffer injustice and not b be able to retaliate. The just is a mean between these; it is not welcomed as good, but valued out of lack of strength to do injustice. Because anyone who could do injustice and be a real man would never contract with anybody not to do or suffer it—he would be crazy. This and of this sort, then, is the nature of justice, Socrates, and such are its natural origins, as the argument has it.

We might especially perceive that those who practice it do so unwillingly, from lack of power to do injustice, if we imagined giving opportunity c to the just and the unjust to do whatever they each may wish; we would then follow along after to see where their desire will in either case lead. Well, we would catch the just man in the very act, going after the same thing as the unjust man due to overreaching, which all nature pursues as good, though forcibly turned aside by law to respect the equal.

The opportunity I especially mean would be this: suppose they both d were given power of the kind people say once belonged to the ancestor of Gyges the Lydian, who was a shepherd serving the then-ruler of Lydia.

There was a great storm and an earthquake and the ground was rent and a chasm opened right where he was keeping his flock; he was astonished at the sight and went down into the chasm, and there saw, among other wonders of which the stories tell, a hollow bronze horse with windowlike openings, through which he peered and saw within a dead body, as it appeared, larger than human size. It wore nothing except a gold ring on its hand, which he took and climbed out.

When the shepherds gathered in their accustomed way to make their monthly report to the king about the state of his flocks, Gyges came too, wearing the ring. Well, sitting with the others, he happened to turn the bezel of the ring around toward himself, to the inside of his hand. When that happened, he became invisible to those sitting right next to him, and they began to speak about him as if they thought he had left. He was surprised, and felt again for the ring to turn the bezel outward, and when he did he became visible. Aware of this, he tested the ring to see if it indeed had this power, and found it to be so: when he turned the bezel inward he became invisible, when outward, visible. Realizing this, he immediately arranged to become one of the messengers sent to the court. He went, seduced the queen, murdered the king with her help, and seized the throne.

Now, suppose there were two such rings, and the just man put on one, the unjust the other. No one would be of such unyielding strength, it would seem, that he should abide in justice and submit to keeping his hands off the belongings of others and not touch them, when it was possible for him to take without fear whatever he pleased from the marketplace, and enter houses and have intercourse with whomever he wished, kill or release from prison anyone he wished, and otherwise act among men as equal to a god. In doing this, the one man would not behave differently from the other: both would go after the same things. And yet, one might claim this is a considerable indication that no one is just willingly, but under compulsion, because he does not suppose it is good for him personally: each will be unjust wherever he thinks it possible to be unjust. For surely every man thinks injustice much more profitable personally than justice—and he thinks truly,

e

360a

b

c

d

so one who offers such an account as this will claim. Since if someone obtained such an opportunity and yet refused to do injustice or touch what belonged to another, those aware of it would think him a most miserable and utter fool, though they would deceitfully praise him in front of each other for fear of suffering injustice themselves. So much for that.

e   As to the actual decision concerning the lives we are discussing, we will be able to decide rightly if and only if we set the most just man over against the most unjust. Well, what is the contrast? This. Let us subtract nothing from the injustice of the unjust man, nor from the justice of the just man, but assume each of the two perfect in his own practice. First, then, make the unjust man like the skilled craftsman—a first-rate pilot, for example, or a doctor fully aware of what is possible and impossible in his art, and able to

361a undertake the one but dismiss the other; but again, should he somehow perhaps slip, adequate to set it right. So also let the unjust man, if he is to be thoroughly unjust, escape detection by going about his crimes in the right way. Whoever gets caught is to be regarded as a bungler; for the extremity of injustice is to seem just without being so. The most perfect injustice, then, is to be given to the perfectly unjust man, and without diminution; rather, he is to be allowed the greatest injustices while providing for himself the

b greatest reputation for justice, and if he should perhaps in some way slip, he must be able to set things right—adequate to speak with persuasive eloquence if accused of any of his crimes, and to use force where force is required, due to his courage and strength and resources of friends and estate.

    Having assumed a man like this, let us stand the just man alongside him in the argument—a simple man and noble, willing, as Aeschylus has it, "not to seem but to be good." Subtract then the seeming. For if he seems to

c be just, he will have honors and gifts for seeming so, and it would then be unclear whether he is such as he is for the sake of the just, or for its gifts and honors. Strip him then of all save justice. Situate him oppositely to the former man: having done nothing unjust, let him have the greatest reputation for injustice, in order that he may be put to the test in respect to justice, and

d not softened by ill repute and what results from it. Instead, let him go his way unwavering till death, seeming to be unjust throughout life but being just, in order that, both men having arrived at an extreme, one of justice, the other of injustice, it may be judged which of the two of them is happier.

Wonderful, my dear Glaucon, I replied. You burnish each of the two men for the judgment as vigorously as a statue.

I do my best, he said. But if the two are like this, it is no longer difficult, I suppose, to explain in argument the sort of life that awaits them. It must be reckoned up. And should the reckoning be unduly coarse, please do not suppose it is me that is speaking, Socrates, but those who praise injustice before justice. They will say this: that being so situated, the just man will be flogged, racked, bound in chains, have his two eyes burnt out, and finally, after suffering every torment, be impaled, and he will know that one must be willing not to be but to seem just. The words Aeschylus used are much more nearly correct of the unjust. For, they will say, it is really the unjust man, because he practices a thing containing truth and does not live by appearance, who is willing not to seem but to be unjust, "reaping the harvest of his mind's deep furrows, from which the fruits of wise counsel grow." First, by seeming just, he rules in his city; next, he marries where he pleases, gives in marriage to whom he will, has business dealings and becomes a partner with whom he wishes, and besides all this gains profit and advantage by not scrupling to do injustice. Entering on contests both public and private, he engrosses and overreaches his opponents, and in overreaching them he becomes rich, benefits his friends, harms his enemies, offers sacrifices to the gods, and sets up votive offerings with due magnificence. He serves both the gods and the men he prefers far better than the just man, so he is also likely to be more dear to the gods than the just man. Thus, Socrates, they say that the life prepared among both gods and men for the unjust man is better than for the just.

ADEIMANTUS SUPPORTS GLAUCON (362D–367E)

After Glaucon said this, I intended to say something again in reply, but his brother Adeimantus said, Socrates, you surely do not think the argument has been sufficiently stated?

Why not? I said.

The thing which especially needs to be discussed has not been mentioned, he replied.

Well, the saying is, "Let brother help brother," I replied. So if Glaucon left something out, defend him. And yet, what he has said is already enough to throw me and make me unable to come to the aid of justice.

e   Nonsense, he said. But listen still: for we must also go through arguments opposite to those he put, in that they praise justice but condemn injustice, in order that what I take Glaucon to mean may be more clear.

Surely when fathers tell and advise their sons, and all who take care of
363a   anyone advise that it is necessary to be just, it is not justice itself they are praising but the good repute derived from it, in order that by seeming to be just, they may gain offices and marriages from the appearance, and all the other things Glaucon described a moment ago as accruing from a good reputation. They carry talk of appearances even further: for they throw in good standing with gods with an ungrudging plenty of blessings to relate, which
b   they say gods give to pious men, as noble Hesiod and Homer claim. Hesiod says that for just men, the gods cause the very oak trees "to bear acorns in the topmost branches and swarms of bees in the middle, and their wool-laden sheep carry the weight of soft fleeces," and many other goods of the sort. Homer says something similar too: "When some blameless and god-fearing king upholds justice, the black earth bears him wheat and barley, his
c   trees are heavy with fruit, his flocks increase, the sea gives fish."[1] Musaeus and his son provide more jocund blessings from the gods to the righteous: for in their story they lead them to the place of the dead, and lay them down crowned with garlands at a banquet prepared for the pious, and then have them pass the whole of time drinking, as though they thought the fairest reward of virtue was an everlasting drunk. Others stretch divine rewards even
d   further: for they say that the pious and oath-keeping man leaves behind children and children's children and a race that will never fail. This and other things of this sort is their encomium on justice. On the other hand,

---

1. *Odyssey* XIX 109–112. The text departs by omission from the received text of Homer, which was not settled until Hellenistic times.

they plunge unrighteous sinners in the place of the dead into something they call mud, and make them carry water in a sieve, and lead them into ill repute while still alive. They tell of every punishment for the unjust which Glaucon ascribed to just men who seem unjust, but they have nothing else to tell. So this is the praise and blame for each of the two.

e

In addition, Socrates, consider another form of story told about justice and injustice, stated both privately and by poets. For they all with a single voice hymn temperance and justice as noble though difficult and irksome, but intemperance and injustice as pleasant and easily possessed, shameful only in appearance and by law and convention. They say that what is unjust is for the most part more profitable than what is just; they count as happy wicked men grown rich and otherwise powerful, and they are cheerfully willing to honor them in public and private, but they despise and look down on those who are in any way weak and poor, though agreeing that they are better men than the others. Most astonishing of all are the stories told about virtue and the gods, namely, that gods distribute misfortune and a bad life to many good men, an opposite apportionment to their opposites. Mendicant seers come to the rich man's door and persuade him that it is possible, with divine power provided by sacrifices and incantations, to remove with pleasant ceremonies any result of his own or his ancestors' injustice. Will he ruin an enemy? He can harm him at little cost, they claim, just or unjust alike, by using certain charms and binding spells to move the gods to serve him. For all these tales they bring on poets as witnesses, some declaiming the easiness of vice, how

364a

b

c

> Evil is readily chosen, and in abundance; the road is easy
> and lies near at hand; the gods have placed much toil on
> the path to virtue,

d

and a road that is long and steep. Others offer Homer to testify that gods can be turned from their purpose by men, because he also says,

> Even the gods are moved by prayer; men turn them from
> wrath with sacrifice and humble prayers, burnt offer-

e   ings and libations, when someone transgresses and does
       wrong.[2]

365a   They produce a babble of books by Musaeus and Orpheus, children of
       the Moon and the Muses, so they claim, according to which they carry on
       their sacrificial liturgies, persuading not only private persons but whole
       cities that perhaps there really is, for people still alive, absolution and pu-
       rification from the results of injustice through sacrifices and sportive plea-
       sures, while for the dead there are what they call initiations, which relieve us
       of the evils there, though terrible things remain for those who do not sacri-
       fice.

       All this, dear Socrates, he said, such and so much of it, is told about
       virtue and vice, and the value men and gods assign them. What do we sup-
       pose hearing it does to the souls of gifted young men, who are well able, as
       it were, to skim over the surface of everything said and draw inferences
       from it about what sort of person one should be and how to proceed to lead
b   the best possible life. Reckoning from probabilities, he would say to him-
       self, in Pindar's words, "Is it by justice or by crooked deceit that I shall scale
       a higher fortress" and so live out my life in security? For according to what
       is told, it is of no benefit, only manifest toil and loss, for me to be really just
       if I do not also seem so; but if I am unjust and procure for myself an ap-
       pearance of justice, life is said to be divinely sweet. Now, since seeming, as
c   wise men assure me, "conquers even the truth" and is lord of happiness, I
       must turn to it wholly. I must draw round myself an illusory likeness of
       virtue as a front and a façade, but drag behind, "cunning and sly," the fox of
       most wise Archilochus.

       "But surely," someone says, "it is not easy always to escape detection, if
       you are bad." We will reply that nothing else of importance is without trou-
d   ble either. Nevertheless, if we are to be happy, we must proceed on this path
       and follow the tracks of the argument. We will organize secret societies and
       political clubs for purposes of concealment, and there are teachers of per-
       suasion to provide wisdom in public speaking and forensic oratory, from

---

2. *Iliad* IX 497–501. Not the modern text.

which in some cases we shall persuade, in others compel, so that we can overreach and not pay a penalty.

"But surely, it is possible neither to compel the gods nor to escape their notice." Well, if there are no gods, or if they have no concern for human affairs, we need not be concerned to escape their notice. But suppose there are gods and they have care for us. We know or have heard this from nowhere except the songs and genealogies of poets. But those same poets also tell that the gods can be persuaded and propitiated by sacrifices and humble prayers and votive offerings. We must accept both or neither. If both, we ought to do injustice and offer sacrifice from the proceeds. For if we are just, we will go unpunished by the gods but lose the profits of injustice, whereas if we are unjust, we will have those profits and, by prayerful begging when we transgress and sin, persuade them and escape unpunished.

"But will we not pay penalty in the place of the dead, ourselves or our children's children, for the wrong we did here?" No, dear friend, our calculating reasoner will reply: the rites of initiation and the absolving gods have great power, as the greatest cities attest, and the children of gods born as poets and prophets of the gods, who reveal that these things are so.

According to what argument, then, would we still choose justice before extreme injustice? If we possess injustice in company with a spurious decorum, we shall act reasonably in life and death among both gods and men, as the argument is put both by the multitude and the highest authorities.

From all that has been said, then, Socrates, how can anyone with any power of soul or money or body or family consent to honor justice, instead of laughing when he hears her praised? No doubt if someone can show that what we have said is false, if he sufficiently knows that justice is best, he will surely have much sympathy for unjust men, not anger. He knows that, except if someone by reason of a godlike nature spurns the doing of injustice, or abstains from it because he has gained knowledge, no one else is willingly just; rather, it is from cowardice or old age or some other weakness that men condemn the doing of injustice, for lack of power to do it. This is clearly so. For the first person among them to attain power is the first to do injustice, so far as he can.

There is no other cause for all this than the very thing that started the whole argument, and it impelled me and my brother here to say to you, Socrates, that what is surprising on the part of all of you who claim to praise justice, beginning with ancient heroes whose stories have survived down to men of the present time, is that no one has ever condemned injustice or praised justice except for the reputation and honors and rewards deriving from it. But as to what each of the two is in itself, and what it effects by its own power when present in the soul of its possessor, even if it escapes the notice of gods and men—no one has ever yet adequately explained, in poetry or prose, that injustice is the greatest evil the soul can contain within itself, justice the greatest good. For if all of you had so spoken from the beginning and convinced us from our youth, we would not now be on guard against each other's injustice; each of us would be his own best guardian, fearing that by doing injustice he might dwell with greatest evil.

This and perhaps still more than this, Socrates, might be said by Thrasymachus and anyone else about justice and injustice. For myself, I think it a vulgar inversion of the nature and power of the two, but I need not conceal that I am speaking as forcefully as I can because I want to hear the opposite side from you. So please do not only show us that justice is stronger than injustice, but show us what each of the two does in and of itself to him who has it, and that the one is evil, the other good. Take away the appearances, as Glaucon urged. For if you do not subtract from both sides the true appearance and add the false, we will claim you are praising not what is just but what seems so, condemning not what is unjust but what seems so, and you are really advising concealment of wrongdoing: you actually agree with Thrasymachus that the just is someone else's good, the advantage of the stronger, while the unjust is advantageous and profitable to oneself but without advantage to the weaker.

Since you have agreed that justice is among the greatest goods, which are worth possessing for their consequences but much more for themselves alone—like seeing, hearing, thinking and being healthy, and all other goods genuine in their own nature rather than by appearance—please then praise this very thing about justice: how justice in and of itself benefits him who has it, and injustice harms. Leave aside rewards and appearances for others to praise: I would accept that kind of praise of justice and censure of injustice from them, extolling and condemning the appearance and the wages, but I would not accept it from you unless you require me, because you have spent your whole life searching after nothing but this. So do not show us only that justice is stronger than injustice, but also what each of the two does in and of itself to him who has it, and, whether or not it escapes the notice of gods and men, that the one is good, the other evil.

e

JUSTICE WRIT LARGE IN THE STATE (367E-369B)

I listened. I had always admired the nature of Glaucon and Adeimantus, but at this point I was very pleased indeed, and said: Sons you are of that great and good man,[3] and the beginning of the elegy Glaucon's admirer composed when you distinguished yourselves at the Battle of Megara suits you well—"Sons of Ariston, godlike offspring of a glorious sire." That seems to me well said, my friends. For there really is something quite god-like about you, if you are not convinced that injustice is better than justice, and yet can speak this way in behalf of it. I do think you are truly not con-vinced. I infer it from the rest of your manner, though from your words alone I would mistrust you. But the more I trust you, the more I am at a loss what to do. For I do not know how I can help. I think I cannot. A sign of this is that you do not accept what I thought I showed in speaking to Thrasymachus, that justice is better than injustice. On the other hand, I cannot refuse to help either: For I fear it would be impious if I stood by when justice was disparaged, and did not come to her aid while I still had breath in my body and ability to speak. So I must help her as best I can.

368a

b

c

Well, Glaucon and the others begged me by all means to come to her aid and not abandon the argument, but rather to investigate thoroughly what justice and injustice each are, and what the truth is about their respective advantages.

So I said what I thought: The inquiry we are undertaking is not trivial,

3. Ariston, who was also Plato's father, mentioned by name in the first line of the poem to follow. Cf. *Philebus* 36d.

d   but requires sharp sight, as it appears to me. So since we are not clever, I said, I think we should make this sort of inquiry as though we were not very sharp-sighted and someone ordered us to read small letters at a distance. If one next realized that the same letters exist elsewhere, larger and on a larger surface, it would appear to be a stroke of luck, I think, to be able to read those first and in this way examine the smaller, to see if they happen to be the same.

e   Of course, said Adeimantus. But what do you see of this sort in the inquiry about justice, Socrates?

I will tell you, I said. Justice, we say, belongs to one man, but surely also to a whole city?

Of course, he replied.

Now, a city is greater than one man?

Yes, he said.

Perhaps then justice would be larger and easier to understand in what is greater. If you will, then, let us first seek to discover what it is in cities; af-
369a   terward, we will thus also examine it in the individual, looking for the likeness of the greater in the character of the less.

Why, I think that is an excellent suggestion, he said.

Then if we should watch a city come to be in discourse, I replied, we would also see the justice and the injustice of it come to be?

Perhaps, he replied.

So if that happened, there is hope that what we seek would be easier to see?

b   Yes, much easier.

Do you think we should try to go through with it? For I suspect it is no small task. Think about it.

I have, Adeimantus replied. Please continue.

DIVISION OF LABOR AND EXCHANGE (369B–372A)

Well, I suppose a city comes to be, I replied, because we are not each self-sufficient, but lack many things. Do you think there is any other principle for the founding of a city?

None whatever, he replied.

In this way, then, one man associates himself with another for one pur-   c
pose, another for another, because they need many things. And when many
people gather together in one dwelling place as partners and helpers, we call
this settlement a city. Not so?

Certainly.

But one man gives in exchange to another, if he does give something in
exchange or receives it, because he supposes it better for himself?

Certainly.

Come then, I replied, let us make a city in discourse from the beginning.
Our own need will make it, it seems.

Of course.

But surely the first and greatest of our needs is the provision of food for   d
the sake of existence and life.

Indeed so.

Second, then, shelter, and third, clothing and that sort of thing.

Yes.

Come then, I replied. How will the city suffice for this sort of provision?
One man a farmer, another a builder, someone else a weaver? Or shall we
also at this point add a shoemaker, or some other among those who minis-
ter to the needs of the body?

Of course.

So the minimally necessary city would consist of at least four or five
men?

It appears so.   e

Well then, is each one of them to contribute his own work for the common use of all? Must a single farmer, for example, provide food for four people, and spend four times the time and toil to provide food, and share it with
others? Or should he disregard them and produce a quarter of the food for
himself alone, in a quarter of the time, and spend the other three-quarters of   370a
his time producing his house, his cloak and his shoes, doing what is his own
by himself and for himself, without the trouble of sharing with others?

And Adeimantus said, Why, perhaps the former way is easier than the
other, Socrates.

It would not be at all surprising, I replied. It occurred to me even as you spoke that, in the first place, one man is not very like another; they differ in nature, one for one work, another for another.[4] Do you agree?

b   I do.

Well then, would one man do better when working at many arts, or when one man works at one art?

When one man works at one art, he replied.

Furthermore, I think it is also clear that if one allows the right time for a work to pass, it is ruined.

Yes.

Because I suppose what is done refuses to wait upon the leisure of the doer; the doer must attend to what is done, not treat it as a hobby.

c   Necessarily.

It follows that everything is produced in greater quantity, and better and more easily, when one man does one thing according to nature, and at the right time, at leisure from other activities.

Quite so.

Then more than four citizens will be required to provide the things we are speaking of, Adeimantus. For the farmer will not himself, it seems, make his own plow, if it is to be a good one, nor his hoe or any other farm implement. Nor again the builder: he also needs many tools. And so similarly the weaver and the shoemaker. Not so?

True.

Then carpenters and smiths, and many other craftsmen of the sort, will also become partners in our little city, and make it crowded.

Of course.

But it still would not be very big, even if we add cowherds and shepherds and other herdsmen, so that the farmers may have oxen for plowing, and the builders teams to use along with the farmers for hauling, and weavers and shoemakers hides and wool.

4. "Nature" here includes second nature, different natures produced by different training in different arts.

Yes, but it would not be such a little city either, he replied, with all this.

Then again, I replied, it is pretty nearly impossible to establish the city by itself, in a place where it will not need imports.

Yes.

So it will also need still others to bring it what it needs from another city.

Yes.

Furthermore, if the servant goes empty-handed, taking nothing which those others require from those who might provide what they need, he will come back empty-handed.

I think so.

Then they must make not only enough for themselves at home, but also enough, in the right number and kind, for those others of whom they stand in need.

Yes.

Then we will require more farmers and other craftsmen in our city.

Yes.

And specifically, surely, other servants for import and export. These are merchants, are they not?

Yes.

Then we will also need merchants.

Of course.

And if the trade takes place by sea, a whole crowd of others will be needed in addition, knowledgeable in nautical matters.

Quite a crowd.

What about within the city itself? How will they exchange with each other what they each produce? After all, that is why we made a community and founded a city.

Clearly, he replied, they will buy and sell.

Then we will have a marketplace, and currency as a token for the sake of exchange.

Of course.

Suppose then the farmer or some other craftsman brings something which he makes to market, but does not arrive at the same time as those

371a

b

c

who need to exchange with him. Will he sit in the marketplace idled from his own art?

Not at all, he replied. There are people who see it and appoint themselves for this service. In rightly ordered cities, they are pretty much the weakest in body, and useless for doing any other work. They must wait around in the marketplace, exchanging money for the goods of those who need to sell, goods again for the money of all who need to buy.

So this need produces shopkeepers in our city, I replied. Or do we not call shopkeepers those who set up in the marketplace to buy and sell, but merchants those who travel from city to city?

Of course.

Still again, I suppose, there are certain other servants who would scarcely be worth admitting to our society for their intellect, but have strength of body sufficient for purposes of labor. They sell the use of their strength, and since the price is called wages, I suppose they are called wage-laborers. Not so?

Of course.

Then wage-laborers also go to make up the complement of a city, it seems.

I think so.

Well then, Adeimantus, has our city at this point grown so that it's complete?

Perhaps.

Where in it then would justice and injustice be? And with which element among those we have considered does it come to be present?

I cannot think, Socrates, he said, unless in some need those elements themselves have relative to each other.

Why, perhaps you are right, I replied. And it is a question we must face and not shirk.

THE LUXURIOUS STATE (372A–373D)

(Socrates continues) First then let us consider how those who have been so provided will live. They will make bread and wine and clothes and shoes, will they not? And build themselves houses, and in summer heat they will work mostly without clothes and shoes, but in winter they will be adequately clothed and shod. They will be nourished by preparing meal from barley and flour from wheat, kneading the one and baking the other, and they will serve noble cakes and loaves on some arrangement of rushes or clean leaves. They will recline on couches made from boughs of yew and myrtle, and they themselves and their children will feast and drink their wine crowned with wreaths and singing hymns to the gods, delighting in each other's company, not producing children beyond their substance for fear of poverty or war.

b

Glaucon interrupted: You imagine them feasting, it seems—on dry bread?

c

You're right, I replied. I forgot that they will also have relishes—salt, clearly, and olives and cheese. And they will boil root and leaf vegetables of the kind cooked in country stews. And for dessert we will serve them figs and chickpeas and beans, and they will roast myrtle berries and acorns by the fire, and sip their wine in moderation. And in this way passing their lives in peace accompanied by good health, as is likely, they will die in old age and hand on another life of the same sort to their offspring.

d

And he said, But surely, If you were founding a city of pigs, Socrates, what else would you feed them but this?

But how should it be, then, Glaucon? I replied.

What is customary, he said. If they are not going to be uncomfortable, I expect they will lie on couches and dine from tables, and have relishes and desserts as people do now.

Very well, I replied, I understand. We are considering not only how a city comes to be, it seems, but also a luxurious city. Well, maybe that's not all bad; for perhaps we will see how justice and injustice take root in cities by examining a city of this sort. Now, the genuine city is I think as we have described—a city in sound health, as it were. But on the other hand, nothing prevents us, if you wish, from also viewing a city inflamed with fever. Some people, it seems, will be dissatisfied with these things and this way of life. Couches will be added, and tables and other kinds of furniture, and relishes too, and myrrh and incense and courtesans and tarts—all kinds of

e

373a

each of them. In particular, the things we mentioned at first, houses and clothes and shoes, will no longer be limited to what is minimally necessary, but painting and embroidery will be set in motion, and gold and ivory and all that sort of thing possessed. Not so?

b   Yes, he said.

Then we must again make the city larger? For this healthy city is no longer sufficient, but must at this point be swollen in bulk and multitude with things which do not exist in cities for the sake of what is necessary. Hunters and fisherman, for example, and imitators, many dealing with figure and color, many with music and literature—poets and their assistants, reciters and actors and dancers and producers, and manufacturers of all

c   sorts of artifacts, especially for female adornment. In particular, we will need more servants. Or does it not seem we will need tutors and wet nurses, governesses, ladies' maids, barbers, and again, confectioners and cooks? Still further, we will need swineherds; they were not present in the earlier city because there was no need, but they will be needed in this one, and there will also be need for a host of other animals, if people eat them.

d   Of course.

Now, if people lead this sort of life, we will have much more need of doctors than before.

Of course.

WAR AND THE GUARDIANS (373D–374D)

And the territory sufficient to sustain them then will now be insufficient and too small. Do you agree?

Yes, he said.

So we must slice off some of our neighbors' land, if we are going to have enough for plow and pasture—and they in turn must take ours, if they also give themselves over to unlimited acquisition of wealth, overstepping the bounds of what is necessary.

e   Yes, Socrates, he said.

The next thing is, Glaucon, we will be at war. Or how will it be?

That way, he said.

Let us not yet say whether war works an evil or a good, I replied, but only this much: we have discovered an origin for war in those things from which evils both public and private especially arise for cities, when they do arise.

Certainly.

Then a still larger city is required, my friend—not by a little but by a whole army, which will go forth to do battle against invaders in defense of our whole substance and the people we just now described. 374a

Really? he replied. Do they not themselves suffice?

No, I replied, not if we made all the right agreements when forming the city. We agreed, if you recall, that it is impossible for one man to practice many arts well.

True, he said.

Then does not the kind of contest involved in warfare seem to be a mat- b
ter of art? I replied.

Very much so, he said.

Now, is shoemaking more important than the art of war?

Hardly.

But we did not let the shoemaker try to be a farmer or weaver or builder at the same time, but a shoemaker, in order that the work of shoemaking might be done well for us. Similarly, we gave each single one of the others one work for which he was naturally suited and at which he was to work throughout life, at leisure from other activities and not letting slip the right time for doing c
it well. Is it not then of utmost importance that work be done well in matters pertaining to war? Is warfare so easy that any farmer at the same time will be a soldier, and make shoes and practice any other art, whereas not one person would be competent at backgammon or dice if he did not practice it from childhood, but treated it as a hobby? Will anyone who picks up a shield or any d
other of the weapons and tools of war forthwith be competent to fight in heavy armor or any other kind of warfare? Are there any other tools which will produce a craftsman or athlete merely by being picked up, or prove useful to someone who has not acquired knowledge and had sufficient practice?

They would be valuable tools indeed, he replied.

THE GUARDIANS' NATIVE DISPOSITION (374E–376E)

e   Then in as much as the work of the Guardians is of greatest importance, I replied, it would by so much require utmost leisure from other activities, and again, the greatest amount of art and training.

Yes, I think so, he replied.

Does it also require a nature suited to the occupation itself?

Of course.

So it would be our task, it seems, to pick out, if we can, which and what sorts of nature are suitable for guardianship of a city.

Indeed.

Really then, I replied, we have perhaps taken on ourselves no mean task. Nevertheless, it is not to be shirked, so far as ability permits.

375a   No, he said.

Do you suppose then, I replied, in respect to guardianship, that there is any difference in nature between a well-bred young pup and a well-born young lad?

How do you mean?

For example, each of the two must be sharp of perception and quick in pursuit of what he perceives, and strong too, if he must subdue what he has caught.

Why, they require all this, he said.

Yes, and courage too, if they are to fight well.

Of course.

Will a horse or dog or any other animal be courageous if it is not spir-
b   ited? Or have you not realized how irresistible and invincible spirit is? Its presence makes every soul fearless and indomitable in everything.

Yes.

It is clear then what bodily characteristics the Guardian must have.

Yes.

And further, those of his soul—at least that it be spirited.

That too.

Then if their natures are of this sort, Glaucon, I replied, how will they not be savage with one another and the other citizens?

Really, it is not easy to see, he replied.

Nevertheless, they must be hard on their enemies but gentle with their   c
friends. Otherwise, they will not need to wait around for others to destroy
them; they will be beforehand in doing it themselves.

True, he said.

What shall we do, then? I replied. Where shall we find a character at
once gentle and high spirited? For gentle nature is surely opposite to spirited.

It appears so.

A nature deprived of either would never become a good guardian. Yet
they seem incompatible, and thus then it follows that a good guardian is
impossible.

Very likely, he said.   d

I was at a loss, and reflected on what had gone before. We are rightly perplexed, my friend, I said, for we have departed from the image we set before
ourselves.

How do you mean?

We did not realize that there are, after all, natures which have these opposites, of a sort we did not consider.

Where?

One might see it even in other animals, but especially in the animal we
compared to the guardian. For you surely know that it is the natural char-   e
acter of well-bred dogs to be as gentle as possible to those they know and are
accustomed to, but the opposite to those they do not know.

Yes, certainly.

So it is possible, I replied, and the sort of guardian we are seeking is not
contrary to nature.

It seems not.

Now, in addition to being spirited, do you think our future guardian will
in nature still further need to be a philosopher?

How so? he said. I don't understand.   376a

You see it even in dogs, I replied. Indeed, it is worth admiring in the beast.

What's that?

The dog is roused to anger at seeing someone he does not know, without ever having suffered any evil; but he welcomes someone he knows even if he has never experienced anything good at the other's hands. Have you never yet wondered at that?

I had not paid much attention to it before this, he said. But clearly, they do act that way.

But surely this shows a fine trait of his nature, and that it is truly philo-
b   sophical.

How so?

Because, I replied, he distinguishes a friendly from an unfriendly face on no other basis than having learned to know the one but not the other. And yet, if he can distinguish what is his own and what is alien on the basis of knowledge and ignorance, how would he not be a lover of learning?

He must be, he replied.

Again, I said, love of learning and love of wisdom are the same?
c   Yes, he said.

Then we may confidently assume also in man, that if he is to be gentle toward his own and those he knows, he must by nature be a philosopher and lover of learning?

Let's assume it, he said.

Then anyone who is to be a good and noble Guardian of our city will be a lover of wisdom, and spirited and quick and strong in nature.

Most assuredly, he said.

So that is their natural disposition. But how will they be raised and edu-
d   cated? Is it helpful to examine the question relative to discerning the object of our whole inquiry: how justice and injustice come to be present in a city? We must not curtail argument, nor yet draw it out at length.

And Glaucon's brother said, I certainly think this inquiry is helpful in re-spect to that.

Then we surely must not give it up, dear Adeimantus, I replied, even if it happens to be rather lengthy.

No.

Come then. As though telling a story at our leisure, we will educate these men in discourse.
e   Why, so we must.

EDUCATION IN MUSIC AND GYMNASTIC (376E–378E)

What education, then? Or is it hard to find better than what has been discovered by lengthy time? Gymnastic for the body, music and poetry for the soul.

Yes.

Then shall we begin education in music and poetry earlier than gymnastic?

Of course.

You assume that verse belongs to music and poetry, don't you?[5]

I do.

And verse is of two forms, true and false?

Yes.

Then they must be educated in both, but in the false first. 377a

I don't understand what you mean, he said.

You don't understand, I replied, that we first tell children stories? Taken as a whole they are surely false, but there is also truth in them. We use stories with small children even earlier than gymnastic.

That's so.

That's why I said that music and poetry must be taken up before gymnastic.

And rightly, he said.

You know that the beginning of every work is most important, especially b for whatever is young and tender. For it is then most easily shaped, and takes the pattern which one may wish to impose on it.

Indeed so.

Then shall we thus lightly permit the children to hear any chance stories anyone chances to invent, and to take into their souls opinions for the most part contrary to those we think they ought to have when they grow up?

By no means.

First then, it seems, we must supervise the storytellers, accepting what c

5. *mousike:* Any art over which the Muses preside; the periphrasis "music and literature," if awkward, is at least approximately accurate. Poetry was often sung to the accompaniment of instruments.

they do well and rejecting what they don't. We'll persuade nurses and mothers to tell the children only what is acceptable, and to shape their souls with their stories even more than their bodies with their hands. Most of what they tell now has to be discarded.

Why? he said.

In the greater stories we also see the less, I replied, for surely greater and less are the same in pattern and have the same effect. Don't you think so?

d   No doubt, he said. But I don't understand what you mean by greater.

Those Hesiod and Homer told us, and the other poets, I said. For they told people stories and composed falsehoods, and still do.

Of what sort? he replied. And what fault do you find with them?

What should first and most be faulted, I replied, especially if the falsehood is ugly.

What's that?

e   Suppose someone misrepresents the nature of gods and heroes in discourse, like a painter drawing a picture nothing like what he meant to draw.

In fact, he said, it's right to find fault with that sort of thing. But what exactly do we mean?

The first and greatest falsehood, I replied, and concerning matters of utmost importance, is the ugly lie that Uranus did what Hesiod says, and again, how Cronus punished him. And next, the deeds of Cronus and his sufferings at the hands of his son. Even if they were true, I think they should not thus lightly be told to thoughtless youth; they are best passed over in silence. But if they must be told, the fewest possible should hear, as in a mystery, after sacrificing not a pig but some rare and unaffordable victim, so that the least number possible may hear.

In fact, he replied, those are hard stories.

b   Yes, and not to be told in our city, Adeimantus, I said. Nor should a young man hear that he would do nothing extraordinary in committing the extreme of injustice, nor again, that by going to all lengths to punish a father for injustice, he would only be doing what the first and greatest of gods has done.

No, by Zeus, he replied, I don't think such stories are even fit to be told.

No, I replied, nor in general that gods war on gods and plot against each   c
other and fight—at least if we're to have Guardians who consider it dis-
graceful lightly to quarrel with one another—for it is not true. Still less
should stories of the battles of gods and giants be told to them or pictured
in embroidery, or other enmities of gods and heroes, many and various, toward their own kith and kin. But if somehow we can persuade them that
not a single citizen ever quarreled with another, nor is it pious, that's the
sort of thing old men and women should tell to children from the very first,   d
and as the children grow older, the poets also must be compelled to keep
their stories close to this. But as for Hera put in fetters by her son, or Hephaestus hurled from Heaven by his father for trying to save his mother from
a beating, and all the battles among gods which Homer describes—they are
not to be admitted into our city, whether they are meant allegorically or literally. For the child cannot tell the difference between what is allegorical
and what is not, but the opinions he takes in at that age are likely to become   e
indelibly fixed. For which reason, then, we must count it of utmost importance that the stories they first hear should have the best possible effect relative to virtue.

THE GOODNESS OF THE GODS (378E–383C)

Yes, that is reasonable, he said. But suppose someone also asked us just what
stories these are. How would we reply?

And I said, Adeimantus, we are not at present poets, you and I, but   379a
founders of a city. It is up to founders to know the patterns within which
the poets must tell stories, and beyond which they are not permitted to go,
but not, surely, to compose their stories for them.

Right, he said. But exactly what are these patterns in matters of theol-
ogy?

Something of this sort, I replied. Whether in epic or lyric or tragedy, the
god must always be represented as he actually is.

Yes.

Now, the god is really good, and must be so described?

b   Of course.

Furthermore, nothing among good things is harmful?

I think not.

Now, does what is not harmful do harm?

Of course not.

Does what does not harm do anything evil?

Nor that.

What does nothing evil would not be responsible for any evil?

How could it?

Again, the good is beneficial?

Yes.

Therefore, responsible for well-being?

Yes.

So the good is not responsible for all things, but responsible for things that are good; it is not responsible for evils.

c   Exactly so, he said.

So the god, I replied, since good, would not be responsible for all things, as the multitude claims, but responsible for few things among men and not responsible for many. For good things are much fewer among us than evils; and no one else should be held responsible for good things, but it is necessary to seek other causes of evils, not the god.[6]

I think that's very true, he said.

d   Then this error about the gods, I replied, must not be accepted from Homer or any other poet. There is ignorance and folly in his saying that "two urns stand at the threshold of Zeus, filled with destinies, the one of evils, the other of goods," and that him to whom Zeus gives a mixture of both "meets now with evil, now again with good," while him to whom Zeus does not give the mixture but the other unmixed, "him evil drives over the

e   shining earth," or that Zeus is for us "dispenser both of goods and evils." We won't approve if anyone claims that Pandarus's violation of oaths and

6. It will be observed that the expressions "god," "gods," and "the god" are used interchangeably here and throughout the *Republic*. The reference is to the divine generally, unless some particular god is mentioned, and there is no implication of monotheism in the use of the singular.

treaties was brought about by Athena and Zeus; nor strife and contention among gods by Themis and Zeus. Nor again are young people to be allowed to hear, as Aeschylus tells, that "god implants guilt in mortals when he would utterly destroy a house." On the contrary, if someone composes a poem about the sufferings of Niobe, where those lines occur, or about the calamities of the house of Pelops or the Trojan War or anything of the sort, he must not be allowed to say that they are works of god; or, if of god, he must find for them some such account as we are now seeking: he must tell how what the god wrought was just and good, and how they benefited from being punished. The poet is not allowed to tell that those who pay a just penalty are wretched, and that the doer was a god. But if he should say the bad were wretched because they were in need of punishment, and that in paying just penalty they are benefited by the god, it is permitted. But to say that god, who is good, is cause of evils to anyone, must be contended against in every way. No one is to say this in his own city, if it is to be well governed, nor is anyone, young or old, to hear it in verse or prose. Saying it, if it were said, is neither pious, nor of advantage to us, nor in harmony with itself.

I vote with you to approve this law, he said.

This then, I replied, would be one of the laws and patterns within which those who speak about gods will need to speak, and authors will need to compose: the god is not responsible for all things, but for good things.

A very satisfactory law, he said.

What about this as a second? Do you think the god is a magician, able to reveal himself intentionally from time to time in different characters, sometimes changing his own form into a multitude of shapes, sometimes deluding us into thinking he has done so? Or is the god simple, and of all things least likely to depart from his own character?

I can't now say, he said.

Then what about this: If something passes from its own character, must it not necessarily be changed by itself or by another?

Yes.

Now, what is in the best condition is least altered and moved by another?

380a

b

c

d

e

A body by food and drink and toil, for example, and every plant by heat of the sun and winds and similar influences—are not the healthiest and strongest least altered?

381a   Of course.

Wouldn't the wisest and most courageous soul be least disturbed and altered by external influence?

Yes.

So too surely for all that is compound—furniture and houses and clothes. By the same account, those which are well made and in good condition are least altered by time and other affections.

That's so.

b   In general, then, what is well constituted by nature or art or both admits least change by another.

It seems so.

Again, the god and what belongs to the god is in every way best.

Of course.

So the god would scarcely get a multitude of shapes in this way.

No, surely not.

But would he change and alter himself?

Clearly so, he said, if indeed he is altered.

Then he changes himself to what is better and more beautiful, or to what is worse and more ugly than himself?

c   Necessarily to what is worse, he said, if indeed he is altered; for we surely will not say that the god is lacking in beauty or virtue.

You are quite right, I replied. And this being so, Adeimantus, do you think that anyone among gods or men would willingly make himself worse in any way?

Impossible, he said.

So it is also impossible for a god to be willing to alter himself, I replied. Rather, it seems, since they are most beautiful and as good as possible, each of them ever abides simply in his own form.

Quite necessarily, it seems to me, he said.

d   Then my friend, I replied, let no poet tell us that "gods take on all sorts

of disguises, visiting our cities in the likeness of wandering strangers." No
one may tell falsehoods about Proteus and Thetis, nor introduce Hera in
tragedies or elsewhere disguised as a priestess begging alms "for the life-giv-
ing children of Inachus, Argive river." And there are many other such falsehoods they must not tell. Nor again are mothers to be persuaded to scare   e
their children with bad stories—namely, how some gods roam abroad at
night in the guise of many strangers from many lands—in order that they
may not at the same time speak ill of gods and make their children more
cowardly.

No, he said.

But do the gods themselves, I replied, even though they are not such as
to change, use deception and magic to make us think they appear in many
different forms?

Perhaps, he said.

Really? I replied. Would a god be willing to deceive in word or deed by   382a
putting forth a false appearance?

I don't know, he replied.

You don't know, I replied, that all gods and men hate, if it is possible to
say it, what is truly false?

What do you mean? he said.

This, I replied. Everyone refuses to be willingly deceived in the most au-
thoritative part of himself and about the most determinative things; he especially fears to have falsehood there beyond all else.

I still don't understand, he replied.

Because you think I mean something deep and mysterious, I said. I only   b
mean that no one would choose to be deceived and in error in their soul
about things which are, or be ignorant and have and hold what is false there.
They would least accept falsehood and especially hate it in that quarter.

Yes, very much so, he said.

Moreover, it would be quite correct to call what I just now mentioned,
namely, ignorance in the soul of him who is deceived, true falsehood. After
all, an imitation in words of an affection in the soul is a mere image consequent on it, not quite falsehood unmixed. Not so?

c   Of course.

But the real falsehood is hated not only by gods but also by men.

I think so.

What about falsehood in words? When and for whom is it useful, so as not to be worthy of hatred? Isn't it against enemies, and so-called friends, when through madness or some folly they undertake to do something evil, and it then becomes useful as a medicine for averting evil? And in the myths

d   of which we were just now speaking: because we don't know the truth about ancient times, we make the false as much as possible like the true and thus render it useful?

That's quite so, he replied.

How then is falsehood useful to the god? Would he make false likenesses through not knowing the past?

That's ridiculous, he said.

So there's nothing in god of the false poet?

I think not.

e   But would he deceive his enemies out of fear?

Of course not.

Or because of foolishness or madness of friends?

No one foolish or mad is loved by the gods, he said.

So it's not possible that god should deceive for this reason.

No.

So what is spiritual and divine is in every way without falsehood.

Completely so, he said.

So the god is altogether simple and true in word and in deed, and he does not himself change nor deceive others, either by false appearances, or words, or by sending of signs, awake or in dream.

383a   So it also appears to me, now that you say it, he said.

You agree, then, I said, that this is a second pattern within which it is necessary to speak and write about gods: since they are not magicians, they do not change themselves, nor mislead us by falsehoods in word or in deed?

I do agree.

So we'll praise Homer for many things, but not for the sending of that

dream to Agamemnon from Zeus;[7] nor Aeschylus, when he has Thetis tell
how Apollo sang at her wedding and celebrated the happy fortune of her   b
child,

> He predicted my happiness in my children, whose days
> were to be many and unacquainted with disease; and in
> triumph-strain that cheered my soul, he praised my lot,
> blest of the gods. But he who raised this song, present at
> my marriage feast, himself hath slain my son.

When someone says things of that sort about gods, we will be angry: we will   c
not give him a chorus nor allow teachers to use him for the education of the
young, if our Guardians are to become god-fearing and divine in the highest degree possible for man.

I completely agree to these patterns, he said, and would use them as laws.

---

7. *Iliad* II 1–34. In the dream, Zeus promises Agamemnon immediate success if he attacks Troy:
the promise is false.

Book III

386a   Such then, it seems, is what should and should not be heard about gods from childhood upward, I replied, if they are to honor the gods and their parents, and count friendship with one another important.

Yes, I think that is right, he said.

But what if they are to be courageous? Should not the things they are told make them least afraid of death? Or do you believe anyone having in himself this fear could ever become courageous?

b   Certainly not, he replied.

If someone believes that the place of the dead exists, and that it is terrible, do you think he will be unafraid of death, and choose death in battle before defeat and slavery?

Hardly.

It seems then we must undertake to supervise these tales and those who tell them, and require them not so heedlessly to speak ill about the place of the dead, but offer praise, because what they are saying is not true, nor will it benefit those who are to be warriors.

c   Yes, he said.

70

Then beginning with this verse, I replied, we'll expunge all such lines as these:

> I would rather be on earth as the wretched hireling of a
> landless man, than be king over all the dead.

And:

> Graves lie open to men and immortals, ghastly and
> noisome; the very gods shudder before them.

And: d

> Alas! In the House of the Dead there is a soul and a like-
> ness, but no wits in it at all.

And:

> He alone thinks, the rest are flitting shadows.

And:

> His soul fluttered from his limbs and descended to the
> place of the dead, mourning its doom, youth and man-
> hood left behind.

And: 387a

> The soul went below the earth like smoke, gibbering.

And:

> As bats in the depth of an awful cave flit and gibber
> whenever one of them, as they cling together, falls from
> the roof-suspended cluster of them, so they went gibber-
> ing too.

We will beg Homer and the other poets not to be angry if we expunge these   b
lines and all others like them, not because they are not poetical and pleasant
for most people to hear, but because, the more poetical they are, the less

they should be heard by children and by men who must be free, and fear slavery more than death.

Quite so.

Still again, those terrible and frightening names must also all be cast aside—the "Wailing Rivers of Cocytus" and "Hateful Streams of Styx" and "the infernals" and "the withered ones," and other names of this pattern which make all who hear them shudder. Maybe they're good for something else, but we are afraid our Guardians may become overheated from such shivering as this, and become softer than we need them to be.[1]

Yes, he said, and we'd rightly be afraid.

So they should be removed?

Yes.

The opposite pattern is to be followed, in prose and verse?

Clearly so.

And so we will also remove the lamentations and piteous wailings of distinguished men?

Necessarily, he said, given what has gone before.

Consider then whether or not we do right to remove them, I replied. We claim, surely, that a good man will not believe death terrible for another good man who is his friend?

Yes.

So he would not grieve for him, thinking he had suffered something terrible.

Of course not.

Again, we also said that the good man is especially self-sufficient relative to living well, and surpasses the rest in having least need of another.

True, he said.

So to be deprived of a son or a brother, or possessions or anything else of the sort, is least terrible to him.

Yes.

So he also grieves least when such misfortune befalls him, and bears it as lightly as possible.

---

1. The metaphor is from tempering iron.

Of course.

So we would be right to remove the sad lamentations of famous men, and give them instead to women and not even women of the better sort, and the baser sort of men, in order that those whom we claim to be raising   388a
for guardianship of the land may disdain behavior like this.

Yes, he said.

Again then, we will require Homer and other poets not to describe Achilles, son of a goddess,

> lying now on his side, now on his back, and now again
> on his face,

but then standing upright,

> wandering distraught on the shore of the salt sea.

Or as pouring ashes on his head with both hands, and all the other weeping   b
and wailing Homer describes; or Priam, a near kinsman of the gods, begging,

> wallowing in dung, entreating each man by name.

Still further, we'll ask them not to make gods lament and say,   c

> Woe to me, unhappy. Woe that I bore the best of
> children to my sorrow.

And if they are to describe gods, they will not dare to represent the greatest of gods in a manner so unlike himself that he says,

> Alas! with my own eyes I see a man dear to me being
> pursued around the wall; my heart grieves for Hector.

And:

> Woe to me that Sarpedon, dearest of men, is fated to be
> slain by Patroclus, Menoetius's son.

For if our young men seriously listen to such stuff, dear Adeimantus, and   d
do not laugh it to scorn as unworthily said, they would scarcely think it un-

worthy of themselves as men, or be embarrassed if it even occurred to them to say or do such things. On the contrary, they would not be at all ashamed to give way and chant many a lament over small sufferings.

e   Very true, he said.

Yes, but the argument just indicated that this must not be—an argument which must be trusted, until someone persuades us with a better one.

I agree.

Nor again should they be fond of laughter. For when someone gives way to violent laughter, it usually provokes a violent reaction.

I think so, he said.

So it is unacceptable to portray men who are worth anything, much less a god, as overpowered by laughter.

389a   I agree, he replied.

Then we won't accept such things as this from Homer about gods:

> Unquenchable laughter arose among the blessed gods,
> as they saw Hephaestus bustling from room to room.

That's unacceptable, by your account.

b   Call it mine if you will, he said: it is surely not to be accepted.

PRIMARY EDUCATION: TRUTHFULNESS (389B–D)

Again, truth must be counted of utmost importance. For if we were right just now, and falsehood really is useless to gods, and useful to men only as a form of medicine, it is clear that such a thing must be administered by physicians, and not touched by laymen.

Yes, he said.

Then it belongs to the rulers of the city—if indeed to anyone—to deceive enemies or citizens for the benefit of the city. No one else is to touch

c   such a thing. On the contrary, it is an even greater sin for a private citizen to lie to such rulers as these, we shall claim, than for a sick man to lie to his doctor, or an athlete not to tell the truth about his bodily condition to a trainer, or a seaman to say what is not to a pilot about the ship and its crew, or how he himself or any of his fellow sailors is faring.

Very true, he said.

So if the ruler catches anyone else in the city lying, "among the crafts-   d
men, prophet or physician or carpenter," he will punish him for introducing a practice as subversive and destructive to a city as it is to a ship.

Yes, he replied, if deeds follow on word.

PRIMARY EDUCATION: TEMPERANCE (389D–392A)

Again, will not our young people need temperance or self-control?

Of course.

For the majority, temperance mostly consists in obeying rulers, and ruling themselves in the pleasures of food and drink and sex?

I think so.   e

Then I suppose we'll approve the words of Homer's Diomedes:

> My friend, keep silent, and be persuaded by my story.

And what follows:

> The Achaeans, breathing valor, went silently in fear of
> their commanders.

And everything else of the sort.

Yes, excellent.   390a

Then again, what about this:

> You're a wine-bag, with the eyes of a dog, and the heart
> of a deer.

And what about the lines that follow, and all other brash insolence in poetry
or prose, offered by private persons to their rulers?

They're not well said.

No, for in respect to temperance, I think, they're not fit for the young to
hear. But it's hardly to be wondered at if they provide some other kind of
pleasure. Or how does it appear to you?

Thus, he said.

b   Again, it is wrong to make the wisest of men speak as though he thought it the finest thing in the world when,

> Beside them were tables loaded with bread and meat,
> and the cupbearer draws wine from the mixing bowl and
> carries it to fill the cups.

Do you think it's suitable, relative to his own self-control, for a young person to hear this? Or this:

> It is most pitiable to die by hunger, and meet one's doom.

c   Or how Zeus, awake and alone while other gods and men slept, readily forgot everything else he'd planned because he wanted sex, and was so struck by seeing Hera that he refused to go into the bedroom but wanted her right there on the floor, and said he was even more possessed by desire than when they first had intercourse, "unknown to their dear parents"? Or again, how Ares and Aphrodite were chained together by Hephaestus in other circumstances of the same sort.

      No, by Zeus, he replied, it does not appear suitable to me.

d   Yet surely, I replied, if there are examples of steadfast endurance, expressed and done by distinguished men against all odds, they ought to be seen and heard. For instance:

> He struck his chest and rebuked his heart, saying,
> Endure, my heart. You've suffered worse than this.

Quite so, he said.

      Nor are our people allowed to be bribe takers or money lovers.

e   By no means.

      Then they are not to sing that, "Gifts persuade gods, gifts persuade dread kings." Nor is Phoenix, the teacher of Achilles, to be praised for advising Achilles to defend the Achaeans only if he received gifts, and not to put aside his wrath without them. Nor shall we think fit to agree that Achilles himself was such a money lover that he accepted gifts from Agamemnon and, again, refused to release a dead body without ransom.

It's surely not just to praise that sort of thing, he said.   391a

No, I replied. Out of regard for Homer, I shrink from suggesting that it is unholy to say this about Achilles, or be persuaded when others say it—or to believe that he told Apollo:

> You've harmed me, Far-Striker, most malignant of gods;
> I'd punish you, if I but had power.

And how he disobeyed the river Scamander, a god, and was ready to fight it.   b
And again, when he'd already consecrated them to Spercheius, another river, that he said,

> Let me give locks of my hair to the hero Patroclus to
> take with him.

Patroclus was a corpse, and it is not to be believed that Achilles did this. Again, we will deny that he repeatedly dragged Hector around the tomb of Patroclus, and butchered living captives on his funeral pyre—we'll refuse to say any of this is true. Nor will we allow our own children to be persuaded   c
that Achilles, child of a goddess and of Peleus, a most temperate man and a grandson of Zeus, and reared by the most wise Cheiron, was so filled with disturbance that he contained within himself two opposite diseases: a servile love of money, and an arrogant disregard of gods and men.

You're right, he said.

Then let us not be persuaded ourselves, I replied, nor allow it to be said, that Theseus son of Poseidon and Peirithus son of Zeus were thus moved to terrible rapes, nor that any other hero and child of a god ventured to do ter-   d
rible and impious deeds such as now are falsely told of them. Rather, let us compel the poets either to deny that these are their deeds or to deny that they are children of gods, but not to assert both, nor try to persuade our young men that gods may beget evils and that heroes are no better than men. For as we said before, this is neither holy nor true, for we showed,   e
surely, that it is impossible for evils to derive from gods.

Of course.

And moreover, harmful to those who hear them. For every one will have an excuse for being bad himself, if he is persuaded that such were and are the actions of,

> The kindred of the gods, close to Zeus, whose altar to
> Ancestral Zeus, their sire, is high on Mount Ida, and in
> their veins the divine blood has yet to fade.

That is why it is necessary to put a stop to such stories: for fear that they may engender a hearty proclivity to wickedness in our young men.

392a   Quite so, he said.

PRIMARY EDUCATION: JUSTICE NOT YET ASCERTAINABLE (392A–C)

Well then, I replied, what form of story still remains to be marked off, to be told and not told? For we have described how one must speak of gods and demigods and heroes, and those in the place of the dead.

Certainly.

Then what remains is stories about men?

Clearly so.

But it is impossible for us to settle this, at least at present, my friend.

Why?

b   Because we shall say, I presume, that poets and prose writers therefore speak badly about what is most important for men, claiming that many men are happy but unjust, or just but wretched, and that the doing of injustice is profitable if it escapes detection, while justice is another's good and one's own loss. We shall forbid them to say this sort of thing, and order them to tell the opposite both in song and story. Don't you think so?

I'm sure of it, he said.

Then if you agree that I'm right, I'll claim you have agreed about what we have long been seeking?

A fair assumption, he said.

c   Then we will come to agreement about what stories must be told about men only when we have discovered what justice is, and how by nature it profits him who has it, whether he seems just or not.

Very true, he said.

LITERARY FORM AND IMITATION (392C–394D)

Let this then end our discussion of content. I think we must next consider diction or style. We shall then have fully considered what is to be said, and how it is to be said.[2]

Adeimantus replied, I don't understand what you mean.

Yes, but surely you must, I said. Perhaps you may tell better from this: Is   d
not everything said in stories or poetry a narrative of events, past, present, or future?

Yes, what else? he said.

Then does it not proceed either by simple narrative, or through imitation, or both?

This I need to understand more clearly too, he replied.

I seem to be a ridiculously unclear teacher, I replied. Well, like those   e
without ability in speaking, I will not try to make clear to you what I mean in general, but break off a part. Tell me: You know the first lines of the *Iliad*, where the poet says Chryses begged Agamemnon to release his daughter, but Agamemnon was angry, and Chryses, when it did not happen, cursed the Achaeans?

I do.   393a

Then you know that up to and including these lines,

> And prayed to all the Achaeans, and especially Atreus's
> two sons, marshals of the people,

the poet himself is speaking, and does not even try to suggest that anyone else is talking except himself; but next, he speaks as if he himself were Chryses, and does his best to make us think it is not Homer speaking but the   b
priest, an old man. And he composed nearly all the rest of the narrative about what happened at Troy that way, and what was done at Ithaca and the whole of the *Odyssey*.

Of course, he said.

---

2. 392c, 398b. Compare 329c, 394c. I am much indebted, here and in what follows, to Alan C. Bowen, *Plato's Criticism of Harmonic Science* (Toronto, 1977).

Now, it is narrative both when he recites from the several speeches, and when he tells what took place between the speeches?

Of course.

c But when he recites a speech as if he were someone else, shall we not say he then makes his own diction as much as possible like that of the person he has introduced to speak?

Yes, of course.

Now, if someone makes himself like someone else, either in voice or gesture, he imitates the person he makes himself like?

Of course.

Then in this case, as it seems, Homer and other poets effect their narrative through imitation.

Yes.

d But if the poet does not hide himself, then his poetry and narrative are all produced without imitation. And in order that you may not again say you don't understand, I'll tell you how this might happen. For if Homer, in telling how Chryses came bearing ransom for his daughter and as a suppliant to the Achaeans and especially their kings, went on next to speak not as if he'd become Chryses but still as Homer, you know that it wouldn't be imitation but simple narrative. It would go something like this—I'll speak

e without meter, because I'm no poet—

The priest came and prayed the gods to grant them safety in taking Troy, and that they accept compensation and release his daughter out of reverence for the god. When he said this, the rest were in awe and consented, but Agamemnon angrily ordered him to leave immediately and not return again, lest the staff and fillets of the god prove unavailing to his safety. Agamemnon said he'd

394a grow old with Chryses' daughter in Argos before ever he released her, and bid him leave and not provoke him if he meant to return home safely. The old man heard and was frightened and departed in silence, but when he'd left the

camp he prayed at length to Apollo, summoning him by
his eponyms and reminding him and asking requital, if
ever he'd given him anything acceptable either in building of temples or sacrifices of victims. In return for these
things, then, he prayed that the Achaeans pay for his tears
with the god's arrows.

In this way, my friend, I said, it becomes simple narrative without imitation.

I understand, he said.   b

Then understand too, I replied, that the opposite of this also occurs
when one omits the poet's intervening narrative, and retains alternation of
dialogue.

I do understand, he said. Tragedy is like that.

Exactly right, I replied. And now I think I can make clear to you what I
could not before, that one sort of poetry and storytelling consists wholly in
imitation—namely, tragedy and comedy, as you say—but another consists   c
in recital by the poet himself; no doubt you'd find it especially in dithy-
rambs. A third, again, consists in both; this occurs in epic poetry and many
other places too, if you follow me.

Why, I now understand what you meant to say, he said.

And please recall what we said before; content, what is to be said, had already been described, but style or diction, how it is to be said, still needed
to be examined.

Yes, I do recall.

This then is what I meant: we must decide whether we shall allow the   d
poets to imitate in composing narratives, or to imitate some things but not
others, and what sorts of thing in either case—or not to imitate at all.

You're considering, I suspect, whether or not we shall admit tragedy and
comedy into the city, he said.

Perhaps, I replied, but perhaps also something more. I really don't know
yet. We must go in whichever direction the argument, like a wind, carries us.

Well said, he replied.

GUARDIANS NOT PRONE TO IMITATION (394E–398B)

e   Consider then, Adeimantus, whether or not our Guardians should be imitators. Does it not also follow from what went before that one person would
practice one pursuit well, not many, and if he tried, he would deal with
many in such a way as to fail of distinction in all?

Of course.

Then also the same account for imitation? The same person is not as well
able to imitate many things as one?

Of course not.

395a   Then he will scarcely practice a worthwhile pursuit and at the same time
imitate many things and be an imitator, since the same persons cannot even
at the same time imitate well two kinds of imitation which seem closely related to each other, for example, comedy and tragedy. Didn't you call them
imitations just now?

Yes, I did. And you're right: they can't.

Nor again, be a reciter of epic poetry and an actor at the same time.

True.

Nor are the same people even actors in both comedies and tragedies. But
these all are imitations, are they not?

b   Yes.

Moreover, Adeimantus, it appears to me that the nature of man is divided up into even smaller bits than this, so that it is impossible to imitate
many things well, or to do the things themselves of which the imitations are
likenesses.

Very true, he replied.

So if we are to preserve our first account, if our Guardians, released from
all other crafts, must in a very strict sense be craftsmen of freedom for the
c   city and practice nothing that does not bear on this, then they surely would
do nothing else nor imitate it. But if they do imitate, they must imitate
from childhood up what befits them as men who are brave, temperate, pious, free, and all such things. They must not do what is unfree or become
skilled at imitating it, nor anything that is shameful, so that they not gain

the benefit of the reality from the imitation. Or are you not aware that imi- d
tations in respect to posture, speech, and thought, if continued much beyond youth, become established in habit and nature?

Yes, he replied.

Then we will not allow those whom we claim to care about and require
to become good men, I replied, since they are men, to imitate a woman,
young or old, insulting a husband or quarreling with gods and boasting be- e
cause she thinks she is happy, or in misfortunes and possessed by grief and
lamentation—much less a woman sick or in labor or in love.

Certainly not, he replied.

Nor to imitate how male and female slaves act in so far as they are slaves.

Nor that.

Nor bad men either, it seems—cowards, and people doing the opposite
of what we just described, whether drunk or sober, abusing and ridiculing
and speaking shamefully of one another, or any of the other ways such folk 396a
sin in words and deeds against themselves and others. Neither, I think, are
they to form the habit of making themselves like madmen in words or
deeds. For they must recognize madness and wickedness in men and
women, but do none of these things nor imitate them.

Very true, he said.

But are they then to imitate smiths or any other craftsmen? I replied. Or
rowing a galley or giving the time to the oarsmen, or anything else like that?

How could they, he said, if they cannot even to pay attention to such b
things?

Will they imitate horses whinnying and bulls bellowing, and the noise of
rivers and seas, and claps of thunder and all that sort of thing?

Why, it's forbidden them to be mad or to make themselves like madmen,
he said.

If I then understand what you mean, I replied, there is a certain form of
diction and narrative in which a man of genuine good character would ex-
press himself whenever he needs to say something; and a different form c
again, unlike this, which the man opposite him in birth and breeding
would always also persist in using.

What are these forms? he said.

I think the well-ordered man, I replied, when he comes to some speech or action of a good man in his narrative, will report it as though it were his own and not be ashamed at this sort of imitation, especially imitating the good man when he acts steadily and intelligently, but in fewer respects and to a less degree when the good man has been thrown off balance by illness or drunkenness or love or some other misfortune. When it comes to someone beneath him, he will refuse to liken himself seriously to an inferior, unless perhaps briefly when the fellow does something good. He would be ashamed, at once because he is unpracticed in imitating people like that, and because he cannot endure to mold and set himself into the patterns of worse men, since his understanding disdains them except as a joke.

Naturally, he said.

Then he will use narrative of the sort we illustrated a little earlier with those lines from Homer, and his diction will have a share of both imitation and simple narrative, but a small part of imitation in a great deal of speech—or am I wrong?

Indeed not, he said. Such a pattern necessarily belongs to that kind of speaker.

The other kind of speaker, I replied, to the degree that he is the more inferior, will narrate everything and think nothing unworthy of himself; the result is that he will seriously try to imitate everything, and in front of many people—the things we just mentioned, and claps of thunder and sounds of wind and storm, axle and pulley, trumpet and flute and pipe, noises of all sorts of tools, and even the sounds of dogs and sheep and birds. His whole diction, then, will consist in imitation by sound and gesture, with only a small amount of narration.

This too is necessary, he said.

These then are the two forms of diction I meant, I replied.

They surely exist, he said.

Now, one of the two has only slight modulation, and if one assigns suitable pitch[3] and rhythm to the diction, then when someone speaks correctly,

3. *harmonia.*

he speaks almost with the same intonation and in one pitch—for the modulations are slight—and further, in almost the same rhythm.

Exactly so, he said.

What about the other form? Does not it require the opposite, namely, all pitches and all rhythms, if it is in turn to have its own proper expression, because it admits every possible variety of modulation?

Yes, very much so.

Now, all poets, and indeed everyone who says anything, fall into one pattern of diction or the other, or combine something from both?

Necessarily, he said.

Then what shall we do? I replied. Admit them all into the city? Or one of the unmixed kinds, or the mixed kind?

If my vote wins, he said, the unmixed imitator of the good man.

But surely the mixed kind is also pleasing, Adeimantus. And the opposite of your choice, all pitches and all rhythms, is by far the most pleasant to children and their tutors,[4] and to the vast crowd.

Yes, it is.

But perhaps you would say it does not accord with our constitution, I replied, because it is not possible among us for a man to be double or multiple, since each does but one thing.

No, it does not accord.

Then that is why only in such a city as this will we find that the shoemaker is a shoemaker, and not a pilot in addition to his shoemaking, the farmer a farmer, and not a judge in addition to his farming, the soldier a soldier, and not a businessman in addition to his soldiering, and so on.

True, he said.

A man then, as it seems, who is able by his wisdom to assume every kind of character and imitate every sort of thing, if he came into our city wishing to show himself off along with his poems—we would bow down before him as before a sweet and holy wonder, but we would also say that there is no such man among us in our city, nor is it lawful. We would anoint his head with myrrh, crown him with fillets of wool, and send him to another

4. Who were usually slaves.

city. As for ourselves, we would employ for our benefit more austere and less
b   charming poets and storytellers, who would imitate for us the diction of
people of good character; the content of what they recite would conform to
the patterns we enacted at the beginning, when we undertook to educate
soldiers.

I would certainly do so, he said, if it were up to me.

Now, my friend, I said, we've perhaps finished with the part of literature
and music concerned with speeches and stories; for we have described what
is be said and how it is to be said, content and style.

I agree, he said.

MUSIC AND IMITATION IN MODE AND METER (398C–400C)

c   Next then, I replied, what remains is concerned with the character of song
and melodies?

Clearly so.

Well, at this point anybody might discover what should be said about
how they ought to be, if indeed we are to be in concord with what we said
before.

And Glaucon laughed. Well, Socrates, he said, I am afraid "anybody"
does not include me: I cannot sufficiently at present make out what sort of
thing we ought to say, though I do have my suspicions.

d   But surely, I replied, you in the first place can say this: that song is composed of three elements, verse, mode, and rhythm.

Yes, he said, I can at least say that.

Now as to the verse, it surely does not differ at all from speech not sung,
in that it must conform to the same patterns we just prescribed, and in the
same way.

True, he said.

Again, the mode and rhythm must follow the verse.

Of course.

However, we said we needed no dirges and lamentations in verse?

No.

e   Then what are the dirgelike modes? Tell me—you're a musician.

Mixed Lydian and Stretched Lydian, he said, and some others of the sort.

Then they're to be discarded, I replied. They're useless even for women who must be good, let alone men.

Of course.

Again, drunkenness is utterly unsuitable for Guardians, and softness and laziness.

Certainly.

Then what modes are soft and convivial?

Ionian, and certain Lydian modes called slack, he replied.

Then can they be used for warriors, my friend?   399a

Not at all, he said. But you perhaps have only the Dorian and Phrygian left.

I don't know the modes, I said, but leave me that mode which would fittingly imitate the tones and accents of a courageous man in warlike deed and all violent business, a man who when he fails and goes to wounds or death, or falls into any other misfortune, steadfastly and unflinchingly de-   b
fends himself against his fate. And leave me again another mode, that of a man engaged in peaceful action, action not constrained but voluntary, either persuading someone and asking for something, or praying to a god or instructing and admonishing a man, or conversely, submitting himself to instruction or persuasion by another, and in consequence acting reasonably and without arrogance but with temperate restraint in all this, and accepting of the outcome. Leave these two modes and no others, one constrained,   c
one voluntary, which will best imitate the accents of brave and temperate men in misfortune and prosperity.

Why, you're asking me to leave none other than those I just now mentioned, he replied.

So we will have no need in our songs and melodies, I replied, of many-stringed instruments capable of encompassing all modes.

It does not appear so to me, he said.

So we will not support craftsmen of triangular lyres and Lydian harps, or other instruments many in string and multiple in mode.

Apparently not.   d

Again, will you admit flute makers or flutists into the city? Isn't the flute[5] the most many-toned of instruments? Are not other panharmonic instruments which allow modulation into all modes mere imitations of a flute?

Clearly so, he replied.

Then lyre and cithara are left you for use in the city, I replied. And again in the fields, shepherds will have a pipe.

e   So at any rate the argument signifies to us, he said.

Yes, I replied, and we are hardly innovating, my friend, in preferring Apollo, and the instruments of Apollo, to Marsias[6] and his.

No, emphatically not, he replied.

By the Dog,[7] I said, we have again, quite unawares, cleansed and purified a city we just described as luxurious.

Yes, and we are wise to do so, he replied.

Come then, I said. Let us cleanse and purify the remainder. For following then on the modes, we have the rhythms—not to pursue them in all their variety or every kind of meter, but to determine the rhythms of a brave and ordered life. Once we discern them, we will compel meter and melody also to follow the verse[8] of such a life, not verse the meter and melody. It is your job, as with the modes, to say what these rhythms might be.

400a

Why really, he said, I cannot tell. For I have observed, and I can say that there are three given forms from which the feet are woven,[9] just as there are four forms in the musical notes from which the modes all derive.[10] But which sort is an imitation of what sort of life, I cannot tell.

b   Why, we will also consult with Damon,[11] I replied, about what meters

5. The *aulos* was not in fact a flute, but a double-reed instrument similar perhaps in sound to an oboe, though of higher pitch, and sometimes played in pairs.

6. That is, Dionysus.

7. The dog-god of Egypt, a characteristic (and emphatic) Socratic oath. See IX 592a, *Apology* 21e, *Phaedo* 99a, *Gorgias* 481b.

8. *logos,* not only the verse but the reason and ratio or proportion of such a life.

9. Presumably, these forms are the kinds of feet formed by the ratios 2:2, 3:2, and 2:1, in either order. Thus, for example, 2:1 is the form of both trochee and iamb.

10. The fourth (4:3), fifth (3:2), octave (2:1), and tone, which define the perfect consonances of all natural scales and thus by derivation all modes.

11. Damon is several times mentioned in the dialogues as a musical expert. *Laches* 200a, b, 197d,

suit illiberality and insolence, or madness and other evils, and what rhythms are to be left for their opposites. I think I've heard him speak obscurely of a certain composite meter he called "martial," yes, and of both a dactylic and a heroic meter. I don't know how he arranged them, but he made the rise [*arsis*] and fall [*thesis*] equal, ending with a short and a long. I think he also spoke of an iambic foot and called another trochaic, assigning them longs and shorts. And in some of these I think he praised and criticized the tempo of the foot quite as much as the rhythms themselves—or else some combination of them, for I cannot tell—but as I said, let us refer this to Damon, for it requires a lengthy account. You agree?

Yes, emphatically, he said.

THE MORAL EFFECT OF MUSIC (400C–403C)

But you are able to determine this, at least, that gracefulness and clumsiness attend on excellence of rhythm and the lack of it.

Of course.

Moreover, excellence of rhythm follows on beauty of diction and becomes like it, and the lack of it on the opposite. So similarly for tunefulness and discord, if indeed, as we were just now saying, rhythm and mode follow on the verse, not the verse on them.

Why, certainly, they should follow on the verse, he replied.

What about the pattern of diction, and the verse? I replied. Does it not follow on character of soul?

Of course.

And the others follow on the diction?

Yes.

So gracefulness of verse and diction, excellence of musical form and rhythm, all attend upon goodness of nature—not the foolishness we eu-

---

180c–d, *Alcibiades* I 118c, IV 424c. He is here suggested as an authority on the ethical effect of various rhythms. A pupil of the sophist Prodicus, he is perhaps expert in music as Prodicus was expert in distinguishing the meaning of words.

phemistically call "good nature,"[12] but character well and truly founded on understanding.

Yes, certainly, he said.

Then our young men must everywhere pursue these things, if they are to do what is their own.[13]

Yes, they must.

401a   But surely, painting and all such crafts are full of them, and so are weaving and embroidery and architecture and also all production of other artifacts, and still further the nature of bodies and of other growing things; for gracefulness or the lack of it is present in all of them. Clumsiness and discord and lack of rhythm are akin to bad speech and bad character, but their opposites are akin to and imitations of the opposite, a good and temperate character.

b   Perfectly true, he said.

Is it then only the poets we must supervise? Is it only they whom we must compel to render the image of good character in their works or not work among us? Or must the other craftsmen be supervised too, and forbidden to embody bad character and intemperance and servile gracelessness either in the images belonging to painting and sculpture or in architecture, or any other product of their craftsmanship? Anyone who cannot must not be allowed to practice his craftsmanship among us, in order that our Guardians may not be nurtured among images of vice, as in an evil pasture where little

c   by little and day by day they repeatedly graze and feed until, unawares, they gather into their own soul from many sources a single thing constitutive of great evil. Rather, we must seek craftsmen with the natural ability to search out the nature of what is beautiful and graceful, in order that our young men may benefit from everything, as dwelling in a healthy climate, whence, like a breeze bearing health from happy regions, some influence from noble works

d   falls on eyes or ears from childhood upward, leading them, unawares, into likeness and friendship and concord with the beauty of reason.

12. *euetheia.* Cf. I 343c.

13. *to auto prattein,* "do their own job," "perform their own function," or (dare one say it?) "do their own thing." This anticipates the definition of justice in Book IV. Cf. 443c–d.

Best by far that they be so nurtured, he said.

Then this is why, Glaucon, I replied, education in music and poetry is of such sovereign importance: rhythm and attunement sink especially deep into the innermost soul and take the strongest hold there, bearing graceful- ness to it and making it graceful, if and only if one has been rightly nur- tured. And again: he who there has been nurtured as he should is quickest to perceive and rightly reject the deficiencies of what is ill fashioned or ill grown; his delight is in the praise of beautiful things. Accepting them into his soul and nourished thereby, he becomes noble and good. What is ugly he would rightly hate and despise while still young, before he is able to grasp the reason. When reason comes, a man so nurtured would welcome it, recognizing it through its special kinship to himself.

I agree, he said. This is the purpose of education in music and poetry.

It is as when we were learning to read, I replied. We became proficient when we recognized the elements or letters, which are few, in all that con- tained and carried them, and did not discount them as if they were beneath notice, in small words or large; we were eager to distinguish them every- where because we supposed we would not read until we could do so.[14]

True.

So too for images of letters? If they appear somewhere in water or in mir- rors, we will not know the images until we know the letters themselves—it belongs to the same art and study.

Of course.

Then am I not also right in saying that in the same way, we will never be musical, neither ourselves nor the Guardians we claim we must educate, until we recognize the forms of temperance and courage and liberality and high-mindedness and all that is akin to them, and also their opposites wherever they occur, and notice them and images of them in those things in which they are present, and discount them in neither small things nor large, but suppose them to belong to the same art and study?

14. For other uses of the analogy of letters and syllables to elements and compounds, see *Cratylus* 393d, *Theaetetus* 206a, *Philebus* 18c, *Politicus* 278a.

Quite necessary, he said.

d   Now, when beautiful character in the soul coincides with outward form, I replied, when they are in concord and agreement because they have a share of the same pattern, it would be a most beautiful sight for him who is able to see?

Yes, very much so.

And surely what is most beautiful is most lovable?

Of course.

Then a person educated in music and poetry would most especially love such people as these. He would not love someone full of discord.

No, he said, at least not if there were some defect of soul. But if it were only in the body, he would abide it and so be willing to welcome him.

e   I see, I replied. It is that you are or have been in love with such persons, and I agree. But tell me: Is excessive pleasure at all compatible with temperance?

How could it be? he said. It disturbs the mind no less than pain.

Or compatible with the rest of virtue?

403a   By no means.

But with arrogance and intemperance?

Most especially.

Can you mention any greater and keener pleasure than sex?

I cannot, he replied, nor any more insane.

But right love temperately and musically loves what is orderly and beautiful?[15]

Very much so, he replied.

Then nothing of madness, nothing akin to licentiousness, must approach right love?

No.

b   So sexual pleasure itself must not approach it. Lover and beloved, if they love and are loved rightly, must have nothing to do with it.

---

15. An example of the cognate nominative, subject and verb expressing the same idea, a common construction in Platonic Greek: love loves, argument argues, thought thinks, opinion opines. This is not a nominative with passive verb corresponding to the cognate accusative with active verb, but a distinct grammatical construction.

Most emphatically not, Socrates.

Thus then, it seems, in the city we are founding, you will legislate that a lover may be with his beloved and kiss and touch him as though he were a son, for honorable reasons and with his consent, but otherwise so associate with anyone he genuinely cares about that he will never even seem to go further than this. Otherwise, he will be blamed for uncultivated coarseness and lack of good taste.

Yes, he said.   c

Then does it now appear to you, I replied, that our account of music is complete? At any rate, it has ended where it ought to end: what has to do with music and poetry must surely end in love of the beautiful.

I agree, he said.

GYMNASTIC (403C–404E)

After music, our young people are to be educated in gymnastic.

Of course.

In this too they must be strictly nurtured throughout life, from child-   d
hood up. Things stand thus, I think—but you must consider it too. It doesn't appear to me that a sound body by its own virtue makes a good soul, but on the contrary, a good soul by its own virtue provides the best possible body. How does it appear to you?

I think so too.

Then if we sufficiently serve the mind, we would turn over to it matters requiring accurate reflection about the body; we do right merely to indicate the patterns, in order not to speak at length.

Of course.   e

Well, we said they must avoid drunkenness. For it is surely permitted anyone rather than a Guardian to get drunk and not know where on earth he is.

Yes, it is ridiculous for the Guardian to need a guard, he replied.

Then what about food? These men are competitors in the greatest of contests, are they not?

Yes.

Then do people in training follow a regimen suitable for them?

Perhaps.

But isn't this a somewhat drowsy condition, I replied, and precarious for health?[16] Don't you see people in training sleeping their life away; and if they depart from their prescribed regimen even a little, they often fall seriously ill?

Yes.

Then a more clever kind of training is required for our athletes of war, I replied. They must be as watchful as dogs and exceptionally quick to see and hear, and since they will undergo many changes of water and many different kinds of food on campaign, and extremes of heat and cold, they must not be in precarious health.

b So it appears to me.

Then the best gymnastic would be somewhat akin to the music we described a little while ago?

How do you mean?

Good gymnastic is surely also simple gymnastic, especially as it concerns war.

In what way?

One might learn it even from Homer, I replied. You know that in the feastings of his heroes on campaign, he does not serve them fish even though they are on the shores of the Hellespont, nor boiled meat, but only roasts, which are especially convenient for soldiers. For it is everywhere easier just to light a fire, one may claim, rather than carry pots and pans around with you.

Indeed so.

Nor again does Homer ever mention sweets, I think. Other people in training know that anyone who intends to be in good bodily condition must stay away from all that sort of thing.

16. Cornford quotes Hippocrates, *Aphorisms* I 3: "In athletes a perfect condition that is at its highest pitch is treacherous. Such conditions cannot remain the same or be at rest and . . . the only possible change is for the worse" (trans. W. H. S. Jones).

Yes, he said. They know and rightly stay away.

If indeed you think this is right, my friend, you apparently do not ap-   d
prove of a Syracusan table, or a Sicilian variety of relishes.

No, I don't.

So for men who intend to be in good bodily condition, you would also
object to a Corinthian maid as a mistress?[17]

Very much so.

And Attic tarts, which seem so dainty?

Necessarily.

In general, I suppose, we would rightly compare this sort of food and
regimen to melodies and songs composed in all modes and every kind of
rhythm.

Of course.   e

Variety there bred intemperance, and from that, disease. Simplicity in
music produces temperance in souls, and in gymnastic, health in bodies.

Very true, he said.

JUSTICE AND THE DUTY OF HEALTH (405A-408C)

When intemperance and diseases prevail in a city, are not courtrooms and   405a
clinics constantly open? Advocacy and medicine put on solemn airs, when
even many free men are quite serious about them.

Inevitably.

Can you have any greater indication in a city of shamefully bad education than need for eminently skilled doctors and judges, not only by common workmen but also by those who claim to have been raised in the posture of freedom? Does it not seem shameful, and a great indication of lack   b
of education, to be compelled to use justice imported from others as masters and judges, at a loss for resources of one's own?

Of all things most shameful, he said.

But do you not think it even more shameful, I replied, when somebody

17. Corinth into classical times retained temple prostitution, practiced by girls before marriage.

not only spends most of his life in courtrooms as plaintiff and defendant, but out of vulgar pride actually congratulates himself on this very thing,

c thinking he is clever at the doing of injustice and up to every twist and turn, constantly backtracking and wiggling so that he is not punished, and this for trivial or worthless ends—ignorant of how much nobler and better it is to order one's own life so that one has no need of a drowsy judge?

That is actually more shameful still, he said.

d But to need a doctor, I replied—not for wounds or by contracting some seasonal disorder, but through laziness and the sort of regimen we have described, filling oneself with winds and humors like marsh gas in stagnant water, compelling the subtle Asclepiads to apply to diseases such names as flatulence and catarrh—does not that seem shameful?

Indeed it does, he said. These are truly new and strange names for diseases.

e Not, I think, the kind Asclepius used, to judge from his sons at Troy, I replied. When Eurypolus was wounded, they did not fault the woman who gave him Pramnian wine well sprinkled with barley meal and grated

406a cheese—an inflammatory mixture, one might think—nor did they criticize Patroclus, who was treating him.

Certainly a strange drink to give someone in that condition, he said.

Not if you understand, I said, that before the time of Herodicus, as they say, the Asclepiads did not use this new kind of medicine which coddles diseases. Herodicus was a trainer, and when he lost his health he mixed gymnastic with medicine, and first and most especially tormented himself and afterward a great many others.

b In what way? he said.

By prolonging his own death, I replied. He closely followed the course of his illness, which was mortal; he could not cure himself, I think, so he lived out his whole life doctoring himself, without leisure for anything else. In torment if he departed at all from his accustomed regimen, he won by his skill the prize of old age, and died hard.

A noble prize for his art indeed, he said.

c Yes, I replied, and appropriate for someone who didn't realize that it was not out of ignorance or inexperience in this form of medicine that Asclepius did not reveal it to his sons. He knew that among all well-governed people, there is some particular work ordered for each person in the city which he is bound to do, and no leisure for anyone to be sick throughout life and doctor himself. We are aware that is ridiculous for craftsmen. We are unaware that it is also ridiculous for people who are rich and regarded as happy.

How so? he said.

When a carpenter is sick, I replied, he expects from his doctor an emetic or a drug to purge the disease, or to get rid of it by use of cautery or the knife. But if somebody orders a long regimen for him, wraps felt bandages around his head and all that goes with it, he is quick to say that he has not leisure to be sick and it is not worth living that way, attending to an illness while neglecting his work. He next says goodbye to that sort of doctor and goes back to his accustomed regimen, and regains his health and lives, doing what is his own; if his body does not bear up under it, he dies and is released from troubles.

Yes, it seems suitable for such a man to use medicine that way, he said.

Because there is work for him to do, I replied, and it is not worth living unless he does it?

Clearly, he said.

But the rich, we say, have no such appointed work, to make life intolerable if a man is compelled to stay away from it.

No, at least so it is said.

Do you not listen to Phocylides? I replied. He says a man should practice virtue when he has got enough to live on.

Yes, he said, and I should think even sooner.

Let's not fight with him about it, I said, but rather determine for ourselves whether virtue must be practiced by the rich man, with life not worth living if he does not practice it, or whether nursing a disease hinders paying attention to carpentry and the other arts but is no hindrance at all to following Phocylides' advice.

Why really, he replied, this excessive care of the body, which goes beyond

d

e

407a

b

the requirements of sound regimen, is pretty nearly the greatest hindrance of all. It is troublesome in managing a household, in military service, and in the holding of public office.

c   But the most important thing, surely, is that it makes it difficult to engage in any sort of learning or reflection and self-examination, if one is always worrying about headaches and dizziness and blames philosophy as the cause of it. So wherever virtue is practiced in this way and approved as fit for its office, excessive care is in every way a hindrance: it makes a man think he's always sick, and he never stops worrying about his body.

Very likely, he said.

Then let us claim that Asclepius also knew this, and to benefit those who by nature and regimen were healthy of body but had some determinable disease within, he revealed the art of medicine for them and for their condition. He cast out their diseases with drugs and surgery and ordered them to follow their usual regimen, so as not to harm the interests of the city. But with bodies generally diseased within, he did not try to produce a long bad life for a man by studied regimens, nicely calculated doses, and evacuations, or allow his patients to beget offspring likely to be of the same sort. He didn't think he should treat a man who was incapable of his established course of life, because it profited neither himself nor his city.

Quite a statesman, your Asclepius, he said.

Clearly, I replied. And because he was, do you not see that his sons proved themselves good warriors at Troy, and practiced the art of medicine as I have described? You recall how "they sucked the blood and applied mild medicines" to the wound Pandarus inflicted on Menelaus, but they no more prescribed what he should eat or drink afterward than they did for Eurypylus; they doubtless thought their medicines would suffice to heal men who were healthy and well-ordered in regimen before being wounded, even if they drank wine mixed with barley meal and cheese, right on the spot. But if a man was sickly by nature and intemperate, they did not think it profitable either to himself or others to live, or that the art was meant for such men, or that they should be treated—not even if they were richer than Midas.

Very clever, these sons of Asclepius, by your account, he said.

Suitably so, I replied. And yet both the tragic poets and Pindar are un-convinced. They claim Asclepius was a son of Apollo but was persuaded by money to heal a rich man at the point of death, for which he was struck by the thunderbolt. But from what was said before, we cannot accept both: if   c the son of a god, we will claim, he was not avaricious; if avaricious, he was not the son of a god.

PHYSICIANS AND JUDGES (408C–410A)

Quite right, he replied. But what do you say about this, Socrates? Must we not have good physicians in our city? The best physicians, surely, are those who have handled the greatest number of cases, well and sick alike; the best judges, again, would be those who have associated with the most varied kinds of natures.

Yes, I said—that is, if they are really good. But do you know who I think   d they are?

If you tell me, he said.

Why, I will try, I replied. But you asked about unlike things in the same question.

How so? he said.

The most skilled physicians, I said, are those who begin in childhood, and in addition to learning the art by dealing with the greatest possible number of the sickest possible bodies, themselves suffer from every disease and are not by nature very healthy. I do not think they treat body with body,   e for then their bodies could never be or have been bad. Rather, they treat body with soul, which cannot treat anything properly if it is or has been bad.

Correct, he said.

Yes, but a judge, my friend, governs soul by soul. His soul cannot have   409a been reared from youth in association with vicious souls and itself have gone through the commission of every kind of crime and injustice, so that, as with diseases of body, it quickly infers from itself the crimes of others.

Rather, it must itself have been inexperienced and untainted by bad habits while young, if it is to be noble and good, and soundly judge what things are right. That is why good and decent people, when young, appear simple-minded and easily deceived by wrongdoers: they have within themselves no standards of like affection with the wicked.

b   Yes, he said, that is very much how they are.

For that reason, I replied, the good judge must not be young but old, having come late to learning what injustice is. He does not perceive it as akin to what is present in his own soul, but through long study as an alien thing in alien souls. He discerns the nature of evil by knowledge, without kindred experience.

c   Such a judge seems to be most noble, he said.

Yes, and good, I replied, which is what you were asking about. For whoever has a good soul is good. But that clever and suspicious fellow, who has himself done many injustices and considers himself wise and cunning when he associates with his equals, appears clever because he is always on guard, his eyes fixed on the standards within himself. But when he comes in contact with good men who have grown older, he appears foolish with his un-

d   timely suspicions and ignorance of healthy character, because he does not possess a standard of that sort. He seems more wise than ignorant to himself and others only because he more often meets with bad men than good.

Quite true, he said.

Then it is not this sort of person who should be sought as a good and wise judge, I replied, but the other. For vice will never know both itself and virtue, but virtue in an educated nature will in time gain knowledge at once of itself and vice. So it is he, I think, not the bad man, who turns out to be wise.

e   I agree, he said.

Then you will also establish by law in our city a medical art along with courts of the sort we have described, which will treat the bodies and souls of

410a   those among our citizens whose nature is sound. Those unsound of body will be allowed to die; those ill-natured and incurable they will themselves put to death.

That appears best both for those so afflicted and for the city, he replied.

As for the young, then, I replied, it is clear that they will be careful not to need a court, by using that simple music which we said engenders temperance.

Yes, he said.

ALL EDUCATION IS FOR THE SOUL (410B-412B)

Then if someone educated in music and poetry pursues the same track in gymnastic, he will choose to have no need of medicine beyond what is minimally necessary?   b

I think so.

Yes, and he will even undertake the labors of gymnastic exercise with a view to the spirited form of his nature, rousing it by his exertions, rather than to bodily strength, unlike other athletes, who diet and train for the sake of strength?

Quite right, he said.

Then Glaucon, I replied, those who established education in music and gymnastic did not do so, as some suppose, to serve body with the one, soul with the other.   c

But why, then? he said.

They established both primarily for the sake of the soul, I replied.

How so?

Have you not noticed, I said, the disposition of mind of those who deal with gymnastic throughout their life, but refuse to touch music and poetry? Or again, the state of mind of those oppositely disposed?

What are you talking about? he said.

Ferocious hardness, and oversoft gentleness, I replied.   d

I've certainly noticed, he said, that those who apply themselves to gymnastic unmixed turn out more fierce than they ought to be, while those who apply themselves only to music become softer than is good for them.

Surely it is the spirited form of our nature which produces ferocity, I replied, and, rightly trained, courage. But if stretched tighter than it should be, it is likely to become hard and tough.

I agree, he said.

e   But then is not the philosophical nature gentle? If relaxed too much it becomes softer than it should be, but gentle and well ordered if properly nurtured?

That is so.

Yes, but we claim the Guardians must have both these natures.

Yes.

So it is necessary to fit them together with each other?

Of course.

And the soul is temperate and courageous from attunement?

411a   Of course.

But cowardly and savage without it?

Very.

Then when someone gives himself up to music and allows the charm of the flute to play upon him, and to pour into his soul through his ears as through a funnel those sweet, soft, dirgelike modes we just described— when he passes his whole life humming and made joyous by the song—he

b   at first, if he had any spirit, softens and tempers it like iron, and makes it useful instead of useless and hard. But when he persists in yielding to enchantment, and does not give over, he dissolves till he quite melts away his spirit and as it were cuts the very sinews of his soul, making himself "a soft warrior."

Indeed, he said.

If he were spiritless in nature to begin with, I replied, he will reach this point quickly. But if spirited, then by making his spirit weak he would make it unsteady, quick to flare in anger over trifles and as quickly quenched. So he would have become quick-tempered and irascible instead of spirited, and full of discontent.

c   Exactly so.

What if he toils at gymnastic and dines very well, but does not touch music and philosophy? At first, being in good bodily condition, he is filled with pride and spirit, and becomes more courageous than he was before.

Yes.

What if he does nothing else, and has no intercourse with Muses at all?   d
Even if there were some love of learning present in his soul, still, because his
soul has acquired no taste for learning or inquiry and has no share of reasoning or any other music, it becomes weak, deaf and blind, because it is
not aroused or nurtured, nor are its perceptions purified and cleansed.

That's so, he said.

Such a person comes to hate both music and argument, I think. He no
longer makes use of persuasion through speech, but in everything achieves
his ends by force and savagery like a wild beast, and lives out his graceless   e
life in ignorance accompanied by an ill-proportioned awkwardness.

This is quite true, he replied.

But it seems god has given the two arts of music and gymnastic to
mankind, I would claim, not for soul and body except incidentally, but for
the spirited and the philosophical elements of the soul, in order that they
may be fitted to each other by being properly stretched and relaxed.

In fact, it does seem so, he said.   412a

So we would quite rightly claim that he who best combines gymnastic
with music and applies them in most fitting measure to his soul is most perfectly musical and attuned, far more so than one who merely brings into
unison the strings of a lyre.

Yes, very likely, Socrates, he said.

Then there will always be need for an overseer of this sort in our city, if
the constitution is to be preserved?

Most certainly, the greatest possible need.   b

The Constitution (III 412b–IV 427c)

SELECTION OF THE GUARDIANS (412B–414B)

These then are the outlines of their education and nurture. For with such
people as these, why go into detail about dances and hunting and the chase,
and athletic contests and horseraces? It is pretty clear what patterns they
should follow; they are no longer hard to discover.

Perhaps not, he replied.

Very well, I replied. What must we decide next? Who among them shall rule and be ruled?

c   Of course.

Now, it is clear that the rulers should be older, those ruled younger?

Yes.

And that the best among them should rule?

That too.

The best farmers are most skilled at farming?

Yes.

But now, since they must be the best guardians, they are most skilled at guarding a city?

Yes.

Then they must be wise and capable in this, and again, concerned for the city?

d   That's so.

But one is most concerned for what he most especially loves.

Necessarily.

And further, he would most especially love that whose interests he believed to be the same as his own, and if he supposed he himself would fare well if and only if it fared well too.

That's so, he said.

Then we must select from among other guardians those men who especially appear to us, throughout their whole lives, to act with all eagerness for what they believe is the advantage of the city, and refuse in any way to do what is not so.

e   Yes, for they are suitable, he said.

I think they must be observed then at every stage of life, to see if they are good Guardians of this conviction, and do not by compulsion or beguilement cast aside unawares the opinion that they must do what is best for the city.

What do you mean by "casting aside"? he said.

I will tell you, I said. It appears to me that an opinion departs from a mind either voluntarily or involuntarily: voluntarily when the false is changed by learning, involuntarily when any truth is changed.

I understand about the voluntary, he said, but I need to learn about the   413a
involuntary.

Well then, I said, do you not believe that people are involuntarily deprived of good things, but voluntarily deprived of evils? Is not being deceived about the truth an evil, but possessing truth a good? Do you not
think that to possess truth is to judge things that are?

Why, you are right, he replied, and I do think that people are deprived of
true opinion involuntarily.

Then they suffer this by theft, or bewitchment, or compulsion.   b

Now I don't understand at all, he said.

Maybe I am speaking in too high-flown a manner, I replied. I say it is
theft when people change their convictions and forget because they have
been deprived of them unawares, some by time, others by argument. Do
you understand now?

Yes.

I say it is compulsion, when pain or suffering causes people to change
their judgment.

This too I understand, he said, and you are right.

But you would say it is bewitchment, I suppose, when people are caused   c
to change their judgment after being seduced by pleasure or terrified by
fear.

Yes, he replied. It seems that all deceit is a kind of bewitchment.

Then as I was just saying, we must inquire who are best guardians of
their own conviction that they must always do what they judge best for
their city. We must observe them from childhood up, setting before them
tasks in which they might especially forget this and be deceived. Only those
who are mindful and hard to deceive are to be selected; those who are not
must be rejected. Agreed?

Yes.   d

Again, they must be subjected to toils and pains and struggles, where we
must watch for these same things.

Right, he said.

Now as a third form of trial, I replied, we must observe how they deal
with bewitchment. Even as one leads colts to loud noises to see whether

they are skittish, so our young men must be brought to terrors and again
thrown into pleasures, testing them much more severely than gold an-
nealed in fire. If a young man appears hard to bewitch and graceful in everything, a good guardian of himself and of the music he has learned, if he
shows excellence of rhythm and attunement in all this, then he is such as to
be most useful to himself and to his city. One who is constantly tested in
childhood, youth, and manhood, and comes through unscathed, must be
established as a ruler of the city and a guardian, and given rewards while
living and after death, allotted highest honors in funeral rites and other
memorials. Whoever is not of this sort must be rejected. Such then, Glaucon, I said, is the manner of selection and appointment of the rulers and
Guardians, I think, stated in outline though not in detail.

It also appears much the same to me, he replied.

Then these are truly the men it is most right to call complete Guardians,
against enemies without and countrymen within, so that the one will not
wish, and the other will not have power to do harm? The young people we
were just now calling Guardians are auxiliaries, helpers in carrying out the
judgments of the rulers.

I think so, he said.

THE MYTH OF THE METALS (414B–415D)

How might we then devise one of those needful falsehoods we were just
mentioning? I replied. A single noble and generous fiction, to persuade especially the rulers themselves, but if not, the rest of the city?

What sort of fiction? he said.

Nothing new, I replied, only a kind of Phoenician tale[18] about something which has already happened in many places, as the poets tell and have
persuaded us. But it has not happened among us, nor do I know if it could
have happened. It would take a great deal of persuasion to believe.

18. Because it is about Cadmus, of Phoenician origin, who sowed the dragon's teeth from which
the Thebans sprang.

You seem hesitant to tell it, he said.

You will think me quite reasonably hesitant, I replied, when I do.

Go on, he said. Do not be afraid.

I say, then—and yet, I do not know how I dare say it or what words to use: d
I will try first to persuade the rulers themselves and the soldiers, and then the
rest of the city too, that what they thought they experienced—namely, that
we reared and educated them—all happened as it were in a dream, when they
themselves were in truth beneath the earth, being formed and nurtured
within it, while their weapons and the rest of their equipment were being   e
fashioned as well. When they were once fully completed, Earth, who is their
mother, brought them forth, and now they must take counsel for the defense
of their country as for a mother and nurse, if anyone comes against it, and
consider the rest of their fellow citizens as brothers born of Earth.

No wonder you kept your fiction quiet so long, he said.

Quite reasonably, I replied. Nevertheless, hear also the remainder of the   415a
tale. "You in this city are all brothers," we shall say, as we tell them the tale.
"But the god, in fashioning those among you who are competent to rule,
mixed gold into them at their birth, whereby they are most precious, and
silver into the auxiliaries; and iron and bronze into the farmers and the
other craftsmen. Now because you are all akin, you will mostly beget children like yourselves, but it is possible that a silver child should be born of   b
gold, or a golden child born of silver, and so all the rest from one another.
To those who rule, then, the god first and especially announces that there is
nothing of which they shall be such good guardians, or guard so carefully, as
the intermixture of metals in the souls of their offspring. If their own offspring are born alloyed with bronze or iron, they will assign it the grade ap-   c
propriate to its nature and thrust it out among craftsmen or farmers without pity. And again, if any born from the latter are alloyed with silver or
gold, they will honor them and lead them up, some to guardianship, others
as auxiliaries, because of a prophecy that the city will be destroyed when
guarded by iron or bronze." Can you persuade them of this story?

No, he said, at least not they themselves. But maybe their sons and their   d
descendents and the rest who come after.

Why, that would be good too, I replied. It would make them care more for their city and for each other. I pretty well see what you mean.

THE GUARDIANS: COMMUNAL PROPERTY AND HOUSING (415D–417B)

(Socrates continues) This then shall be as tradition may determine. But let us arm these sons of Earth and lead them forth under the command of their rulers. When they arrive at the site of the city, let them look to the best place to pitch their camp, a place from which they may best contain those within if any should refuse to obey the laws, and ward off those without, if an enemy should come down like a wolf on the fold. Once camp is pitched and they have sacrificed as they ought, let them construct their quarters. Agreed?

e

Yes, he said.

Now, those must be sufficient to keep out winter storm and summer heat?

Of course. I think you mean houses, he said.

Yes, I replied, but for soldiers, not businessmen.

416a

How do you say one differs from the other? he asked.

I will try to tell you, I replied. It is of all things most terrible and most shameful for shepherds to raise dogs to guard their flocks in such a way that, from intemperance or hunger, or other evil habit, the dogs undertake to harm the sheep and become like wolves instead of dogs.

Terrible? he replied. Of course it is.

b

Then one must in every way guard against the auxiliaries acting that way toward the citizens, since they are stronger, and becoming savage masters instead of kindly allies.

Yes, he said.

Now, they would have been provided with the most important of safeguards, if they have really been well educated.

But surely they have, he said.

Perhaps that is not to be too confidently affirmed, dear Glaucon, I said.[19] But we can certainly affirm what we were just saying, that they must have the right education, whatever it is, if they are to have what is most important for being gentle with themselves and those they guard.

Yes, he replied.   c

In addition to this education, a reasonable man would claim that they should be provided with such dwellings and other property as would not prevent them from being the best guardians possible nor incite them to do harm to the other citizens.

Yes, and he will be right.   d

Consider then, I said, whether they ought to live and be housed in some such way as this: First, none to possess any private property except strict necessities. Next, none to have any dwelling or storehouse not open to anyone who wishes to enter. Provisions needed by temperate and courageous men in training for war to be received from other citizens as pay for being   e
Guardians, in the exact amount needed for the year. Common meals, and living together as though on campaign. They are told that they always have in their soul divine gold and silver from gods and no need of the human kind in addition, that it is impious to sully possession of the former by mixing it with mortal dross, because many unholy things are occasioned by the   417a
popular currency,[20] but what is present within them is undefiled. Alone among those in the city, they are forbidden to touch or handle gold and silver or even be under the same roof with it, or to wear it or drink from vessels made of it. In this way they would preserve themselves and the city. But if ever they come to possess for themselves private land and houses and currency, they will be householders and farmers instead of Guardians, and will have become masters and enemies of their fellow citizens instead of allies.   b
They will then pass their whole lives hating and being hated, plotting and being plotted against, in much greater and better-founded fear of enemies

19. Because justice has not yet been discovered.
20. *nomisma:* money, coin, but also anything sanctioned by custom or use—currency.

within than those without, and at that point running themselves and the rest of the city to the very verge of ruin. For all these reasons, I said, may we not claim that this is how the Guardians ought to be provided with dwellings and the rest, and give it as law?

Certainly, Glaucon replied.

Book IV

And Adeimantus interrupted and said, Well, what defense will you offer,   419a
Socrates, if someone claims you are not making these people very happy,
and this through their own doing? The city in truth belongs to them, yet
they enjoy nothing good from the city. For example, others own fields and
build fine big houses and have suitable furnishings for them, and offer private sacrifices to gods and entertain guest-friends from abroad; they especially possess the things you were just now mentioning, gold and silver and
everything else customary for those who intend to be happy. But these people, he would say, simply appear to be like hired auxiliaries, stationed in the
city for no other purpose but to stand guard.

Yes, I replied, and what's more, for subsistence alone; they do not even   420a
receive pay in addition to their provisions, as others do, so it will not be possible for them to journey abroad as private citizens if they wish, or give presents to courtesans, or spend money in whatever direction they please, as
those who are thought to be happy do. You are omitting these and a host of
other such counts from your indictment.

Why, let those be brought as charges too, he replied.

Then what is our defense, you ask?

b   Yes.

I think we will discover what must be said by continuing on the same path, I replied. For we will say that it would not be at all surprising if they are thus also most happy, even though we are not founding the city so that some one particular class will be surpassingly happy, but so that the city will be as happy as possible as a whole. For we supposed it would be in a city of

c   this sort that we would especially find justice, and injustice again in the worst constituted, and that after viewing them we might judge of what we have long been seeking. So now, as we suppose, we are shaping the happy city, not by setting some few people apart in it and assuming that they are happy, but as a whole; we will examine the opposite city presently. It is as though we were painting statues, and someone came along and criticized us for not applying the most beautiful pigments to the most beautiful parts of the statue—for not having painted the eyes crimson instead of black, say, because they are most beautiful. We would think it a reasonable defense to

d   say to him, "My friend, please do not suppose that we must paint eyes so beautiful that they do not even look like eyes, nor again the other parts, but consider whether by giving what is fitting to each, we make beautiful the whole. In the same way now, please do not compel us to attach to the Guardians a kind of happiness which would make them anything else but

e   Guardians. For we also know how to clothe our farmers in royal robes, crown them with gold, and bid them work the soil at their pleasure; how to make our potters recline on couches by the fire as at a banquet, passing the wine and feasting, their wheel set beside them to potter with as they please; and we know how to make everybody else happy in the same way, so that the whole city may indeed be happy. But please don't urge us to do it, be-

421a   cause should we obey you, the farmer will not be a farmer nor the potter a potter, nor will anyone else have any shape from which a city arises. It is of less account for the others: a shoe stitcher gone wrong and corrupted, pre-tending to be what he is not, is hardly a threat to a city. But if Guardians of laws and a city are not in fact Guardians but only seem so, you surely see that they can reduce a city to utter ruin; but again, they alone have the op-

portunity to govern it well and make it happy." So if we are making Guard-   b
ians in very truth, men least likely to do harm to the city, but he is describing
something different, he must mean something other than a city—perhaps
some farmers happily feasting as at a rural festival but not in a city. We must
consider, then, whether we are establishing the Guardians in order to secure
the greatest possible happiness for them, or whether we must rather look to
the city as a whole to see if happiness is present in it, and whether these
auxiliaries and Guardians must be compelled and persuaded to act so that
they will be the best possible craftsmen of their own work, and so for all the   c
rest. In this way, with the whole city flourishing under good government,
each class may come to partake of the share of happiness its nature allows.

    Why, I think that is an excellent reply, he said.

THE TWO CITIES (421C–423D)

Then will you also think I speak properly on a kindred point? I replied.

    What, in particular?

    Consider, again, whether other workmen are corrupted by the following   d
so that they also become bad.

    What do you have in mind?

    Wealth and poverty, I replied.

    How so?

    As follows. Do you think a potter, once become rich, is still willing to at-
tend to his art?

    Hardly, he said.

    He will become more idle and less careful than before?

    Yes, by a great deal.

    So he becomes a worse potter?

    Again, by a great deal, he said.

    On the other hand, if due to poverty he cannot provide himself with
tools or anything else which pertains to his art, the product will be worse
produced, and his sons or others whom he may teach will learn to be infe-   e
rior workmen?

Of course.

Then the products of the arts, as well as the artists themselves, are made worse by both poverty and wealth?

It appears so.

Then we have found other things, it seems, which the Guardians must never in any way allow to creep into the city undetected.

Which are?

422a Wealth and poverty, I replied. Because the one produces luxury, idleness, and innovation, the other, in addition to innovation, slavish neglect and bad workmanship.

Quite so, he said. But, Socrates, how will our city be able to wage war, when it has not got the resources—especially if it is compelled to fight a great and wealthy enemy?

Clearly it is harder against one of them, I replied, easier against two.

b What do you mean? he replied.

In the first place, I said, if they do have to fight, they will surely themselves be athletes of war fighting against rich men?

Yes, that's so, he said.

Well now, Adeimantus, I replied, do you not think that one boxer, trained for it and in the peak of condition, might easily fight a pair of men who are not boxers, but rich and fat?

Not at the same time perhaps, he said.

c Not even if he could retreat, and then turn and punch whichever came up first? I replied. And do this repeatedly, in the burning sun? Could not he handle an even greater number?

Of course, he said. There would be nothing surprising in it.

But do you think the rich, by knowledge and experience, have more skill in boxing than in warfare?

No, he said.

So probably our athletes will easily fight two or three times their own number.

I agree with you, he said: for I think you are right.

d What if they should send envoys to the other city to state the truth: "We have no use for gold or silver, nor is it allowed us, but it is allowed you. So if you join us as allies, you have what belongs to the others." Do you think anyone hearing this would choose to make war on tough, lean dogs, instead of joining the dogs against fat, tender sheep?

No, I do not. But if the wealth of the others is collected in one city, will that not be dangerous to the city which is not rich?

You are happy, I replied, in thinking there is any other city worthy of the name, except the kind we are founding.

But why? he said.

We ought to address the others more grandly, I replied: for each of them is not a city but a whole multitude of cities, as the joke has it.[1] There are at least two if there are any, the city of the rich and the city of the poor, and they are at war with each other. But there are many other cities in each of these two. If you refer to them as one, you will be altogether mistaken, but if you refer to them as many and give the resources and power or even the persons of some of them to others, you will have many allies and few enemies. And as long as your city is governed temperately, as we just now prescribed, it will be greatest—I don't mean in reputation but greatest in very truth, even if it should number only a thousand defenders. For you will not thus easily find a great city in Greece or anywhere else which is one, but many many times larger than this that seem so. Or do you think otherwise?

No, I certainly do not, he said.

Then this is surely be the best indication for our rulers, I replied, in distinguishing how large to make the city and how much territory should be marked off for a city of that size, and to let the rest go.

What is the indication? he asked.

This, I think, I replied: that it should grow to the point where its increase allows it to be one, but not beyond.

Yes, excellent, he said.

Then we will also issue this further command to the Guardians: to be

e

423a

b

c

1. The play here is on "making many out of one"—as with dropping a pot.

careful that the city not be too small or only seemingly great, but sufficient and one.

No doubt a trivial order! he said.

Yes, and here is one still more trivial, I replied. We mentioned it before when we said that if any inferior offspring are born of the Guardians, they must be sent away to the others, and if a superior is born from the others, he must be sent to the Guardians. This meant to make clear that the other citizens must be put to that one single task for which they are naturally suited, so that each may become not many but one by the one practice which is his own, and thus the whole city will grow to be one, not many.

An even smaller order than the other!! he said.

MUSIC AND THE CONSTITUTION (423D–425C)

Still, my dear Adeimantus, I replied, we are not issuing them a multitude of important commands, as one might think. All are inconsiderable, if only they guard the proverbial "one great thing"—or rather instead of great, sufficient.

What is that? he said.

Education and nurture, I replied. For if they are well-educated and reasonable men, they will easily see through all these things and others too—everything we are now leaving out, the possession of wives, and marriages, and the procreation of children—because in these it is necessary to act, as far as possible, according to the proverb that "friends have all things in common."

Yes, and most correctly, he said.

Furthermore, I said, a constitution, if once properly set in motion, continues to grow as in a circle. For when sound nurture and education are preserved, they produce excellent natures, and again, sound natures grow still better by receiving this sort of education, especially in respect to breeding, as with other animals.[2]

---

2. Plato assumes the inheritance of acquired characteristics.

Likely enough, he said.   b

Put briefly, then, those charged with care of the city must hold fast to this, so that the city may not be corrupted unawares; but beyond all else, they must guard against innovation in gymnastic and music contrary to the established order, and to the best of their ability be on guard lest when someone says that people care more "for the newest song on the singer's lips," the poet may be understand to mean not new songs but a new style of singing, and to commend it. One must not praise such a thing, nor so in-   c terpret the poet, but guard against changing to a new form of music, as endangering the whole. For styles of music are nowhere disturbed without disturbing the most important laws and customs of political order—as Damon says and I believe.

Count me among those persuaded too, said Adeimantus.

Then it seems it is surely here, in music, I replied, where the Guardians   d must erect their watchtower.

At any rate, this kind of lawlessness readily creeps in unobserved, he said.

Yes, I said, as mere play that supposedly does no harm.

Nor does it, he said, except that little by little it establishes itself and quietly spreads to manners and practices; from there, grown great, it steps forth into contracts and business dealings between man and man, whence it pro-   e ceeds with much licentiousness to laws and constitutions, Socrates, until in the end it overturns and perverts all things public and private.

Very well, I replied. Is it really so?

I think it is, he said.

Then as we were saying to begin with, our children must have a share from the very first of more law-abiding play, because if it is lawless and they become like it, they cannot grow into serious and law-abiding men.

Of course, he said.   425a

But when children make a good beginning in their play, they receive lawful order through their music, and the result is the opposite of before; it follows them in everything and causes them to flourish, and straightens anything in the city which before was cast down.

True enough, he said.

And so they rediscover the apparently trivial customs, I said, which their predecessors had altogether done away with.

Such as?

b   Fitting silence on the part of the young in the presence of their elders, and when to sit and rise, and proper service to parents, and hairstyles and garments and shoes and bodily posture in general, and everything else of the sort. Don't you think?

Yes.

But it is silly to enact laws about them, I suppose. For surely they do not arise, nor would they be maintained, by spoken and written enactments.

Of course not.

And in any event, Adeimantus, I said, such things follow from the kind of education with which one begins: does not like always call forth like?

c   Certainly, he said.

In the end then, I suppose we would say, it issues in some one single complete and vigorous result, either good or perhaps the opposite.

Of course, he replied.

For these reasons then, I said, I would not undertake to legislate such matters further.

Reasonably enough, he said.

FUTILITY OF MUCH LEGISLATION (425C–428A)

But again, what about commercial arrangements involving contracts, I said—the deals people make with each other in the marketplace, and if you
d   will, tradesmen's contracts, and actions for defamation and assault, and procedures for bringing suit and impaneling juries, and payment and assessment of market taxes or customs duties required, or again, market regulations in general for city or police or harbor, or anything else of the sort. Shall we venture to legislate them?

Why, it is not worth it, he said, to issue orders to good and noble men. They will easily discover for themselves, surely, most of what needs to be legislated.

Yes, my friend, I said, at least if god grants them preservation of the laws   e
we have previously explained.

If not, he replied, they will pass their whole lives constantly enacting and
amending a multitude of such regulations, expecting to attain what is best.

You mean, I said, they will live like sick people who refuse to abandon a
bad regimen due to intemperance.

Exactly.

What a delightful way to live! They get nothing from their doctoring ex-   426a
cept to make their diseases more varied and severe, forever hoping that if
only someone will advise a drug, they will be cured by it.

Exactly so, he said, for that kind of patient.

Well then, I replied. Aren't they especially charming in their belief that
whoever tells them the truth is their own worst enemy? Namely, that until
they put a stop to their drunkenness and gluttony and lechery and idleness,
neither drugs nor surgery nor cautery, no, nor spells and amulets or anything of the sort will do them any good at all.

Not very charming, he said. There is no charm in being angry at good   b
advice.

It seems you're no admirer of such folk, I said.

Most certainly not.

Then you will not admire a whole city which acts as we just described.
Do not badly constituted cities appear to you to behave in the same way,
when they enjoin their citizens not to disturb the established order of the   c
city as a whole, on pain of death to whoever does so? Among cities so constituted, whoever serves them by being most obsequiously clever in anticipating and satisfying their wishes will then be a fine fellow, wise in great
matters, and honored by them.

I agree. I think they do act that way, he said, and I do not approve in the
slightest.

No? Then what about people willing and eager to serve such cities?   d
Don't you admire their pliable courage?

I do, he said. Except when they fool themselves and think they are in
truth statesmen because they are praised by the multitude.

What? Don't you make allowances for them? I replied. Do you think it is possible for a man who does not know how to measure, if he is told by many others of the same sort that he is four cubits tall,³ not to believe it of himself?

e   Of course not, he said.

Then do not be so hard on them. In fact, people like this are surely the most charming of all: they constantly enact laws of the sort we just described and amend them, forever thinking they will find an end to cheating in business and the other evils I just now mentioned, unaware that they are really cutting off the heads of a hydra.

427a   Yes, he said, that is all they are doing.

Well, I replied, I should have thought that the genuine lawgiver ought not busy himself with a form of laws and a constitution such as this, whether in a well- or badly constituted city. Not in the one, because some laws can be discovered by anybody and others added spontaneously from previous provisions. Not in the other, because it is useless and of no effect.

b   Then what still remains for us in the matter of legislation? he said.

And I said, For us, nothing. But certainly for the Apollo at Delphi, legal enactments of the first importance.

Of what sort? he replied.

Founding of temples, and sacrifices, and other services to gods and demigods and heroes; and again, burial of the dead, and all services required to propitiate those in the other world. For we do not know such things as this, and in founding a city we will be persuaded by no one else, if we have

c   good sense, nor consult any other religious adviser except the god of our fathers. For this god at Delphi, seated at the navel of the earth, is surely in such matters as this the ancestral religious adviser for all mankind.⁴

You are right, he said. It must so be done.

3. Six feet. The Greek cubit was approximately eighteen inches.

4. The Delphic oracle was presided over by Apollo, and its site contained the navel, a rock believed to be the center of the earth. Responses were given by the Pythia, a priestess who spoke in a state of ecstasy induced by divine possession, perhaps induced by drugs: it was assumed that it was not the Pythia who spoke, but Apollo who spoke through her. The answers were of-

Political Virtue (427c–435a)

At this point then, son of Ariston, I replied, the city is founded. Next, look
within it. Provide yourself with sufficient light from any source you can,   d
and summon your brother and Polemarchus and the others, to see whether
we can somehow discern where justice is, and where injustice, and how the
two differ from each other, and which must be possessed by him who is to
be happy, whether or not it escapes notice of all gods and men.

Nonsense, said Glaucon. You promised to inquire yourself, because you
thought it would be impious in you not to come to the aid of justice by
every means in your power.

You're right to remind me, I said, and it must be done that way. But you   e
too must take part.

Why, so we will, he said.

I hope then to find it in the following way, I replied: I think our city, if
indeed it has been rightly founded, is completely good.

Necessarily, he said.

Then clearly it is wise and courageous and temperate and just.

Yes.

Now, if we find some of these in it, the remainder will be what has not
been found?

Of course.   428a

Then even as with any other four things, if we were seeking some one of
them in anything whatever, it would suffice for us whenever we recognized
that first; but if we recognized the other three before it, we would recognize
what we are seeking from this very fact; for it is clear that nothing was still
left other than the remainder.

You're right, he said.

Then we must inquire in the same way about these, since they happen to
be four?

Clearly so.

---

ten riddling and required careful interpretation—for example, the Pythia's claim that Socrates
was the wisest man in Greece (*Apology* 21a–23b).

POLITICAL WISDOM (428A–429A)

And first then, I think, wisdom is evident in it. And there appears to be
something strange about it.

b   Why? he replied.

The city we have described is really wise, I think. For it is well counseled,
is it not?

Yes.

And surely this very thing, good counsel, is clearly a kind of knowledge;
for no doubt people are not well counseled by ignorance, but by knowledge.

Agreed.

But there are many varied kinds of knowledge in the city.

Of course.

c   Is the city then to be described as wise and well-counseled through
knowledge of building?

Not at all through that, he said, but only as skilled in building.

So a city is not to be called wise due to the knowledge which would take
counsel about the best condition of wooden implements?

Hardly.

Nor implements of brass, nor anything else of the sort?

Nor that, he said.

Again, a city is not to be called wise due to knowledge about how to
grow plants from the earth, but only skilled in farming?

I think so.

Well then, I replied, is there any knowledge among any of the citizens in
the city we have just founded which takes counsel not about some particular thing in the city, but about the city itself as a whole, and what sort of relations it may best have toward itself and other cities?

d   Of course there is.

What is it, I said, and in whom?

This art of guardianship, he replied, and in these rulers we just named
perfect Guardians.

Then what do you call the city through this knowledge?

Well counseled, he said, and really wise.

Do you think there will be present in our city more smiths than these genuine Guardians? I said.

Many more smiths, he replied.

e

Then also, among all others named to be something after the knowledge they possess, these would be fewest? I said.

Of course.

So a city founded according to nature would be wise as a whole by the smallest class and least part of itself, and by the knowledge in it by which it governs and rules. And this, it seems, is by nature a kind least numerous, to which is allotted a share of that knowledge which alone among others should be called wisdom.

Very true, he said.

429a

Then I don't know but we've found one of the four, and where in the city it resides.

It seems to me, at any rate, sufficiently discovered, he said.

POLITICAL COURAGE (429A–430C)

Again, it is not very hard to discern courage itself, through which such a city as this must be called courageous, and that part of the city in which it is situated.

How so?

b

Who would look to anything else in saying that a city is cowardly or courageous, I replied, except to this part which defends it and goes to war on its behalf?

No one would look to anything else, he said.

No, I said, for I don't suppose that whether the others in it are cowardly or brave would be determinative of one quality or the other.

No.

And so, a city is courageous by a part of itself, and through having in that part power to preserve in all circumstances the opinion that things to be

c

feared are the same and of the same sort as the lawgiver prescribed in education. Or don't you call this courage?

I didn't quite understand what you said. Please repeat it.

I am saying that courage is a kind of preservation, I said.

What sort of preservation?

That of the opinion produced by law, through education, about things to be feared: what they are, and of what sort. By preservation in all circumstances, I meant preserving it in the midst of pains and pleasures and desires and fears, and not casting it out. I'll compare it to what I think it is like, if you wish.

d   Please do.

Well, you know that dyers, I replied, when they wish to dye wool so that it is purple, first select only pure white wool from among the many different colors; next, they carefully prepare it to take the dye in its full brilliance, and thus, then, they dip it. What is dyed in this way becomes indelibly
e   fixed, and washing it, with soap or without, cannot dull its brilliance. But you also know what happens if one dyes other colors, and does not prepare the wool beforehand.

I do know, he said. It looks washed out and ridiculous.

Understand then, that to the best of our ability, I replied, we were also doing just this sort of thing when we selected the soldiers and educated
430a   them in music and gymnastic. You must suppose we were contriving nothing other than how they might best be persuaded to take the color of our laws like a dye, in order that their opinion, most especially about what is to be feared, might become indelibly fixed through their having a suitable nature and upbringing, the dye not washed out of them even by such solvents as pleasure provides—more terrible to effect this than lye and ashes—and pain and fear and desire, terrible beyond all other solvents. This sort of
b   power and preservation of right and lawful opinion in all circumstances about things which are and are not to be feared, I assume to be and call courage, unless you have something else to suggest.

Why, not at all, he replied. For I think you believe that right opinion about these same things, produced without education, the sort characteristic of a beast or a slave, is not quite fully legitimate, and you call it something other than courage.

Quite true, I replied.

Then I accept this to be courage.

c

In fact, accept it at least as political courage, I replied, and you will be right. If you wish, we will later discuss it better. For right now, we are after not courage but justice. So relative to that search, this, I think, is enough.

Why, very good, he said.

POLITICAL TEMPERANCE (430D–432B)

Two things then remain to be discerned in the city, I said: temperance, and the aim of our whole inquiry, justice.

d

Of course.

How might we discover justice, so that we may no longer be troubled about temperance?

For my part, I don't know, nor would I wish justice to come to light first, he said, if we shall then no longer inquire about temperance. So if you wish to gratify me, please examine this before that.

Why certainly, I replied—if it is not unjust in me to do so.

e

Go on then, he said.

Very well, I said. As it looks from here, at least, temperance is more like a kind of concord and attunement than the previous virtues.

How so?

Temperance is surely a kind of good order and mastery of certain pleasures and desires, I replied, as people say when they speak of being "master of oneself."[5] I am not quite sure how they mean that, but certain other expressions of this sort also appear to point in the same direction, don't they?

Most certainly, he said.

---

5. Or, "stronger than oneself."

Is not "master of oneself" ridiculous? For anyone stronger than himself would also be weaker than himself, and the weaker stronger. For it is the same person described in all this.

Of course.

But it appears to me that this expression means there is something better within the man himself, having to do with his soul, I replied, and something worse, and when what is by nature better governs the worse, that is what is meant by "master of oneself." It is a term of praise, at any rate. But when due to bad upbringing or some evil association, what is better and smaller is overcome by the multitude of what is worse, the expression condemns it as a disgrace, and calls anyone in this condition weaker than himself and intemperate.

In fact, it does seem so, he said.

Look then to our new city, I replied, and you will find one of these present in it: you will claim it is justly described as master of itself, since that in which the better rules the worse must be called temperate and stronger than itself.

Why, I do see it. You're right, he said.

Moreover, the many multifarious desires and pleasures and pains are especially found in children and women and slaves, and in the inferior multitude said to be free.

Of course.

But the simple and moderate desires led by reflection and accompanied by reason and right opinion you will meet with in but few, and those few best in nature and best educated.

True, he said.

You also see it in your city: the desires there present in the inferior multitude are governed by the desires and wisdom present in the superior few.

Yes, he said.

So if any city must be described as stronger than pleasures and desires and itself, this one is.

Certainly, he said.

Now, is it not also temperate in respect to all these?

431a

b

c

d

Yes indeed, he said.

Again, if indeed the same opinion about who must rule is also present in rulers and ruled in any other city, it would also be present in this. Don't you think so?

Yes, quite emphatically, he said.   e

Then in which among the citizens will you say temperance is present, when it is so? In the rulers, or those ruled?

In both, surely, he said.

You see then, I replied, that we were quite right to suspect just now that temperance may be likened to a kind of attunement.

How so?

Because it is not like courage and wisdom, whose presence in some par-   432a
ticular part makes the city wise or courageous. Temperance does not act like that: it is literally stretched through the whole, providing a perfect conso-
nance of weakest and strongest and what is in between, whether in wisdom or if you will in strength and number, or wealth or anything of the sort. So we would very rightly claim that this unanimity is temperance: a concord of better and worse according to nature as to which should rule in a city and in each individual.

I quite agree, he said.   b

POLITICAL JUSTICE (432B–433E)

Very well, I replied. We have discerned three forms in the city—at least that is our present opinion. What then would the remaining form[6] be, through which a city would partake of virtue? For it is clear this is justice.

Yes.

Well, Glaucon, at this point we have to be like hunters surrounding a thicket, and pay close attention that justice does not somehow escape and vanish undetected. For it is evident that it is in here somewhere. So look close, and if somehow you see it before I do, tell me.

6. Form = species.

c   I might wish! he said. But you do better to treat me instead as a follower who can see what is pointed out to him.

Follow along, then, I answered, and wish me luck.

I will, he replied. Only lead on.

Why really, I said, the place appears dark and tangled. At any rate, it is obscure and hard to search. Still, we must go on.

d   Yes, he said.

I took a look and said, There, Glaucon. There! We have found its track, and I think it will not escape us.

Good news, he replied.

But surely, I answered, we have been very stupid.

How so?

It appears it has been rolling around at our feet from the beginning, my friend, and we didn't even see it. We behaved quite ridiculously. Even as people sometimes search for what they already hold in their hands, so we too did not look, but kept staring off into the distance; that is perhaps why it escaped our notice.

e   What do you mean? he said.

This, I replied. It seems to me that we have actually been speaking and hearing of it for some time, and did not understand that in a way we were ourselves talking about it.

A lengthy prelude, he said, for someone eager to hear.

433a   Listen then, I replied, and see if there is perhaps something in what I say. What we from the beginning assumed had to be done throughout, when we were founding the city, that, I think, or some form of it, is justice. We surely assumed and repeatedly said, if you recall, that each individual ought to have one single occupation in the city for which his nature is most suited.

Yes, we did say that.

And again, that justice is doing what is one's own and not interfering or meddling in many things—this we've heard from many others, and often said ourselves.

b   Yes, we have.

Then, my friend, I replied, this doing what is one's own, when it happens to occur in a certain way, is justice. Do you know from what I infer this?

No, tell me, he said.

Among what we have considered in the city, I replied, namely, temperance and courage and wisdom, I think this is the underlying remainder: it provides all of those with their power so that they come to be present, and when they come to be present, it preserves them as long as it is present. We also said that justice would be the remainder among them if we found the other three.

Necessarily, he said.

Again, I replied, suppose we had to judge which of these, when it came to be present, will especially make our city good. It would be hard to decide whether it is unanimity among the rulers and ruled, or preservation of lawful opinion in our soldiers about what things are and are not to be feared, or wisdom and guardianship in the rulers. Or is it especially this that makes it good: that in child and woman, in slave and freeman and craftsman, in ruler and ruled, each, being one, does what is his own and does not interfere or meddle in many things?

Hard to decide, no doubt, he said.

Then it seems the power of each person in it to do what is his own contends on equal terms with its wisdom and temperance and courage, relative to the virtue of a city.

Indeed, he said.

Now, what contends on equal terms with them in respect to the virtue of a city, you would assume to be justice?

Most certainly.

LEGAL JUSTICE (433E–434A)

Consider then whether it also seems so in this respect: Will you require the rulers in the city to act as judges in lawsuits?

Of course.

Will they render judgment desiring anything whatever except that each person not have what belongs to another, nor be deprived of his own?

No, only that.

Supposing it to be just?

Yes.

And so in this too, in some way the having and doing of what is kindred and one's own would be agreed to be justice.

434a   That is so.

POLITICAL INJUSTICE (434A–435A)

See then if you also concur with me in this. Suppose a builder undertakes to produce the works of a shoemaker, or a shoemaker of a builder, or suppose they exchange tools with each other, or honors, or even that the same person undertakes to practice both. Do you think interchanging everything else would greatly harm the city?

Not much, he said.

But when, I think, a craftsman or someone by nature a businessman is
b   afterward raised up by wealth or majorities or strength or any other such thing, and undertakes to enter the military form;[7] or when someone among the military, though unequal to it, undertakes to go into the form of the counselors and Guardians, and they interchange tools and honors; or when the same person undertakes to do all this at the same time—then I suppose you think this change, this interference and meddling in many things, is destructive to the city.

Very much so.

c   So meddling interference among these three kinds, and changing into one another, is the greatest harm to the city, and would most rightly be described as an extreme of wrongdoing.

Exactly so.

---

7. Form = class or part.

You will not deny that the greatest wrongdoing against one's own city is injustice?

Of course not, he said.

So this is injustice. Again, let us say this: minding one's own affairs on the part of the economic, auxiliary, and Guardian kinds, each doing what is its own in the city, is the opposite of that; it is justice, and would make the city just.

I quite agree, he said.

Let us not yet assert it quite fixedly, I replied. But if it is agreed that this form,[8] when it enters into each individual human being, is there also justice, we will at that point concede—for what more is there to say? If not, we will look for something else. But for now, let us bring the inquiry to an end. We supposed that it would be easier to discern what justice is in a single person if we first undertook to view it in something larger which contained it. And it seemed to us that this was a city, so we founded the best we could, well knowing that justice would be present in the good city. Let us then refer what there came to light back to the individual, and if it agrees, it will be well. But if something different reveals itself in the individual, we will go back to the city again and put it to the test; perhaps if we examine them side by side and rub them together like firesticks, we will cause justice to flash forth. And when it has become manifest, we will firmly establish it in our midst.

Why, you describe an excellent way, he said, and it should so be done.

The Structure of the Human Soul (435a–441c)

JUSTICE IN THE INDIVIDUAL AND THE "LONGER WAY" (435A–D)

Now, I replied, if one calls what is larger and what is smaller the same, do they happen to be unlike or like in the respect in which they are called the same?

Like, he said.

8. That is, minding one's own affairs: doing what is properly and peculiarly one's own.

b   And so, a just man will not differ at all from a just city in respect to the form of justice itself, but will be like it?

Yes, he said.

But again, a city seemed just when three kinds of nature were present in it, and each did what is its own. And again, it seemed temperate and courageous and wise through certain other affections and dispositions of these same kinds.

True, he said.

And so, my friend, we will thus also expect the individual to have these
c   same forms in his own soul, and rightly expect the same names for them as those for the city, because of the same affections.

Quite necessarily, he said.

Here again, we have fallen into a trifling inquiry about soul, my friend, I replied: whether it has in itself these three forms or not.

It hardly seems trifling to me, he said. For perhaps the saying that noble things are difficult is true, Socrates.

Apparently, I replied. Be assured, Glaucon, that in my opinion we will never grasp it accurately by such methods as we are now using in argu-
d   ment—for another way, longer and more complex, leads to that—but perhaps, however, on a level with our previous statements and inquiries.

Isn't that to be welcomed? he said. At least for the present, it would be quite enough for me.

Why, it will also very nearly satisfy me, I said.

Then do not give up, he replied. Continue to inquire.

THE INCOMPATIBILITY OF OPPOSITES (435E–437A)

e   Well, I replied, isn't it necessary to agree that the same forms and characters present in the city are present in each of us? For they surely did not arrive there from anywhere else: it would be ridiculous to suppose that the spirited form did not come to be present in cities from private persons who also have this attribute, like people in Thrace and Scythia and pretty generally the region to the north of us. Or the love of learning, which we might claim to have place especially among us, or the love of money, which one might say exists especially in people in Egypt and among the Phoenicians.

Indeed, he said.

This then is so, I replied, and not difficult.

Of course not.

But it is difficult to know whether we do each of these by the same thing, or, since they are three, one by one and another by another. Do we learn by one among the parts in us, and become angry by another, but again, desire the pleasures of nutrition and reproduction and their kindred by some third? Or do we act with respect to each of them by the whole soul, when we are moved to act? This will be difficult to distinguish at a proper level.

I agree, he said.

Then let us undertake to determine whether they are the same as each other, or different, in the following way.

How?

It is clear that the same thing will refuse to do or suffer opposites at the same time in respect to the same thing and relative to the same thing, so that if we find this occurring somewhere among them, we will know that they were not the same, but more than one.

Very well.

Consider this, then:

Please go on, he replied.

Is it possible, I said, for the same thing to stand still and be moved at the same time with respect to the same thing?

Not at all.

Let us then agree still more precisely, lest we somehow fall into dispute as we proceed. For if someone said of a man standing still but moving his hands and head, that the same man stands still and moves at the same time, we would not, I suppose, deem it necessary to speak that way, but rather to say that something of his stands still, but something else moves. Not so?

Yes.

Then again, suppose he who says this carries the pleasantry still further, and in his cleverness suggests that tops stand still and move as a whole at the

436a

b

c

d

same time, when the peg is fixed in the same place and they revolve around it, or indeed when anything else does this by moving in a circle in the same seat. We would not accept it, because such things are not then both at rest and in motion with respect to the same things in themselves; on the con-

e   trary, we would say they have within themselves an axis and a circumference, and with respect to the axis they stand still, for it is not inclined, but with respect to the circumference they are moved in a circle, and when the axis of rotation is inclined and they revolve right to left or front to back at the same time, they then do not stand still at all.

Yes, that's right, he said.

So nothing said of this sort will disturb us, or any the more persuade us that something, being the same, would ever suffer, or be, or produce opposites at the same time with respect to the same thing and relative to the same thing.

437a   I agree, he said.

Nevertheless, I replied, in order that we not be compelled to enter upon all these kinds of dispute and establish by drawn-out discussion that they are not true, let us assume that this is so and proceed. We agree that if ever it turns out otherwise than this, all that follows for us from this will have been loosed and undone.

Why, we must do this, he said.

INWARD ASSENT AND DENIAL (437B–D)

b   Well then, I replied, assent to denial, wanting to get something to refusing it, accepting to rejecting—you would assume that all such things are opposites to each other, whether active or passive? For in this it will make no difference.

Why, of course they are opposites, he replied.

What about thirst and hunger and the desires generally, I replied, and again, willing and wishing? Would you not put all of these somewhere

c   among those forms just now mentioned? For example, will you not say either that the soul of one who desires ever strives after that which he desires, or draws to itself that which it may wish to get for itself, or again, in so far as it is willing that something be provided to it, nods assent to itself as though to an inward question, longing for it to come to be?

Yes.

Then shall we not also put not wishing and not willing or not desiring into rejection and repulsion from the soul, and into all that is opposite to the former?

Of course.   d

DESIRE CORRELATIVE WITH ITS OBJECTS (437D–439B)

But since this is so, shall we say that there is a form[9] which consists of desires, and most conspicuous among them what we call thirst and hunger?

Yes, he replied.

Now, the one is for drink, the other for food?

Yes.

Then in so far as it is thirst, is it for any more than that of which we say it would be a desire in the soul? Is thirst, for example, thirst for hot drink or cold, much or little, or in a word for drink of some particular kind? If a certain heat is present in addition to the thirst, it would produce in addition the desire for what is cold; if coldness is present, the desire for what is hot; if   e
through presence of greatness the thirst is great, it will produce the desire for much, if small, for little. But thirst by itself is never desire for anything other than its object, drink by itself, and again, hunger for food.

That's so, he said. Each desire by itself is only for its object, that of which it is; it is of one kind or another because of things present in addition.

Let no one then catch us off guard, I replied, and disturb us with the ob-   438a
jection that no one desires drink but good drink, and not food but good

---

9. The suggestion that *eidos* here means "class" involves a mistranslation: the reference, as context makes clear, is to a part of the soul.

food. For everyone (it is argued) desires good things: if then thirst is a desire, it would be for good drink or whatever else of which it is a desire, and so in other cases.[10]

Perhaps there is something in that, he said.

But surely, I replied, among things such as to be *for* or *of* or *than* something, those of a certain kind are for or of or than a certain kind, I think, whereas each by itself is for its own object alone.[11]

b   I do not understand, he said.

You do not understand, I said, that the greater is such as to be greater of or than something?

Of course.

Of the less?

Yes.

And much greater, greater than much less?

Yes.

And again, once greater than once less, and will be greater than will be less?

To be sure, he said.

c   Isn't this so also for more relative to fewer, double relative to half, and everything of that sort; and again, heavier relative to lighter, faster relative to slower, and still again, hot things relative to cold and everything like that?

Of course.

What about kinds of knowledge? Is it not the same way? Knowledge by itself is knowledge of what is knowable by itself, or whatever it is one should assume knowledge is of; but knowledge of a certain sort and kind is of a certain sort and kind of object.[12] I mean this: when knowledge of house build-

d

10. All men desire the good (*Gorgias* 468a, *Meno* 77cff., *Symposium* 204e, *Republic* III 413a, VI 505d). But this is of the very nature of desire, not an added or supervening qualification of desires.

11. Cornford translates: "Yes, he agreed, each desire, just in itself, is simply for its own natural object. When the object is of such and such a particular kind, the desire will be correspondingly qualified."

12. Or, "is of what is of a certain sort or kind." The relational genitive here becomes both definitory and objective.

ing arose, did it not so differ from other kinds of knowledge that it was called the art of house building?

Certainly.

Because it is of a certain kind, different from any other?

Yes.

Now, it became of a certain kind because it was of a certain kind of object? And so for the other arts and kinds of knowledge?

That is so.

Then if you perhaps now understand, I replied, please state this as what I meant before in saying that everything which is for or of or than something is, by itself alone, such as to be of or for its own correlative alone; but if it is of a certain sort, it is also of a certain sort of thing.[13] I don't at all mean that they are of the same sort as the things they are of—that knowledge of health and disease is therefore healthy and diseased, and knowledge of goods and evils good and evil. But when knowledge is not only of that of which it is knowledge, but of a certain kind of thing, namely health and disease, it then itself also becomes a certain kind of knowledge, and this causes it no longer to be called knowledge simply, but the medical art, since it is in addition knowledge of a certain kind.

e

I understand, he said, and I think that is so.

What about thirst, then? I replied. Will you not put it among the things which are of something? Thirst is surely for—?

439a

Yes, he replied: for drink.

Then a certain kind of thirst is also for a certain kind of drink, though thirst by itself is neither for much nor little, good nor bad, nor in a word for any certain sort of thing. On the contrary: thirst by itself is of drink by itself alone.

Quite so.

So the soul of someone thirsty, in so far as it thirsts, wishes nothing except to drink, and longs for this and is impelled to it.

Clearly so.

b

---

13. Cornford translates: "This, then, if you understand me now, is what I meant by saying that, where there are two correlatives, the one is qualified if, and only if, the other is so." In terms of propositional content, this is a literal translation.

REASON AND APPETITE (439B – E)

Then if ever anything holds back the soul when it is thirsty, there would be something different in it from what is itself thirsty and leads it like a wild beast to drink? For surely, we say, the same thing cannot behave in opposite ways at the same time concerning the same thing by the same part of itself.

Of course not.

So I suppose it is not well said of the archer that his hands at the same time draw the bow toward him and push it away. Rather, one hand pulls, the other pushes.

c   Quite so, he said.

May we then say that people sometimes refuse to drink when thirsty?

Of course, he said. Many do, and often.

Then what should one say about them? I asked. That what bids them drink is present in their soul, but what forbids it is also present, as other than and overmastering what bids?

I think so, he said.

d   Now, does not what forbids this come to be present from reflection, when it comes to be present, while what pulls and hauls is engendered through passions and diseases?

It appears so.

Then it is not unreasonable for us to regard them as two, and different from each other, I replied, and to describe that by which the soul reflects as reflective; that by which it loves and hungers and thirsts and is aflutter with other desires is unreflective and appetitive, a companion to various replenishments and pleasures.

e   We might very properly believe so, he said.

SPIRIT (439E–441C)

Then let us distinguish these two forms as present in the soul, I said. But is there then also a third, spirit, by which we are angry? Or is it of like nature to one of these two?

Perhaps to the one, the appetitive, he said.

But I once heard a story I believe, I replied: How Leontius son of Aglaion, coming up from the Piraeus under the outer north wall, perceived corpses laid out near the gallows. He wanted to look, and at the same time he was disgusted with himself and turned away; he fought with himself for awhile and covered his face, but, overcome by the desire, he held his eyes wide open and ran up to the corpses and said, "Look, damn you. Take your fill of the lovely sight."

440a

I've heard that story myself, he said.

But surely this story indicates, I said, that anger sometimes wars against the desires, as one kind of thing against another.

Yes, he said.

We perceive this elsewhere in many places, I said. When desires compel someone contrary to reflection, he blames himself and is angry at the compulsion within, and as though there were two political factions, doesn't the spirit of such a person becomes an ally of reason? But as to spirit making common cause with the desires when reason decides spirit should not oppose it[14]—I suppose you would deny you ever perceived such a thing occurring in yourself or in anyone else.

b

Emphatically, he said.

What about when someone supposes he has done injustice? I replied. The more noble he is, the less capable he is of anger at suffering hunger or cold or anything of the sort at the hands of a person whom he supposes justly imposes them, and as I claim, his spirit refuses to be roused against him.

c

True, he said.

What about when someone believes he has suffered injustice? Does not his spirit seethe with anger within him, and become the ally of what he

14. The translation seems required, but inconsistent with such passages as VIII 553cff. (cf. 441a), where spirit does in fact join with the desires against reason. This is an indication of the provisional character of the reasoning, and the need for a "longer way." At 440e, spirit is a natural auxiliary to reason unless corrupted by bad upbringing.

thinks is just? Persevering through hunger and cold and all else of the sort,
d the noble spirit endures and triumphs, and does not give over until it suc-
ceeds or dies, or is called back and calmed by the voice of reason within, like
a dog being called off by a shepherd?

It certainly seems very much as you say, he replied. And indeed, we
imagined the auxiliaries in our city as like dogs who obey the rulers as shepherds of the city.

You understand what I mean to say very well, I replied. But do you also
understand this in addition?

e What?

That the spirited form appears to us opposite to what it did a moment
ago: for then we supposed it was something appetitive, but now we claim it
is far removed from that, but instead takes up arms on the side of reflection
in the party-strife of the soul.

Quite so, he said.

Then is it also different from reflection, or is it a form of it, so that there
are not three but two forms in a soul, reflection and appetite? Or even as
441a there were three kinds contained in the city, money makers, auxiliaries,
and advisers, is there thus also this third kind in a soul, the spirited form,
by nature an auxiliary to reflection if it is not corrupted by bad upbringing?

It is necessarily a third, he said.

Yes, I replied, if it proves to be something other than reflection, as it has
also proved a different thing from appetite.

Why, that's not hard to show, he said. In fact, one can see it in children:
they are full of anger and spirit straight from birth, and some, I think, never
do get a share of reason, while the majority come to it late.

b Yes, I replied, you're quite right. Again, one can see that what you're saying is true among wild beasts. There is also the testimony of Homer which
I quoted before: "He struck his chest and rebuked his heart"; here Homer
clearly has made one thing strike another, what has calculated the better
and worse striking what is unreasonably angry.

c You're quite right, he said.

Justice in the Individual Soul (441c–445e)

VIRTUES THE SAME IN SOUL AND STATE (441C–442D)

And so, with difficulty, we have made it through, I replied. We are properly agreed that the same kinds are present in city and in the soul of each individual, equal in number.

That is so.

Then at this point, it is necessary that as and whereby a city was wise, so also and thereby the private citizen is wise?

Of course.

And whereby and as a private citizen is courageous, thereby and so a city also is courageous, and in like manner both possess all else relative to virtue?

Necessarily.

Then Glaucon, I suppose we will say that a man is just in the same way in which a city is also just.

This too is quite necessary.

But we surely have not somehow forgotten that a city is just by the three kinds in it each doing what is its own?

I doubt it has been forgotten, he said.

So we must remember that each of us also will be just and do what is his own when each of the kinds in us does its own.

We must indeed, he replied.

Now, it pertains to reflection to rule, because it is wise and exercises forethought in behalf of the whole soul; and to the spirited form to be its servant and ally.

Of course.

Then isn't it as we were saying? Mixture of music and gymnastic will cause them to be in concord, stretching and nourishing the one with noble words and studies, slackening and calming the other with mode and rhythm, making it gentle.

Exactly so, he replied.

And when these two are nurtured in this way, when they have studied and been educated in what is truly their own, let them be set over the appetitive—which is surely the most numerous part of the soul in each individual, and by nature most insatiably covetous of money. These two will watch it closely, lest it be filled with the pleasures of the body, so-called, and become multitudinous and strong and not do what is its own, but undertake to enslave and rule what its kind ought not rule, and turn the whole of life completely upside down.

b   Of course, he said.

Then, I replied, won't these two most nobly stand guard in behalf of the whole soul and body against enemies from without—the one taking counsel, the other giving battle, following its ruler, and by its courage bringing what has been advised to a successful conclusion?

That's so.

c   And so, I suppose we call each individual courageous by this part, when his spirited form preserves through pains and pleasures what was and was not pronounced by reasoning to be fearful.

Yes, rightly, he said.

But wise by that small part which rules in him and announces this, and also has knowledge within itself of what is for the advantage of the whole community consisting of the three together, and of each.

Of course.

Is it not temperate by their friendship and concord, when what rules and the two which are ruled share the conviction that reflection ought to rule, and that they should not take part against it?

d   Temperance both of city and private citizen, at any rate, is surely no other than this, he replied.

But again, it will be just by that which we often say, and in that way?[15]

Quite necessarily.

JUSTICE IN ACTION (442D–443B)

Well then, I said. Is justice somehow blurred and indistinct for us? Does it seem to be at all other than what it appeared to be in the city?

---

15. That is, by doing what is its own, performing its proper function.

I think not, he said.

If anything in our soul still disputes this, I replied, we might completely confirm it by applying commonplace tests.

Of what sort?

e

For example, suppose we had to agree concerning this city and the person who in nature and upbringing is like it, whether it seems that, should he accept gold or silver on deposit, such a person might embezzle it. Do you think anyone would suppose he would do it, rather than others not of his kind?

Not at all, he said.

443a

Then he would also be clear of temple robberies and thefts and betrayals, whether privately of friends or publicly of cities?

Yes.

And again, clear of any sort of faithlessness in respect to oaths or other kinds of agreement?

Of course.

Again, adultery and neglect of parents and denial of due service to the gods will belong to anyone rather than such a man as this?

Emphatically, he said.

Now, the cause of all this is that each of the elements in him does what is its own in the matter of ruling and being ruled?

b

That and nothing else.

Do you still look for justice to be anything other than that power which produces men and cities of this sort?

Most certainly not, he said.

THE INWARDNESS OF JUSTICE (443B–444A)

So our dream is fulfilled. We said we suspected right from the start, in founding the city, that we had providentially hit upon a principle and pattern of justice.

Indeed.

c

There really was after all a kind of image of justice, Glaucon—which is why it was useful—in the principle that it is right for someone by nature a shoemaker to make shoes and do nothing else, and for the builder to build, and so on.

It appears so.

d The truth, as it seems, was that justice is something of this sort: not concerned with the external action of things which are one's own, but with the inward, as truly concerned with one's self and things which belong to one's self. The just man does not allow any element in himself to do what properly belongs to another, nor the kinds in his soul to meddle and interfere with each other; on the contrary, he sets in good order what is really akin and achieves self-governance. He introduces beauty and order and becomes a friend to himself, bringing the three elements into attunement as though they were literally the three defining terms of a musical scale, bottom, top, and mean;[16] and if there are other terms in between, he binds them all to-

e gether and becomes, from many, completely one.[17] Temperate and attuned, he at this point so acts, whether he acts concerning possession of money or care of body, or in anything political, or private business transactions. In all these he believes and calls just and proper those actions which preserve and help produce this disposition, and wisdom the knowledge which presides over this kind of action, but unjust an action which might ever tend to destroy it, and again folly the opinion which presides over it.

444a Completely true, Socrates, he said.

Very well then, I replied. We would not be utterly deceived, I suppose, if we claim to have discovered the just man and the just city, and the justice which happens to be in them?

Emphatically not, he said.

Shall we claim it, then?

Yes.

16. The reference is to the perfect consonances of Greek music: the lowest and highest terms may be taken to define the octave (1:2, cf. 432a–b, 617b); the mean in relation to the lower term of the octave then defines the fourth (4:3), and in relation to the higher, the fifth (3:2). The "lowest" string on the harp was highest in pitch; the top string lowest in pitch. Despite ancient conjectures (cf. Plutarch, *Platonic Questions* 1008a–e), it is not here specified which parts of the soul correspond to what pitches.

17. The unity achieved is that of a scale or mode.

JUSTICE IS HEALTH OF SOUL, INJUSTICE DISEASE OF SOUL (444A–E)

Let it be so, then, I replied. Next, I suppose, we must examine injustice.

Clearly.

Then injustice must be, in turn, a kind of faction among the three ele-   b
ments, an interference and alien encroachment, an uprising of part of the
soul against the whole so that it may rule in it improperly, since the part is
by nature fit only to be a slave to the ruling kind. I suppose we will say that
such things as these, and the disturbance and wandering of them, are injustice and intemperance and cowardice and folly, and in general, all vice.

Exactly that, he said.

Now, doing unjust things and being unjust, and again, doing just things,   c
are all clearly evident at this point, I replied, if indeed injustice and justice
are thus.

How so?

Because they do not differ at all from health and disease, I replied: as
those are in body, so these are in soul.

In what way? he said.

Healthful things surely cause health to be present, and diseased things
disease.

Yes.

So also, doing just things causes justice to be present, doing unjust
things injustice?

Necessarily.   d

To cause health is to establish the things in the body as governing and
being governed by each other according to nature; disease causes them to
rule and be ruled, one by another, contrary to nature.[18]

Yes.

So again, I said, to cause justice to be present is to establish the parts
within the soul as governing and being governed by each other according to

---

18. The "things in the body" are the four humors, blood, phlegm, yellow bile, and black bile. See
Timaeus 82a ff., Hippocrates, *On the Nature of Man*, iv–v. Plato adopts the theory that disease
is imbalance of these elements, contrary to proper or natural proportion.

nature; injustice causes one of them to rule and be ruled by another contrary to nature.

Exactly so, he said.

So virtue, as it seems, is a kind of health and excellence and good state of soul, but vice is disease and deformity and weakness.

e   That is so.

Now, do not noble practices tend to the possession of virtue, ignoble practices to vice?

Necessarily.

JUSTICE AS PROFITABLE (444E–B)

Then at this point it remains only for us again to inquire, as it seems, if it is

445a   also profitable to act justly and to practice honorable pursuits and to be just, whether anyone is aware what sort of person one is or not. Or is it profitable to do injustice and be unjust, if only one can escape punishment and not become better by being chastised?

Why Socrates, he said, it appears to me that the inquiry at this point becomes ridiculous. Life does not seem worth living when the bodily nature is ruined, not even with all kinds of food and drink and all wealth and every kind of office. Will it then perhaps be worth living when the very nature of

b   that by which we live is disturbed and corrupted, if only one can do whatever he pleases except what will release him from vice and injustice and cause him to possess justice and virtue, given that each of the two has been shown to be such as we have described?

It is indeed ridiculous, I replied. Nevertheless, since we have reached this point, we must not give up until we can discern with utmost clarity that this is so.

Most emphatically, he said, we must not give up.

VIRTUES, VICES, AND CONSTITUTIONS (445C–E)

c   Come now, I replied, in order that you may see how many forms vice also has which I think are worth examining.

I'm with you, he said. Please continue.

Why really, I replied, since we have ascended to this height of argument, it appears to me, as from a watchtower, that there is one form of virtue, but indefinitely many forms of vice, some four among them especially worthy of remark.

How do you mean? he said.

There are perhaps as many patterns of soul, I said, as there are patterns of constitution having distinct forms.

How many, then?

Five constitutions, I replied, and five patterns of soul.   d

What are they? he said.

I say that what we have described is one pattern of constitution, I replied, though it might admit two names: if a single superior man arose among the rulers, it would be called monarchy, if more than one, aristocracy.

True, he said.

So this is one form I mean, I replied: for whether one or more than one is present, they would scarcely disturb any of the laws of the city worth mentioning, if they make use of the upbringing and education we de-   e scribed.

Very likely, he said.

Book V

449a Here then is the sort of city and constitution I call good and right, and the sort of man. But if this is right, then the others are bad and wrong, both the organization of cities and the fashioning of character of soul among private citizens. There are four forms of vice.

What are they? he said.

I was about to go through them in order and tell how it appeared to me
b each derives from the other. But Polemarchus—he was seated a little farther away than Adeimantus—reached out his hand and took Adeimantus's cloak by the shoulder from above and drew Adeimantus to him, and leaned forward and bent his head and whispered something, of which we heard nothing else except this:

Shall we let it go then? he said. Or what shall we do?

Certainly not, said Adeimantus, at that point raising his voice.

And I said, What is it, in particular, that you are not letting go?

You, he said.

c Why, in particular?

We think you're shirking, he said. You have cheated us out of a whole

148

form[1] of the argument, and not the least important, in order to avoid explaining it. You seem to have thought we would not notice your casual remark about women and children, namely, that it is clear to all that friends will have things in common.

Well, isn't that right, Adeimantus? I said.

Yes, he replied. But this word "right," as in other cases, needs an account. What is the manner of community? For there might be many kinds. So please don't pass over whichever kind you mean; because we have been waiting for some time, thinking you would surely mention the begetting of children and their upbringing and nurture once born, and this whole community of women and children which you speak of. For we think it makes a big difference in a constitution, and indeed the whole difference, whether or not these things occur rightly. Now then, since you are undertaking to explain another constitution before sufficiently explaining this one, it has seemed best to us, as you heard, not to release you until you explain all this as you did the others.

I vote for this too, said Glaucon.

Without more ado, Socrates, consider it carried unanimously, said Thrasymachus.

Why are you treating me like this! I said. You are stirring up a discussion about the constitution again, as though from the beginning! I thought at this point I was done, and welcomed it, delighted if one might accept things as then stated. You do not know what a swarm of arguments you are stirring up now by your demand; I saw it and then passed on by for fear it would produce a great crowd of troubles.

What did you think? replied Thrasymachus. That these people have came here to smelt fool's gold and not listen to a discussion?[2]

Yes, but a discussion of reasonable length, I said.

---

1. Form = part.

2. Thrasymachus is here portrayed as converted to Socratic discussion, having passed beyond the stage of *elenchus*, refutation, to common inquiry, but there is still a certain coarseness in his manner. "To smelt gold" was proverbial for those who fail of their expectations, and specifically of those attempting to derive gold from baser ore. Cf. 336e.

Surely for men of good sense, Socrates, said Glaucon, the reasonable length for hearing such discussions as this is the whole of life. But never mind about us. You must not weary of explaining what you think about this subject—what kind of community of women and children there will be among our Guardians, and their nurture while still young in the interval between birth and schooling, which indeed seems a particularly difficult period. Please try to tell how it should be.

It is not easy to explain, my friend, I replied: it raises many doubts, more than anything we have so far discussed. In fact, one might doubt that what we suggest is possible, and even if it were ever so possible, still doubt that it would be for the best. So there is a certain hesitancy in touching it, dear friend, for fear the argument should seem to be an unreal wish.

Don't hesitate, he replied. Your hearers will not be unsympathetic, nor incredulous or ill inclined.

Is your remark intended to encourage me, my friend? I asked.

Yes, he said.

Well, you are doing exactly the opposite, I replied. If I were convinced I knew what I am talking about, your encouragement would be a fine thing: if one knows the truth, there is no risk in speaking among wise and valued friends about things of utmost importance and value. But to fashion arguments while in doubt and still in search, which indeed I now do, is frightening and dangerous. It is not that I fear being laughed at—that is childish. But if I slip and miss the truth in matters about which it is of utmost importance not to slip, I may not only fall myself but take my friends down with me. I hope that Nemesis will not distribute punishment to me, Glaucon, for what I am about to say: for in fact, I expect it is a lesser offense to kill someone involuntarily than to mislead him about what institutions are noble, good, and just. It is preferable to run this risk among enemies than friends, so you must not encourage me.

And Glaucon laughed. No, Socrates, he said. If we suffer anything untoward at the hands of the argument, we will absolve you as though of homicide and hold you guiltless of intent to deceive. Speak with confidence.

Well, I said, the law does say that one who is absolved is in that respect guiltless. If there, then likely enough here.[3]

Please do go on, he said.

EQUALITY OF MEN AND WOMEN (451B—457B)

We must now return to discuss what perhaps should have been dealt with in proper order before, I said. Still, perhaps it is right to bring the women on stage this way, after the male drama is done, especially since you request it. For men born and educated as we described, the only right possession and treatment of women and children, in my opinion, consists in proceeding according to that impulse which we first communicated. We no doubt undertook in discourse to establish these men as guardians of a flock.

Yes.

Then let us follow that out and assign the corresponding birth and nurture, to see if it suits or not.

What do you mean? he said.

This: do we think female watchdogs should join in guarding what the males guard, and hunt and do other things in common with them? Or should they be kept at home as though incapable because they bear and raise the pups, while the males have all the work of caring for the flock?

All things in common, he said. Except we treat them as physically weaker, and the males stronger.

Then is it possible to use any animal for the same purposes, I said, if you do not provide the same nurture and education?

No.

So if we are to use women and men for the same purposes, they must also be taught the same things.

Yes.

c

d

e

452a

---

3. Homicide was a religious offense, as involving pollution and purification; jurisdiction over it in Athens belonged to the King Archon, who was also a priest.

Men were given music and gymnastic.

Yes.

So these two arts must also be given to women, along with the things that pertain to war. They must be treated the same way.

That seems to follow, he replied.

Perhaps many things about the subject we are now discussing, if done as prescribed, I said, would appear ridiculous, as contrary to custom.

Yes, he said.

What do you see as most ridiculous? I replied. Obviously, women exercising naked in the palaestra along with the men. Not only the young women, but older women too, like old men in the gymnasium who still love exercise even when they're wrinkled and not very pleasant to look at.

Certainly, he said. As things now stand, at least, it would appear ridiculous.

Now that we have raised the subject, I replied, we must not be afraid of the variety and number of entertaining jokes that might be directed at this sort of change—about women's exercise, and the training of their minds, and not least about their bearing arms, and riding horseback.

You're right, he said.

Now that we have begun, we must proceed to the rougher provisions of the law, after begging the jokers not to do what is their own but to be serious. We will remind them that it has been no long time since it seemed ugly and ridiculous to the Greeks to see men naked, even as it does to the majority of barbarians now, and that when the Cretans and later the Spartans first began to exercise naked, the humorists of the time were able to poke fun at it all. Agreed?

Yes.

But I suppose when practice had shown that it was better to strip rather than cover everything up, what seemed a visual joke ceased to be funny, because it was proved by reasonable arguments to be best. This shows that only a fool believes anything ridiculous except evil, or tries to raise a laugh by ridiculing any sight except that of folly and evil, or seriously sets up any standard of beauty except the good.

Most assuredly, he said.

The first thing to be agreed concerning these proposals is whether or not they are possible. It must be open to anyone, humorously or in earnest, to dispute whether female human nature can share all tasks with the male sex, or none, or some tasks but not others, and this especially concerning military service. Isn't that the best way to begin, as also likely to conduce to the best end?

Very much so, he said.

Would you like us to argue in behalf of those others against ourselves, I said, so that the opposing argument is not attacked without defenders?

Nothing prevents it, he said.

Let us then say in their behalf: "No one else has to argue against you, Socrates and Glaucon. You agreed to begin with, in founding your city, that everyone must do the one thing which according to nature is his own." We did agree, I suppose?

Of course.

"Isn't it true that a woman is completely different in nature from a man?"

We can scarcely deny it.

"Now, it is proper to assign different work to each according to their nature?"

Certainly.

"Then how is it you are not now making a mistake and contradicting yourselves, in claiming that men and women must do the same things when they have a completely separate nature?" Do you have any defense to that, my friend?

Not very easily at the moment, he said. But I shall beg you, and I do beg you, to put our side of the case, whatever it is.

These and many other such objections I long foresaw, Glaucon, I replied. That's why I was afraid, and shrank from touching on the law about possession of women and raising of children.

It certainly does not seem easy, he said.

Nor is it, I replied. Still, the fact is that whether one falls into a small plunge-pool or the middle of the greatest ocean, he still has to swim for it.

Indeed.

So we too must swim and try to save ourselves from the argument, hoping a dolphin may bear us up, or for some other unexpected salvation.[4]

e   It seems so, he said.

Come then, I replied, let us see whether we cannot somehow find a way out. We agreed that a different nature should pursue a different occupation, and that the nature of a woman and a man is different. But now we are saying that different natures should pursue the same occupation. Is that the charge against us?

Exactly.

454a   How extraordinary, Glaucon, I replied, is the power of disputation.

Why so?

Because many people seem to fall into it even against their will, I said. They think they are conversing rather than being contentious, through inability to divide what is under investigation in their discussion according to forms. Instead, they chase after verbal contradiction of what is said in terms of words alone, and use eristic against one another instead of dialectic.

Yes, he said, that is how most people are. But surely that is not at present relevant to us?

b   Certainly it is, I replied. At least, we are caught up in disputation against our will.

How so?

We are insisting very boldly and eristically, according to the very name, that different natures should not engage in the same pursuits. But when we assigned different pursuits to a different nature and the same pursuits to the same nature, we did not at all consider what form of difference and sameness of nature, and the relevance of distinguishing them.

No, he said, we did not.

c   It seems we can accordingly ask ourselves, I said, whether the same nature and not the opposite belongs to bald and long-haired men, and when

---

4. The musician Arion leaped overboard to escape the treachery of Corinthian sailors and was carried ashore by a dolphin. Herodotus i 24.

we agree it is the opposite, refuse to allow long-haired men to cobble if bald men are cobblers, or bald men to cobble if those others are cobblers.

That would be utterly ridiculous, he said.

Ridiculous for any reason except this? That we did not assume any and every sameness and difference in nature, I said, but looked only for that form of otherness and similarity which is relevant to the occupations themselves? For example, if both are medical and have a medical mind, we say that a man and a woman have the same nature. Don't you agree?

I do.

But a physician and a carpenter have a different nature?

Of course.

Then if the gender of men and women appears to make a difference relative to some art or other occupation, I replied, we will say it must be assigned to one or the other. But if they appear to differ only in this, that male begets and female gives birth, we will say this does not at all show that woman differs from man relative to what we are discussing; we will still suppose that the Guardians and their women must pursue the same occupations.

And rightly, he said.

Then we next invite anyone who says the opposite to teach us just this: relative to what art or occupation, in the establishing of a city, is the nature of woman and man not the same but different?

A fair question, surely.

Perhaps then someone else also might say what you were saying a little while ago, that it is not easy to give a satisfactory answer on the spot, but not at all difficult upon reflection.

Yes.

Would you have us then beg anyone who raises such objections to follow us, if we can somehow show him that there is no occupation peculiar to a woman in the management of a city?

Of course.

"Come then and answer," we will say to him. "When you were speaking in this way, of one person being naturally talented in something, another

not, did you not mean that the one would learn it easily, the other with difficulty? And that the one would discover for himself the greater part of what
he learns after only brief instruction, while the other would not retain what
he learned even after lengthy instruction and study? And that the bodily
powers of the one would adequately serve the mind, but of the other would
oppose it?" Is there any other way than this by which you distinguish someone who is naturally talented in anything from someone who is not?

No one will say otherwise, he replied.

Then do you know of any human practice in which the male sex is not
superior in all this to the female? Shall we speak at length, and talk about
weaving and cake baking and vegetable cooking—where the female sex certainly seems to amount to something, and its defeat is most ridiculous?

It is true, he said: the one sex is generally much superior to the other in
almost everything. No doubt many women are better than many men in
many things; but on the whole, it is as you say.

So no single occupation in the management of a city, my friend, belongs
to a woman because she is a woman, nor a man because he is a man. On the
contrary, natural gifts are scattered alike among both kinds of animals; according to nature, a woman has a share in all occupations a man does,
though for the most part a woman is physically weaker than a man.

Of course.

Then shall we assign everything to men, nothing to women?

How can we?

Rather, I suppose, we will claim it is possible for one woman to be by nature medical but another not, one musical but another unmusical.

Of course.

Can we then deny that one woman is athletic or warlike, another un-
warlike and unathletic?

I think not.

And again, one loves wisdom, another hates it? And one is spirited, another spiritless?

That is so too.

So one woman may be fit for guardianship, another not. Isn't this also the sort of nature for men we selected as fit for guardianship?

Yes.

And so, the same sort of nature belongs to women and men in respect to guardianship of a city, except in so far as one is weaker or stronger.

It appears so.

And so, women of this nature must be selected to dwell and share guard-   b
ianship with men of this nature, since they are competent and akin to them in nature.

Of course.

But the same occupations are to be assigned to the same natures?

Yes.

So we are back to our former position: we agree that it is not contrary to nature for the women of the guardians to be given training in music and gymnastic.

Most certainly.

So we were not legislating impossibilities or empty hopes, since we   c
framed the law according to nature. Rather, it is present practices contrary to this, it seems, which are contrary to nature.

Yes.

Now, our inquiry was whether our proposals are possible and best?

It was.

And it is agreed they are possible?

Yes.

Then it is next to be agreed they are best?

Clearly.

Then as to women becoming fit for guardianship, we will not provide one education for men and another for women, since the nature dealt with is the same.

Agreed.   d

Then what is your opinion about this:

What?

Deciding whether one man is better and another worse. Or do you believe they're all alike?

Not at all.

Then in the city we are founding, who do you think are made better men—the Guardians by receiving the education we have described, or cobblers educated only by their cobbling?

A ridiculous question, he said.

I agree, I said. These Guardians are best among other citizens?

e   By far, he said.

And their women will be best among other women?

This too by far, he said.

Is anything better for a city than that the best possible men and women should come to be present in it?

There is not.

This will be produced when music and gymnastic are conjoined, as we have explained?

457a   Of course.

So the institution we prescribed is not only possible for a city, but also best.

True.

Then the women among the Guardians must strip for exercise, since they will clothe themselves with virtue instead of garments, and take common part in war and the other duties of Guardians concerning the city, and perform no others. Of these duties, lighter tasks are to be given women than men because of the physical weakness of their sex. But the fellow who

b   laughs at naked women exercising for the sake of what is best "plucks unripe wisdom from the fruit of laughter." He does not know what it is he is laughing at, it seems, nor even what he is doing. For surely the most beautiful thing that is said or has ever been said is that what is beneficial is beautiful and what is harmful ugly.

Exactly so.

ABOLITION OF THE FAMILY AND THE UNITY OF
THE CITY (457B–466D)

We may claim to have escaped one wave, as it were, in speaking about the law relating to women; so that we are not completely swamped by our assumption that male and female Guardians should have all pursuits in common. Rather, the argument in some sense agrees with itself, for it states what is both possible and beneficial.

It is surely no small wave you are escaping, he said.

You will not say it is big when you see this next one, I replied.

Go on then, he said. Let's see it.

A law, I think, follows on this and the rest of what preceded it, I replied: What is it?

That all the women belong in common to all the men, and none shall live privately with any man. And again that children are common; parent shall not know his own offspring, nor child his parent.

This is much more doubtful than the other, he said, both in its possibility and its benefit.

I do not think there would be controversy about the benefit, I replied, because community of wives and of children would be an immense good, if it were possible. But I do think very considerable controversy might arise over whether or not it is possible.

There might be quite a bit of controversy about both, he replied.

Combined arguments, you mean? I replied. I thought I could escape the one, and that if it seemed to you beneficial, it would only remain for me to say whether or not it is possible.

But you got caught attempting to escape, he replied, and you must render an account of both.

The penalty must be paid, I replied. But do me this favor. Let me take a holiday, like a lazy-minded man accustomed to feast on his own thoughts as he walks alone. In fact, such people as that, even before they discover how to get something they want, pass it by in order not to be burdened by deliberating about whether or not it is possible. They assume what they wish as

c

d

e

458a

given, and then arrange what remains and delight in following out what
they will do if it occurs—making a lazy soul lazier still. Well, at this point I
am getting soft myself: I want to postpone the issue of possibility and examine it later. I will assume it, for now, and if you allow me, I will consider
how the rulers will arrange these matters in practice, and why if carried into
effect it would be of utmost benefit to the city and its Guardians. I will examine this with you first, and the possibility afterward, if you agree.

Of course I agree, he said. Please go on.

I suppose then, I replied, that if the rulers are to be worthy of the name,
and their auxiliaries too, they will issue orders, and the others will carry
them out. They will follow the laws in some things, and imitate them in all
the other matters we have left to their discretion.

Very likely, he said.

You are their lawgiver, I replied. As you selected the men, so you will also
select the women, providing a like nature so far as possible. But because
they have houses and meals in common, with nothing of the kind privately
possessed by any, they will be together; and being mixed together both in
exercises and in the rest of their rearing, they will be led by an inborn necessity, I think, to sexual intercourse. Don't you think that is a necessary
consequence?

Yes, he replied. Not a geometrical but an erotic necessity—which perhaps for most people is more keenly persuasive and compelling.

Indeed, I replied. But the next point, Glaucon, is that irregular intercourse or anything of the sort is unholy in a happy city, and the rulers will
not allow it.

Because it is wrong, he said.

Clearly then, we will next make marriages as sacred as we possibly can.
But it is the most beneficial which is sacred.

Certainly.

How then will they be most beneficial? Tell me, Glaucon: I see you keep
quite a considerable number of hunting dogs and game cocks. Have you
paid attention to their breeding?

How do you mean? he said.

In the first place, even though they are all of good pedigree, do not some of them turn out better than the rest?

Yes.

Then do you breed from all alike, or are you concerned as much as possible to breed from the best?

From the best.b

From the very young or the very old? Or as much as possible from those at their peak?

At their peak.

And if they were not bred this way, you believe your strain of dogs and birds would be the worse for it?

Yes, he said.

What do you think about horses, and your other animals? I replied. Is it any different?

That's absurd, he said.

Good heavens, my friend, I replied. If it is like this for the human race as well, how emphatic is our need for highest skill in our rulers!

Of course, he said. What about it?c

They will have to use a considerable dose of medicine, I replied. We believe that even an inferior doctor suffices if bodies don't need medicine but will respond to a diet. But when medication is required, we know that a more redoubtable doctor is required.

True. But what are you after?

This, I replied. The rulers will need to use a quite considerable amount of falsehood and deception for the benefit of those ruled. But we said, I d think, that all such things are useful only in the form of medicine.

Yes, and rightly, he said.

Well, this sound principle seems no less important to marriage and childbearing.

How so?

It follows from what has been agreed, I said, that if the flock is to be kept in peak condition, best must be mated to best as often as possible, worst to worst oppositely, and the offspring of the one raised but not the other. And e that all this is taking place must be unknown except to the rulers themselves, if, again, the herd of Guardians is to be kept as free as possible from internal strife.

Quite right, he said.

Then we must institute certain festivals and sacrifices at which we will bring together brides and bridegrooms, and our poets must compose hymns suitable to the weddings that take place. The number of marriages we will make over to the rulers, in order that they may as far as possible preserve the same number of people, taking into account wars and diseases and everything of the sort, and our city so far as possible not become too great or too small.

Right, he said.

Then a clever system of lots must be devised, I suppose, so that at each pairing, the inferior fellow we mentioned will blame chance, not the rulers.

Yes, he said.

And we must give privileges to those among the young who are good in war or elsewhere, and especially more generous permission for intercourse with the women, in order that at the same time too, with this excuse, the greatest possible number of children may be sown from this sort of parent.

Right.

Then too, as offspring continue to be born, officials appointed for this purpose will receive them, men or women or both—for men and women no doubt share common offices.

Yes.

They will take the offspring of good parents, I think, and carry them to the nursery, to nurses who dwell separately in another part of the city. But the offspring of inferior parents, or any others who may perhaps be born defective, they will conceal in a secret and out-of-the-way place, as is proper.[5]

Yes, if the race of Guardians is to be kept pure, he said.

Then too, they will also supervise nursing. They will lead mothers to the

5. The reference is to infanticide by exposure.

nursery when their breasts are full, using every device so that none will be aware of her own; and they will provide wet nurses if the mothers do not have enough milk, and supervise the mothers themselves so that they suckle a measured time, giving over to nurses, wet and dry, the wakeful nights and other toils.

Your description makes childbearing extremely easy for the women of the Guardians, he said.

It should be, I replied. But let us explain what we proposed in due order. We said that offspring must be born of parents at their peak.

True.

You agree that their peak reasonably extends twenty years for a woman, thirty for a man?

Which years? he said.

A woman should bear children for the city from twenty to forty, I replied. A man should beget for the city after he's passed "the racer's peak of swiftness,"[6] up to the age of fifty-five.

Yes, he said, that's the peak for both sexes, in body and mind.

Then if anyone older or younger than this should touch begetting of children for the commonwealth, we will claim his mistake is neither holy nor just, because he is raising up a child for the city which, if it escapes detection, will have been conceived unattended by the prayers and sacrifices which priests and priestesses and the whole city offer for every marriage, in order that the offspring may be born ever more virtuous and useful than their virtuous and useful parents. The child will have been conceived in darkness accompanied by dire incontinence.

Yes, he said.

The same law, I said, if anyone still of an age to procreate touches women of that age without a ruler bringing them together: we will say he foists upon the city an unauthorized and unhallowed bastard.

Very rightly, he said.

6. As a racehorse is put to stud only after he has ceased to run. In the *Laws* (VI 785b) men are to marry between thirty and thirty-five, women between sixteen and twenty; marriage and the procreation of children are civil duties (773e–774a).

c But I suppose when the men and women have passed the age of begetting, we will leave them free to have intercourse with whom they please, except lineal parents and descendents, daughter and mother and granddaughter and grandmother, and for women again, son and father and grandson or grandfather, and this only after they have been ordered to do all they can not to bring even a single thing so conceived into the light, but if it should be born, if it somehow forces its way, to deal with it as of a kind not to be reared.

d That too is reasonable. But how will they recognize one another's fathers and daughters and the relations you just now mentioned?

They will not, I replied. Instead, a man will call all offspring born in and between the seventh and tenth months after his marriage his sons if male, his daughters if female, and they will call him father. Their offspring, defined in the same way, he will call grandchildren, and they will address members of his group in turn as grandfathers and grandmothers. Those born in the time during which their mothers and fathers were engaged in

e begetting children will call each other brothers and sisters, with the result that, as we were just saying, they do not touch each other. But the law will allow intercourse between brothers and sisters, if the lot falls this way and the Delphic Oracle approves.

Quite right, he replied.

This then, Glaucon, and of this sort, is the community of wives and children for the guardians of your city. It must next be established by argument that it conforms to the rest of the constitution, and is much the best. Do you agree?

462a Emphatically, he replied.

Then is not the first step this? To ask ourselves what we can claim as the greatest good in founding a city, at which the lawgiver must aim in giving laws, and what the greatest evil? And next, to consider whether what we have just described fits the footprints of the good but not the evil?

I heartily agree, he replied.

Can we state any greater evil for a city than what rends it asunder and makes it many instead of one? Or a greater good than what binds it together and makes it one?

We cannot.   b

Now, a community of pleasure and pain binds it together when, so far as possible, all citizens rejoice and are pained about equally on the same occasions of gain and loss?

Certainly, he said.

But private feelings produce disunion, when some are much grieved while others greatly rejoice at the same events affecting the city and those in it?

Of course.   c

This sort of thing happens when words such as "mine" and "not mine" are not uttered in unison in the city? And the same for "another's"?

Quite so.

But that city is best governed in which the greatest number of people agree in applying "mine" and "not mine" to the same things in the same way?

Yes, very much so.

Then which is closest to a single person? For example, when one of us hurts his finger, the whole community stretched throughout the body toward the soul, organized into one ordered whole by what governs in it, is   d
made aware; and though only a part suffers, it all feels pain at the same time as a whole; and so we say the man has a pain in his finger. The same account for all else belonging to the man, for any part suffering pain or eased by pleasure.

Yes, he said. And as for your question, the best governed city is most nearly like this.

Then I suppose when anything happens to one of its citizens, for good   e
or ill, such a city will claim the part affected as especially its own, and share as a whole in its joy or sorrow.

Necessarily, he said, if its laws are good.

It is now time to return to our own city, I replied, and consider whether it most especially contains what was agreed in our argument, or whether some other city has more.

We must do so, he said.

Now, there are surely also rulers and common people in other cities as   463a
well as in this.

Yes.

They will all address each other as citizens?

Of course.

But what do the common people in other cities call their rulers, besides citizens?

In most cities, masters; but in democracies they use this same name, rulers.

b   What about the common people in our own city? What do they say the rulers are, besides citizens?

Preservers and protectors, he said.

What do the rulers call the people?

Employers and maintainers.

What do those who rule in other cities call the people?

Slaves, he said.

What do the rulers call each other?

Fellow rulers, he said.

And ours?

Fellow Guardians.

Can you then say whether any rulers in other cities describe some of
c   their fellow rulers as kin, others as strangers?

Yes, many do.

They consider and claim their kin as their own, strangers as alien?

Yes.

What about these Guardians of yours? Could any of them consider or describe a fellow Guardian as a stranger?

Not at all, he said. For he will consider everyone he meets as a brother or sister or father or mother or son or daughter, or their descendent or forebear.

Very good, I replied. Still, tell me this too: will you legislate that they are kindred only in name, or also that in every action they must act according
d   to their names—treating fathers with all lawful reverence and care and the obedience due parents? Otherwise, it will be worse before both gods or men, because if anyone does other than this, he acts neither piously nor

justly. Is it these maxims, or others, do you think, that they will constantly repeat in the ears of the children from the very first, both about fathers who may be pointed out to them, and their other kin?

These, he said. It would be ridiculous if mere names of kinship issued from their mouths without deeds.

e

So in this city beyond all others, when any one person fares well or ill, they will all pronounce in unison the words we just mentioned: "Mine fares well," or "Mine fares ill."

Very true, he replied.

Now, we said that feeling pleasure and pain in common accompanies these words and this judgment.

464a

And we were right.

Then our citizens will have a common share in the same thing, which they will name "mine." Because they share it in common, they will in this way have a community of pleasure and pain.

Yes, very much so.

Now, a cause of this, besides our other institutions, is the community of wives and children among the Guardians?

Most especially, he said.

Again, we agreed that this is a very great good for the city. We compared a well-governed city to how a body is relative to a part of itself in the matter of pleasure and pain.

b

Yes, and we agreed rightly.

So community of children and wives among the auxiliaries has appeared as a cause of very great good to the city.

Indeed, he said.

Moreover, this agrees with what we said before. We said they must not have private houses or land or any possession, but receive support from the others as wages for their guardianship and all consume it in common, if they are really to be Guardians.

c

Right, he said

Is it not then as I claim, that what was said before and is being said now makes them more genuine Guardians still, and causes them not to tear the

city apart, with different people calling not the same but different things
"mine"? This one hauls to his own house whatever he can possess apart from
the rest, another something else to his; they have different wives and children, and they introduce the private pleasures and pains of private individuals. They should all rather have one judgment about what is their own,
and all aim at the same goal, sharing so far as possible a like experience of
pleasure and pain.

Quite so, he said.

Then lawsuits and prosecutions will all but vanish from among them?
They possess nothing private except their bodies; the rest is common.
Whence it is that they are free of those quarrels which set men at odds,
through possession of money, or children and kin.

They will quite necessarily be rid of that, he said.

Nor again would there rightly be actions for battery or assault among
them: for we will claim it right and proper that men of the same age defend
themselves against each other, compelling them to keep in condition.

Right, he said.

Actually, I replied, this law is also right because, if someone is angry at
someone else and satisfies his anger in this way, he is far less likely to proceed to a greater quarrel.

Of course.

An older person, however, will be authorized to rule over and correct all
younger persons.

Clearly.

Again, a younger person will likely never undertake to use force or strike
an older person unless the rulers command it, nor, I think, offer any other
kind of disrespect. A pair of sufficient guardians will prevent it: fear and reverence—reverence restraining him from laying hands on anyone he regards
as a parent, fear that others will come to the aid of the person affected, some
as sons, some as brothers or fathers.

Yes, that follows, he said.

Then the laws secure that these men will everywhere live in peace with
one another.

Much peace, yes.

But if they are free from quarrels among themselves, there is no danger whatever that the rest of the city will be divided against them or against itself.

Of course not.

I actually shrink from mentioning the petty evils they would be rid of, because it is unseemly: the poor man's flattery of the rich, all the lack of means and suffering involved in raising a family and getting the money required to support a houschold—now borrowing, now denying the debt, using every means to scrape together enough for wives and servants to spend. All the things they suffer in these matters, such and so many, are surely obvious and ignoble and unworthy of discussion, my friend.

Obvious even to a blind man, he said.

They will be clear of all this, and live a life more blessed than the blessed life lived by Olympic victors.

In what way?

Olympic victors are happy through but a small part of what the Guardians have, whose victory is more noble and public subsistence more complete. The victory the Guardians gain is salvation for the whole city, and the prize they receive for themselves and their children is public subsistence and all else that life requires. They are honored by their city while they live, and in death share a worthy grave.

Noble honors indeed.

Do you recall then, I replied, that someone in the preceding argument, I don't know who, objected that we weren't making the Guardians happy, because even though it was possible for them to have everything that belonged to the citizens, they had nothing? We replied that if it so fell out, we would examine this afterward, but that we were then making our Guardians guardians and our city the happiest we could, rather than looking to any one group in it and trying to make it happy.

I do remember, he said.

Then the life of the auxiliaries, since it has turned out to be far nobler and better than that of an Olympic victor, does not at all compare with the life of shoemakers or any other craftsmen or farmers.

b   I think not, he said.

But rather, it is right to repeat here what I said before: that if the Guardian undertakes to become happy in such a way that he is not even a guardian, if a life so measured and firmly secured and, as we claim, best, does not please him, but an irrational and sportive opinion about happiness descends upon him and impels him to use his power to appropriate everything in the city for himself, then he will know that Hesiod was really wise in saying that half is more than whole.[7]

c   If he takes my advice, he said, he will abide in this life.

You concede, then, I said, the community of women with men which we have described, in education and children and in guardianship of the rest of the citizens? Both while in the city and at war, they must stand guard and hunt together like a pack of dogs, and so far as possible have everything in

d   common. In doing this, they will act for the best, not contrary to the nature of the female relative to the male, but in accord with the natural community of the two relative to each other.

I agree, he said.

THE USAGES OF WAR (466D–471C)

Then it remains to determine, I replied, whether this kind of community can be established among men, as among other animals, and how it is possible.

You anticipate the question I was about to raise, he said.

e   As to warfare, I suppose, it is clear how they will conduct military affairs, I said.

How? he replied.

They will campaign in common, and lead children grown up enough to war, so that, like the children of other craftsmen, they see the things they

467a will spend their lives practicing. Besides observing, they will serve and assist in all that has to do with war, and help their fathers and mothers. Aren't you

---

7. "Fools, who do not know by how much half is more than whole, or what advantage there may be in mallow and asphodel." *Works and Days,* 40, cf. *Laws* 690e. Mallow and asphodel were common Greek flowers; Cornford suggests "buttercups and daisies."

aware, in the arts, how the children of potters, for example, assist and watch for a long time before they touch the wheel?

Indeed.

Are they to be educated by experience and observation in what is to be their own business more carefully than the Guardians?

That would be ridiculous, he said.

Moreover, every animal fights better in the presence of its offspring.　　b

That's so. But there is no small risk, Socrates, as likes to happen in war, that they will be defeated and lose their children in addition to themselves, making it impossible for the rest of the city to recover.

True, I replied. But do you believe that never being at risk is the first thing one must prepare against?

Not at all.

If risk must be incurred, will it not be where, if all goes well, they will be the better for it?

Clearly so.　　c

Do you suppose it makes scant difference and isn't worth the risk, if children who are to be soldiers observe what pertains to war?

Why, it certainly does make a difference, relative to what you are saying.

So we must start there, and make the children spectators of war. But it would be well also to devise means for their safety.

Yes.

In the first place, I replied, their fathers, so far as humanly possible, will not be ignorant but knowledgeable about which campaigns are hazardous and which not.

Very likely, he said.　　d

They will lead them to the one kind and take care to avoid the other?

Right.

And they will surely set over them as officers, I said, not the most inferior, but those most competent to lead and teach because of age and experience.[8]

Properly so.

---

8. The ordinary overseer of children in Athens was a slave, but here a distinguished soldier.

Still, we will grant that the unexpected often happens.

Yes.

Then to guard against it, my friend, the children must be given wings from the start, so that if there is need, they can escape by flying.

e   What do you mean? he said.

They must be mounted and taught to ride as young as possible, I replied, and led to the scene on horseback—not on spirited warhorses, but on the fastest and most biddable. They will in this way best see their own proper work, and if there is any need, they will be safely preserved in following their older leaders.

I think you are right, he said.

468a   What about the conduct of military affairs? I said. How are the soldiers to behave toward themselves and their enemies?

Tell me what you think.

Any of them who leaves his post or throws away his arms or does anything like that out of cowardice, I said, must be demoted to a craftsman or farmer.

Of course.

Anyone taken alive by the enemy we will give to his captors as a present, to use their prey as they please?

b   Indeed.

But don't you think someone who distinguishes himself by his valor should first be crowned in the field by the youths and boys who accompany the campaign, each in turn?

I do.

And congratulated by handshakes?

That too.

I suppose then you will not also agree about this, I said.

What?

Kissing and being kissed by them.

c   Best of all, he said. Yes, and I add to the law that while on this campaign, no one he wants to kiss is allowed to refuse, so that if anybody is in love with someone, male or female, he will be more eager to win the prize for valor.

Excellent, I replied. And we have already said that opportunities for marriage will be more numerous for the brave than for others and they will more frequently be chosen for it than the rest, in order that as many children as possible may be born from this kind of person.

Yes, he replied.

Moreover, according to Homer, it is also right to honor good and brave young men in the following way: Homer says that when Ajax distinguished himself in battle, "he was honored with the whole saddle of beef from rib to rump"—this being thought the appropriate honor for a brave young man in his prime, from which comes at once increase of honor and of strength.

d

Exactly right, he said.

So we will at least be persuaded by Homer in this, I said. In fact, we will honor them not only in so far as they show themselves to be good and brave, with songs and the honors we have just described at sacrifices and all such occasions, but also "with brimming cup, and meat, and seat of honor," so that by honoring good and brave men and women, we may at the same time continue to train them.

e

Excellently put, he said.

Very well. Among those killed on campaign, will we not say, first, that those who died with distinction belong to a golden race?

Most certainly.

We will be persuaded by Hesiod that when someone of such a race dies, "They are called pure spirits dwelling on the earth, kindly deliverances from harm, guardians of speech-given men."

469a

Yes.

So we will inquire of the god how we ought to bury divine and godlike men, and with what distinctions, and in this we will do as he prescribes.

How could we not?

For the rest of time, we will in this way care for and reverence their graves as though divine. And we will offer the same observances when someone judged surpassingly good in his life dies in old age, or in any other manner?

b

It is just to do so, he said.

But how will our soldiers act toward their enemies?

In what respect?

First in the matter of slavery. Does it seem just for Greek cities to enslave Greeks? Or should they refuse so far as possible to allow any other city to do it, and introduce the practice of sparing the Greek race for fear of being reduced to slavery by the barbarians?

c   It is altogether better to spare them, he said.

So they are not themselves to hold any Greek as a slave, or advise other Greeks to do so.

Of course not, he said. They would in this way resist the barbarians but keep hands off themselves.

Again, I said, when they have won, is it a noble thing to strip the dead, except for weapons? Is not that an excuse for cowards not to advance against someone who is continuing to fight, as though they were doing their duty by kneeling over a corpse? Many an army has been destroyed by this sort of pillage.

Yes.

Does it not also seem slavish and avaricious to plunder a corpse, and the mark of a womanish and petty mind to treat a dead body as the enemy when the enemy has flown, leaving behind only the instrument by which he fought? Do you think people who act this way behave any better than dogs who growl at the stone that hit them, but don't touch the person who threw it?

Not a bit, he said.

So plundering of corpses must not be permitted, or refusal to allow taking up of bodies.

Most emphatically, he said.

Nor shall we carry weapons to the temples to dedicate as trophies, I suppose, especially those of Greeks, at least if we are concerned for the goodwill of other Greeks. We will rather fear some sort of pollution in carrying such things to a temple from among our own kind, unless the god[9] specifically pronounces otherwise.

d

e

470a

---

9. That is, the Oracle at Delphi, who spoke for Apollo.

Quite right, he said.

What about laying waste to Greek land and burning houses? How will you deal with that?

I would gladly hear you declare your opinion, he said.

Why, it seems to me they must not do either of those things, I said, but only remove the annual crop. Shall I tell you why?   b

Of course.

It appears to me that, even as we have two names, war and faction, so there are also two things, two different kinds of disagreement. The two I mean are disagreement between what is kindred and related, and what is alien and strange. Faction is the term for the enmity of what is kindred, war for the enmity of what is alien.

Not an unreasonable distinction, he said.

Then consider whether this is reasonable too. For I say the Greek race is   c
kindred to itself and related, but strange and alien to the barbarian.

Well put, he said.

So when Greeks war against barbarians and barbarians against Greeks, we will say they are by nature enemies and this enmity is to be called war. But when Greeks fight Greeks, they are by nature friends; Greece is sick with faction in such circumstances, and this kind of enmity should be   d
called faction.

I agree that it should be so regarded, he said.

Consider then in what now is agreed to be faction, I said, where something like this occurs and a city is divided against itself, if each of the two sides lays waste to fields and burns each other's houses, how cursed a thing civil strife seems to be. Neither side loves its city, for otherwise it would never venture to ravage its nurse and mother. But it is reasonable and fair for the victorious party to take away the crops of the vanquished, recogniz-   e
ing that they intend to be reconciled and not always at war.

This state of mind is much more amenable than the other.

Now, I said, the city you're founding—won't it be Greek?

It must be, he said.

Then they will be both brave and gentle?

Very much so.

But not lovers of Greece? They will not regard Greece as kindred and their own, and share with the others a common religion?

Again, very much so.

471a   Then they'll regard the difference between Greeks as faction, because it is among kindred. They will not call it war.

No.

They will therefore differ as intending to be reconciled?

Certainly.

Then they will impose correction in a friendly spirit, but not chastise for purposes of slavery or destruction. They are correctors, not enemies.

Yes, he replied.

Being Greeks, then, they will not lay waste to Greece, nor burn houses, nor agree that everyone in a given city, man, woman, and child, is their en-

b   emy; on the contrary, only a few enemies are ever responsible for their differences. For all these reasons, they will refuse to ravage land or destroy houses, supposing that the majority are friends. They will carry the quarrel only to the point where those responsible are compelled to render satisfaction by those who suffer and are not responsible.

I agree that our citizens should deal with their opponents this way, he said. Only toward barbarians should they act as Greeks now act toward each other.

c   Then may we also set this as law for the Guardians: Do not lay waste to land, nor burn houses?

Let us do so, he said. It is quite as appropriate as the former regulations.

IS THE REPUBLIC POSSIBLE? PHILOSOPHERS MUST
BECOME KINGS (471C–474B)

But Socrates, I think if you're allowed to go on this way, you will never recall the question you earlier set to one side, namely, whether this constitution is possible, and how it is possible. No doubt if it ever came into existence, all manner of good things would accrue to the city which had it—I

can even add something which you left out, that men who know and address each other as fathers and sons and brothers are least likely to desert   d
one another and would best fight their enemies. And if the females also join
the campaign, either drawn up in the same ranks, or even at the rear to
frighten the enemy and act as reserves, I know that by all this they would be
invincible. Yes, and I see good things at home which were left out, all of
which they would have. So accept my agreement that these and countless   e
other benefits would accrue if this constitution came to be, and say no more
about it. Let us at this point try to convince ourselves that the thing is possible, and how it is possible, and let the rest go.

What a sudden attack you make on my argument! I replied. You have no   472a
sympathy for my hesitation. Or perhaps you're unaware that having barely
escaped two waves, you're now sending the biggest and most difficult as the
third. When you see and hear it, you will have more sympathy for my natural reluctance, my fear to state and attempt to examine so paradoxical an
account.

The more you talk like that, he said, the less we will excuse you   b
from telling how this constitution can come to be. Speak and be quick
about it.

First, then, I replied, it is necessary to recall that we came here seeking
what justice is, and injustice.

Yes. What about it? he replied.

Nothing. Except, if we discover what justice is, will we also require that
the just man not differ at all from it, but everywhere be as justice is? Or will
we be content if he approximates to it as closely as possible, and partakes of
it in much greater degree than the others?

That will content us, he said.   c

So it was for the sake of a standard or paradigm, I replied, that we sought
to discover what justice is by itself, and the perfectly just man if he came to
exist, and of what sort he would be if he did, and again injustice and the
most unjust man—so that we might look to them to see how they would
appear to us in the matter of happiness and its opposite. We would also be
compelled to agree concerning our own selves, that whoever is most like

them will have an apportionment most like theirs. But our purpose was not to prove it possible for these things to exist.

d   That is true, he said.

Now, if a painter drew a standard or paradigm of what the most beautiful human being would be, and rendered everything in the picture satisfactorily, do you think he would be any less skilled as a painter if he could not also prove it possible for such a person to exist?

Emphatically not, he said.

Well then, are we not constructing in discourse a standard or paradigm of a good city?

e   Of course.

Do you think we'd describe it any less well if we could not prove it possible to found a city so described?

Surely not, he said.

So that is the truth of the matter, I replied. But if, to satisfy you, I must do my best to show how and in what way it would be most possible, you must in turn agree, relative to such a demonstration, that the same principles apply.

What are they?

473a   Can something be acted out in fact exactly as it was spoken in word? Or is it natural for action to touch less of truth and reality than speech, even if most people do not think so?[10] Do you agree, or not?

I do.

Then please do not make me prove that what we have described in discourse must in all respects be realized in fact.[11] On the contrary, if we can discover how a city might be founded most nearly approximating to what has been described, we will claim to have discovered what you require: that it is possible. Will attaining that satisfy you? It surely would me.

---

10. Shorey points out that Plato here rejects the usual contrast of words and deeds, with its assumed superiority of deeds to words.

11. In *Laws* V (739b–d), the best constitution answers to that of *Republic* IV and V, where friends have all things in common, and is that of a city inhabited by gods or children of gods; the *Laws* describes a second-best city, inhabited by men.

Yes, and me, he said.   b

Then next, it seems, we must try to seek out and show what defect in
cities now prevents them from being thus governed, and what least change
would bring a city to this kind of constitution—best a single change, or
two, or at least the fewest in number and smallest in effect.

By all means, he said.   c

There is one change, I replied, which I think I can show would accomplish this. Not a small change, however, nor an easy one, but possible.

What is it? he said.

I am at the very crest of what we likened to the greatest wave, I replied.
Nevertheless, it shall be told, even if it completely drowns us in laughter like
a wave of ridicule and scorn. Consider what I am about to say.

Go on, he said.

Unless philosophers become kings in their cities, I replied, or those now
called kings and potentates legitimately and sufficiently come to love wis-   d
dom; unless political power and philosophy coincide in the same person,
while the many natures which now proceed separately, each apart from the
other, are of necessity prevented, there can be no surcease from evils, dear
Glaucon, for cities nor I think for the human race. Nor will this constitution we have now described in discourse ever till then grow to its full stature e
and see the light of day. I have long shrunk from saying this, for I saw how
very paradoxical it would be: it is not easy to see that there is no other way
to attain happiness, private or public.

And he replied, After delivering yourself of a claim like this, Socrates, you
must expect a number of by no means contemptible opponents to throw off
their cloaks and strip, as it were, pick up whatever weapon is handy, and rush 474a
you—intending wondrous deeds. If you do not ward them off by argument
and escape, you will pay the penalty of really being jeered at.

Well, I replied, are you not responsible for this?

Yes, and a good thing too, he said. I won't desert you, I'll defend you
where I can. I can offer goodwill and encouragement, and perhaps I might
answer your questions more suitably than someone else. Rely on this sup-   b
port. Try to prove to the doubters that it is as you say.

Since you offer so powerful an alliance, I replied, I must try.

PHILOSOPHY AS LOVE OF TRUTH (474B–475C)

(Socrates continues) If we are to escape the people you mention, I think we must define for them the philosophers we dare claim ought to rule. Once this is clear, we can defend ourselves by showing that some people are by nature suited to understand philosophy and rule in a city, while others are unsuited and should follow their leader.

c   Yes, it is time for definition, he said.

Come then. Follow me in this, if we can somehow sufficiently explain it.

Proceed, he said.

Need I remind you, I replied, or do you recall, that when we say a person loves something, then if we are right, it must appear that he does not love this or that part of it, but wants it all?

d   It seems you will have to remind me, he said. I don't quite understand.

It might better suit someone else to say that, Glaucon, I replied: it hardly suits an amorous man to forget that lads in the bloom of youth somehow sting and stir the lover, seem delightful and worth caring about. Don't you act thus toward beautiful boys? This one you praise and call charming because he is snub-nosed; you claim the beak on that one is regal, while the

e   one in between is perfectly proportioned. The swarthy have a manly look, blonds are children of gods, but then again there are the honey-hued—do you think that name is anything but a euphemism invented by a lover who cheerfully puts up with sallowness, if it is on the bloom of youth? In a word, you allege every excuse and any pretext not to discard a single flower in its prime.

475a   If you mean to offer me as an example of how lovers act, he said, I will agree for the sake of the argument.

Do you not see wine lovers acting the same way? I replied. Finding any excuse to delight in every kind of wine?

Very much so.

Yes, and you see it in lovers of honor too, I think. If they cannot be generals, they are lieutenants. If they cannot be honored by more important and serious people, they delight in being honored by nobodies, because they desire honor of any kind.

Quite so. b

Then yes or no: if we say a person is desirous of something, shall we say he desires every form of it, or one form but not another?

Every form, he said.

Then we will also say that the philosopher desires not some kinds of wisdom and not others, but all?

True.

So if someone is finicky about what he learns, especially if he is young and does not yet have a reasoned account of what is or is not useful, we will c not say he is a lover of learning or a philosopher, just as we do not say that someone finicky about food is hungry or desires food; he is not a lover of food, but a picky eater.

Yes, and we will be right.

But if someone cheerfully tastes every subject and goes to learning gladly, and cannot get enough of it, we will rightly say he is a philosopher. Not so?

PHILOSOPHERS AND LOVERS OF SIGHTS AND SOUNDS: THE THEORY OF FORMS (475D–476B)

And Glaucon said, Then many strange folk will be philosophers. For all d lovers of sights and spectacles, it seems to me, are like this, because they delight in learning. And lovers of sounds are among the strangest to rank as philosophers, because they will not willingly engage in arguments and such pursuits as that, but run around to Dionysiac festivals as though they had rented out their ears to every chorus, omitting no performance either in city or country village. Shall we then say that all these are philosophers too? And others who learn other things of this same sort, or practice the minor arts?

No, I said, but they are like philosophers. e

Who do you say are the genuine philosophers? he said.

Those who love the sight and spectacle of truth, I replied.

No doubt, he said. But what do you mean?

It's not easily explained to another, I replied, but I think you will agree with me in this.

What?

Since beautiful is opposite to ugly,[12] they are two.

476a   Of course.

Then since two, each is also one?

Yes.

And the same account for just and unjust, good and evil, and all the forms: each in itself is one, but by communion with actions and bodies and each other, they make their appearance everywhere, and each appears many.

You are right, he said.

In this way, then, I replied, I distinguish separately on one side those
b   whom you just now described as lovers of sights and spectacles and lovers of arts and practical men, and separately again on the other side those with whom the argument is concerned, and whom one alone would rightly call philosophers or lovers of wisdom.

How do you mean? he said.

Lovers of sights and sounds, I replied, surely delight in beautiful tones and colors and figures and all that is fashioned from such things, but their understanding is incapable of seeing and delighting in the nature of the beautiful itself.

Yes, that is certainly so, he said.

WAKING AND DREAMING (476B–D)

But then, would not those able to go to the beautiful itself and see it by itself be very few?
c   Yes indeed.

Then one who acknowledges beautiful things but does not acknowledge beauty by itself, and is unable to follow if someone should lead to the knowledge of it—does it seem to you he lives awake, or in a dream? Con-

---

12. Or "since beauty is opposite to ugliness . . . " The neuter adjective, with or without article,
may be used as equivalent to the corresponding abstract noun.

sider. Is not dreaming just this: believing, whether asleep or awake, that what is like something is not like but the same as what it resembles?

I would certainly say dreaming is of this sort, he replied.

But then someone who believes the opposite of this, that beauty by itself   d is something, and is able to discern both it and the things which partake of it, and neither believes that it is the things which partake of it, nor that the things which partake of it are it—does it seem to you, again, that he lives awake or in a dream?

He is wide awake.

KNOWLEDGE AND OPINION (476D–477B)

Then we would rightly say that the understanding of the one is knowledge, since he knows, but that of the other is opinion, since he judges by appearances.

Of course.

What if this person whom we say judges by appearances but does not know became angry at us, and contended that we do not speak truly? Can we soothe and gently persuade him, while disguising the fact that he is unsound?[13]

We must at least try, he said.   e

Come then, consider what we will say to him. Or would you have us inquire of him in this way, suggesting that if he knows something no one begrudges him; on the contrary, we would be delighted to see that he knows something. But he must please tell us this: does someone who knows, know something or nothing? You answer me in his behalf.

I will answer that he knows something, he said.

Something that is, or is not?

Something that is. For how could something be known if it is not?   477a

Then we are sufficiently assured, from whatever point of view we may

---

13. Or unhealthy. "He who has opinion is, in comparison with the man who knows, not in a healthy state as far as truth is concerned." *Meta.* IV 1008b 30–31, trans. Ross.

examine it, that the perfectly real is perfectly knowable, but what in no way is, is in every way utterly unknowable?

Yes.

Very well. But if there is something such that it both exists and does not exist, would it not lie intermediate between what purely is, and again, what in no way is?

Yes.

Then since knowledge is directed to what is, but ignorance of necessity to what is not, something intermediate between knowledge and ignorance must also be sought, if there happens to be such a thing, directed to this intermediate.

b   Of course.

Now, we say that opinion or judgment of appearances is something?

Certainly.

Is it a power other than knowledge, or the same?

Other.

So judgment of appearances is ordered to one object, knowledge to another, each according to its own respective power.[14]

That is so.

KNOWLEDGE AND OPINION ARE POWERS DISTINCT IN OBJECT AND
IN WHAT THEY EFFECT (477B–478D)

Then knowledge is by nature directed to what is, to know what is as it is? But first, it seems to me, we must draw the following distinction.

What?

c   We will say that powers are a certain kind among things which are, by

14. It is here claimed that opinion involves knowledge minus something; it is not infallible, and does not have the real for its object. Compare *Timeaus* 51e–52c. The more popular alternative is that knowledge involves opinion plus something: this is examined in the *Theaetetus,* where knowledge is successively considered as sensation or perception, as true or right opinion, and as true or right opinion with an account. That all of these proposed definitions fail does not imply, since they are not exhaustive, that opinion is not prior to knowledge, or that knowledge is prior to opinion. The *Theaetetus* is not demonstrative but aporetic.

which we and all else are able to do what we are able to do. For example, I count sight and hearing among powers, if perhaps you understand the form I mean to mention.

Why, I do understand, he said.

Hear then what appears to me about them. For of a power I see neither color nor shape belonging to it, nor anything of the sort, as I do with many other things toward which I sometimes look and distinguish some as different from others in my thought. Of a power I look only to this: to what it is directed, and what it effects. It is by this that I came to call each of them a power. If it is ordered to the same object and effects the same thing, I call it the same power; if it is ordered to a different object and effects a different thing, I call it a different power. What about you? What do you do?

That, he said.

Then back again, my friend, I replied: do you claim knowledge is a power, or into what kind do you put it?

Into this kind, he said, and strongest of all powers.

Shall we rank opinion as a power, or as another form?

Not at all, he said. Because that by which we have power to judge is nothing other than opinion.

Yes, but you agreed a little earlier that knowledge and opinion are not the same.

Of course, he said. How could any reasonable person ever assume that what is infallible is the same as what is not infallible?

Excellent, I replied. Clearly then we are agreed that opinion is different from knowledge.

Yes.

So each of them, having a different power, is naturally directed to a different object.

Necessarily.

Knowledge, surely, is directed to what is, to know what is as it is.

Yes.

But opinion, we say, judges?

Yes.

The same thing which knowledge knows? Is the same thing both knowable and opinable, or is that impossible?

Impossible, from what has been agreed, he said, since a different power is naturally directed to a different object, while opinion and knowledge are both powers but each different from the other, as we claim. It follows from this that knowable and opinable cannot be the same.

b Then if what is is knowable, something other than what is would be opinable?

Yes.

Does it judge what is not? Or is it in fact impossible to judge what is not? Think about it. Does not he who judges refer his opinion or judgment *to* something? Is it possible on the contrary to judge but to judge nothing?

Impossible.

But he who judges, judges some one thing?

Yes.

But surely, not being would most rightly be described not as some one thing, but as no thing.

c Of course.

But of necessity we assigned ignorance to not being, knowledge to being?

And rightly, he said.

So it judges neither being nor not being?

No.

So opinion or judgment would neither be ignorance nor knowledge?

It seems not.

Then is it outside these, surpassing knowledge in clarity, or ignorance in unclarity?

Neither.

Does it rather appear to you, I replied, that opinion is darker and more obscure than knowledge, brighter and more evident than ignorance?

Yes, very much so, he said.

d It lies within both extremes?

Yes.

So opinion would be intermediate between them.

Quite so.

THE OBJECTS OF OPINION (478D–480A)

Now, we were saying before that if something should appear such that it at once is and is not, it would lie intermediate between what purely is and what completely is not, and neither knowledge nor ignorance is directed to it, but rather, what appeared intermediate between ignorance and knowledge.

Right.

But now what we call opinion has appeared intermediate between the two?

Yes.

Then it remains for us to discover, it seems, what has a share of both being and not being,[15] and would rightly be addressed as purely neither, in order that, should it appear, we may rightly address it as opinable or judgeable, assigning intermediates to intermediates and extremes to extremes. Not so?

Yes.

Then given these assumptions, I'll say, I call for an answer from our good friend who does not believe in a beautiful by itself, a certain idea of beauty itself ever the same with respect to the same things, but does acknowledge the many beautiful things—that lover of things seen who cannot in any way abide it if someone should claim that the beautiful is one, and the just, and so for the rest. We'll say, "Is there any among these many beautiful things, dear friend, which will not appear ugly? And among just things which will not appear unjust? And among holy things which will not appear unholy?"

No, he said. Rather, they necessarily appear somehow both beautiful and ugly, and so with all the others you ask about.

15. Or, existence and nonexistence, where existence is understood not as quantificational but as a domain of reality.

What about the many doubles? Do they appear any less halves than doubles?

No.

And things which we might say are large, small, light, heavy—will any be addressed as this more than the opposite?

No, he said. On the contrary, each always has both.

Then each of the many things no more is than is not what one might affirm it to be?

c   They seem like the ambiguous stories told at banquets, he said, or the children's riddle about the eunuch who threw at the bat—hinting obscurely at what he threw and on what it sat.[16] In fact, these things are ambiguous, and it is not possible fixedly to conceive any of them to be, or not to be, or both, or neither.

Then how can you deal with them? I replied. Where better to put them than intermediate between reality and what does not exist? For surely they will not appear more obscure than not being, relative to what even more does not exist, nor brighter than being, relative to what even more exists.

d   Quite true, he said.

So we have discovered, it seems, that the many conventional notions of the multitude about beauty, and other things, roll about somewhere between pure being and not being.

Yes, we have.

Yes, but we earlier agreed that if something of this sort appeared, it must be said to be opinable but not knowable, what is capable of intermediate wandering captured by the intermediate power.

Yes, we did.

e   So those who contemplate many beautiful things but do not see the beautiful itself and are unable to follow another who would lead them to it, and many just things but not the just itself, and so in everything—we will

16. A man who was not a man (a eunuch) seeing and not seeing (seeing imperfectly) a bird which was not a bird (a bat) sitting on a branch which was not a branch (a reed) threw a stone which was not a stone (pumice)—and missed.

say that they judge or opine all things, but know nothing of what they judge or opine.

Necessarily, he said.

But again, what about those who contemplate each thing by itself, ever the same in respect to the same things? Will we not say they know but do not judge or opine?

That too is necessary.

Shall we then also say they delight in and love these things to which 480a knowledge is directed, but the others those things to which opinion and judgment are directed? Do we not recall that we said they love and contemplate beautiful sounds and colors and such things as that, but cannot abide the beautiful itself as something which is?

I do recall.

Then we will not strike a false note in calling them lovers of judgment and opinion, rather than lovers of wisdom or philosophers. Will they be angry at us if we say this?

Not if they are persuaded by me, he said; for it is not right to be angry at the truth.

So those who delight in each thing which is by itself must be called lovers of wisdom or philosophers, not lovers of judgment or opinion.

Most certainly.

Book VI

484a Then following out a somewhat lengthy way, Glaucon, I replied, those who are philosophers and those who are not have, with some difficulty, revealed who they each are.

Perhaps the way could not easily have been shortened, he said.

It appears not, I said. At any rate, I think it might have been still better revealed if this were the only thing we had to talk about, and so many other things did not also require explanation in order to discern how a just life differs from an unjust life.

b What is next, then? he said.

What else but what's next in order? I replied. Since philosophers are able to grasp what is always the same with respect to the same things, while those who cannot do this are not philosophers and wander amid manifold and diverse multiplicity, which of them then should be leaders of a city?

How might we fairly respond? he said.

Whichever of the two appear capable of guarding the laws and practices of cities should be established as Guardians, I replied.

c Rightly, he said.

But it is clear, I replied, that a Guardian must not be blind but sharp of sight if he is to guard anything at all.

Of course it is clear, he said.

Then do you think that those really deprived of knowledge of the reality of each thing which is, and who have no clear paradigm or standard in their souls, differ at all from the blind? They cannot, like painters, look to what is most true and ever refer to it yonder and contemplate it as exactly as possible, and thus then, if there is need, establish conventional notions here about things beautiful and just and good, and guard and preserve what has been established. $\quad$ d

No, he replied, it's not much different from being blind.

Shall we then rather establish them as Guardians, or those who know what each reality is, and do not fall short of the others in experience, nor are inferior in any other part of virtue?

If the latter do not fall short in other respects, he said, it would be absurd to choose the others; for it is in this very knowledge that their superiority would mainly consist.

Shall we then tell how it will be possible for the same people to have both $\quad$ 485a the former and the latter?

Of course.

Well as we said to begin with, it is first necessary to understand their nature. I think if we once sufficiently agree on that, we'll also agree that it is possible for the same people to have both, and that no others should lead cities.

How so?

Let us first agree that philosophical natures are always in love with a $\quad$ b study which makes clear to them the nature and reality of what always is, and is not caused to wander by coming to be and passing away.

Agreed.

And further, I replied, that they desire all of it, and will not voluntarily give up any part, small or larger, more valuable or less, even as we formerly described lovers and those ambitious for honor.

You're right, he said.

Then next consider whether people who are to be such as we described necessarily have this additional element in their nature:

c   What?

Lack of falseness and refusal willingly to accept falsehood in any way, but to hate it and desire the truth.

Likely enough, he said.

Not only likely, my friend, but there is every necessity that someone in love by nature delights in everything akin and closely related to what he loves.

Right, he said.

Now, would you find anything more closely related to wisdom than truth?

No, he replied.

Then is it possible for the same nature to love wisdom and love falsehood?

d   Surely not.

So the real lover of learning must, from childhood up, strive as much as possible after all truth.

Certainly.

Again, when the desires set strongly in one direction, we know they flow more weakly by the same amount in others, like a stream diverted into another bed.

Of course.

So when they flow toward learning and everything of that sort, I suppose they would be concerned for the pleasure of the soul alone by itself, and forsake the pleasures obtained through the body, if one is not a pretender but truly a lover of wisdom.

e   Quite necessary.

Such a person would surely be temperate and in no way a lover of money; for he is the last person to take seriously the things for which money is eagerly sought and lavishly spent.

That is so.

486a   Again, if you intend to distinguish a philosophical from an unphilosophical nature, you must also consider this:

What is that?

That you not overlook any share of slavishness. For surely, pettiness of mind is utterly opposite to a soul whose desire is always set on the Whole and the All, human and divine.

Very true, he said.

Do you then think that an understanding lofty enough to contemplate all time and all existence can suppose this our human life a thing of great importance?

Impossible, he replied.

Then indeed, such a person will not believe death something terrible?   b

Hardly.

There is no share of genuine philosophy for a cowardly and slavish nature, it seems.

I think not.

Well then, is it possible that a well-ordered person, neither money-loving nor slavish, neither braggart nor coward, would ever become hard to deal with or unjust?

It is impossible.

So too then, in considering whether or not a person is philosophical in soul, you will observe from youth up whether he is just and kind, or unsociable and wild.

Of course.

Again, you will not omit this, I suppose: c

What is that?

Ease and difficulty in learning. Or do you expect anyone ever to sufficiently love something if he does what he does in pain and with difficulty accomplishes little?

No.

What if he were able to retain nothing of what he learned and was full of forgetfulness? Could he possibly fail to be empty of knowledge?

Of course not.

So he will labor in vain, you think, compelled in the end to hate both himself and this kind of activity?

Of course.

d   Let us not then enroll a forgetful soul among those adequate to pursue philosophy. Let us require a good memory.

Of course.

But surely, we would also deny that graceless awkwardness of nature tends anywhere except to excess and disproportion.

Yes.

Do you believe that truth is akin to excess and disproportion, or to due measure?

To due measure.

Then in addition to the rest, let us seek an understanding naturally measured and graceful, which will easily lead of its own growth to the Idea of each thing which is.

Of course.

e   Now, we think that all we have described is in some way necessary, and follows each upon the other in a soul which intends sufficiently and perfectly to come to have a share of what is?

487a   Most necessarily, he said.

Is there then any way to find fault with a pursuit which one could not sufficiently practice unless he were not by nature of good memory, quick to learn, high-minded, graceful, friendly and akin to truth, and to justice and courage and temperance?

Why, Momus himself[1] could not find fault with it, he said.

But when such people are perfected by education and age, I replied, you would turn the city over only to them?

ADEIMANTUS OBJECTS: PEOPLE THINK PHILOSOPHERS
USELESS (487B – E)

b   And Adeimantus said, No one can gainsay you in this, Socrates. Still, when you talk this way, your hearers are often affected somewhat like this: they believe that through inexperience in question and answer, they are little by

---

1. The spirit of faultfinding.

little led astray by the argument at every question, and when the little mistakes are collected at the end, they turn out to be a big slip and opposite to
what was said at first. Just as less skillful players at backgammon are finally
shut out by clever ones and can't make a move, so also they themselves are   c
finally shut out in this other kind of game where the counters are not peb-
bles but words, and don't have a thing to say—though it's not at all the
more true for being that way. I speak with a view to the present argument.
For as it is, someone might say that he cannot oppose you on any given
question in word, but he sees in deed, among those who turn to philosophy
and continue in it too long instead of taking it up to complete their educa-   d
tion while young and then dropping it, that the greater part become very
strange, not to say rotten, and even those who seem best nevertheless become useless to their cities as an effect of the study you praise.

And I listened and said, Well, do you think those who say this are mistaken?

I don't know, he replied. I'd gladly hear what you think.

You would hear that they appear to me to tell the truth.   e

THE SHIP OF STATE (487E–489D)

Then how can it be proper, he said, to claim that cities will find no surcease
from evils until philosophers—whom we agree are useless to them—rule
in them?

You ask a question, I replied, which needs an answer stated through an
image.

I think you are not unaccustomed to speak through images, he said.

Well, well, I replied. You poke fun at me, after throwing me into an ar-   488a
gument so hard to prove? Then hear the image, so that you may still better
see how hard I strain to draw it. The experience of the best sort of men in relation to their cities is so difficult that nothing else is like it; to defend them
by offering an image, one must collect it from many sources, as painters
mix things up to draw goat-stags and such. Conceive this then as happening on many ships or one. A shipmaster is big and strong beyond everyone

b   else on board, but also a bit deaf and somewhat near-sighted; and his knowledge of navigation is like that too. The sailors quarrel with each other over the helm; each thinks he ought to steer though he has never learned the art and cannot point to a teacher or a time in which he learned. They claim in addition that navigation cannot be taught, and they are ready to cut to pieces anyone who claims it can. They crowd around the shipmaster, beg-

c   ging him, prepared to do anything if only he will turn the rudder over to them. Sometimes, if they do not persuade him, but others do, they kill them or throw them overboard and banish them. Using drugs[2] or drink or something else, they bind the noble shipmaster hand and foot, seize the ship, plunder its stores, and sail on as one might expect, drinking and feast-ing. In addition, they praise and call a man a navigator, a pilot, and a mas-ter of seamanship if only he is clever at persuading or compelling the ship-

d   master to let them govern; anyone not like that they condemn as useless. They do not realize that a genuine pilot must be concerned with the year and its seasons, with sky and stars and winds and all that belongs to his art, if he really intends to be governor of a ship. Neither do they suppose that there is an art or study of steering, whether one wishes it so or not, nor that

e   it is possible to grasp it and therewith the art of the pilot. When things like this occur, don't you believe that sailors on ships managed this way will call the true pilot really a stargazer and an idle babbler, and useless to them?

489a   Indeed, said Adeimantus.

Then you understand what I mean, I replied. I doubt you need examine the image further to see that it is like the disposition of cities toward gen-uine philosophers.

Yes, he said.

Then first teach this image to anyone who is surprised that philosophers are not honored in their cities, and try to persuade him that it would be much more surprising if they were.

---

2. Mandrake, a plant with a large forked root, used as a drug with analgesic and narcotic proper-ties—in effect an opiate. The association of mandrake with fertility—cf. John Donne's "Go and catch a falling star / Get with child a mandrake root"—traced to Genesis 30, is perhaps based on a doctrine of signatures; *mandragoritis* is an epithet of Aphrodite. Adam remarks: "False rulers dull the senses of the Demos by the opiate of Pleasure, and so escape detection."

Why, I will teach it, he said. b

And further, that he is right to claim that the best among those in philosophy are useless to the multitude. However, he is not to blame good men for their uselessness, but rather those who make no use of them. For it is not natural that a pilot should beg sailors to be governed by himself, or for the wise to go to the doors of the rich; whoever invented that bit of cleverness was wrong. The actual truth is that, rich or poor, a sick man must go to the doors of doctors, and all who need to be ruled to the doors of someone capable of ruling; it is not for the ruler to beg those who need ruling to submit to being ruled, if he in truth confers a benefit. But you will not be mistaken in comparing present-day political rulers to the sailors we just described, and those whom they call useless babbling stargazers to true pilots.

Quite right, he said.

In consequence then, and under these conditions, the most noble pursuit is not easily held in high esteem by those who practice occupations opposed to it. But by far the greatest and strongest prejudice against philosophy arises through those who claim to practice it. The accuser of philosophy, you say, claims that most of those who go to her are thoroughly bad, and the best sort useless. And I conceded that is true, did I not?

Yes.

Then we have explained the cause of uselessness of the better sort?

Indeed.

PHILOSOPHY AND CORRUPTION (489D–491E)

Would you have us next explain why the majority are necessarily bad, and try to show, if we can, that philosophy is not responsible for it?

Certainly. e

Then as we speak and listen, let us bear in mind the point from which we began, in explaining what nature is necessary for someone who is to be noble and good. First, the philosopher is guided by truth, if you recall, which 490a he must always and in every way pursue or be an imposter without any share at all of genuine philosophy.

Yes.

Then this is one thing quite contrary to the opinion currently held of him?

Yes indeed, he said.

Then may we not also fairly plead in his defense that the real lover of learning naturally strives toward what is real, and does not linger among the many particular things which are objects of judgment or opinion? Keen and unremitting in his love, he will go on till he touches the nature of each thing which is by itself with that part of his soul which is suited to grasp it. But it is suited to what it is akin. Drawing near it and having intercourse with what is really real, begetting thought and truth, he knows and truly lives and is nourished, and thus, but not before, ceases from his travail.[3]

That is the fairest possible defense, he said.

Now, will such a person delight in any falsehood, or quite the contrary, hate it?

He will hate it, he said.

Then when truth takes the lead, we would never say, I think, that a chorus of evils follows in her train.

Of course not.

But a healthy and just character, attended also by temperance.

Right, he said.

What need, then, to marshal again from the beginning that other chorus which must necessarily belong to the philosophical nature? For you surely recall that it implied courage, high-mindedness, quickness to learn, memory. And you objected that everyone must agree to what we are saying, but if one dismisses the words and looks to those to whom the words refer, they claim to see that some philosophers are useless and the majority afflicted with every kind of evil. Examining the reason for this charge, we reach the present question: Why are most of them bad? That is why we again took up the nature of true philosophers and of necessity defined it.

That's so, he said.

---

3. The explicit sexual imagery of this passage is anticipated in the doctrine of Eros in the *Symposium* (210a–212a) and occurs in the *Phaedrus* (for example, 246e–247d).

Then we must observe the various corruptions of this nature, I replied, and how it is destroyed in many cases while a small remnant escapes— whom indeed people call not wicked but useless. And we must next also observe those who imitate it and establish themselves in the practice of it even though the nature of their souls is such that they have arrived at a practice to which they are unequal—it's too much for them. By their multiple misdoings, they everywhere and among everyone attach to philosophy the kind of reputation you describe.

What corruptions do you mean?

I'll try to explain it to you, I said, if I can. Everyone will agree, I think, that such a nature as this, possessed of all that we just now assigned to it if it is to become perfectly philosophical, arises seldom among men and in few. Don't you agree?

Yes, very much so.

Consider then how many and how great are the kinds of destruction for those few.

What are they?

What is most astonishing of all to hear is that each one of the qualities we praised can destroy the soul which has it, and tear it away from philosophy. I mean courage, temperance, and everything we have discussed.[4]

Astonishing to hear indeed, he said.

Still further, I replied, all other things said to be goods tend also to corrupt and tear at the soul—beauty and wealth and strength of body, powerful family connections in a city, and everything akin to these—you have the outline of what I mean.

I do, he said. And I would gladly learn what you mean more exactly.

Rightly grasp it as a whole, I replied, and what is said of them will not seem astonishing but obvious to you.

What are you suggesting? he said.

___

4. See below, 494b ff. The virtues here are plainly conceived as demotic, not as implicated with wisdom and one another. Compare Kant's opinion that the courage of the villain gives his villainy a deeper dye.

d   Of every seed or growing thing, plant or animal, I replied, we know that if it does not in each case meet with suitable nurture or climate or location, then the stronger it is, the more it falls short of what is proper to it. For surely, evil is more opposite to good than to what is not good.

Of course.

It makes sense, then, I suppose, that the best nature, under conditions of alien nurture, fares worse than its inferior.

Yes.

e   Well then, Adeimantus, I replied, may we thus also say that the best-endowed souls become surpassingly bad when they meet with bad education? Do you think great crimes and unmixed wickedness derive from a petty nature, not from a vigorous nature ruined by its nurture? A weak nature will never be responsible for great things, whether for good or ill.

That's so, he replied.

SOPHISTRY AND THE GREAT BEAST (492A–495B)

492a   Then the philosophical nature we assumed, I think, if it meets with proper instruction, necessarily arrives at all virtue as it grows. But if it is not sown and cultivated and nourished in proper soil, it arrives at all the opposite, unless a god comes to its aid. Or do you also believe, as most people do, that some young men are corrupted by sophists, and that certain sophists corrupt them by private instruction to any extent worth mentioning? On the contrary: are not those who say this themselves the greatest sophists, most perfectly educating young and old, men and women, fashioning them to be of the sort they wish?

b   When does this occur, then? he replied.

When the collected multitude is seated together in assemblies or courtrooms, or theaters or army camps or any other public gathering, I said. They condemn with much tumult some of the things said or done, and praise others, in either case excessively; they bellow and clap till the very stones of the place echo and redouble the tumult of their ignorant praise

c   and blame. In such circumstances, where is the young man's heart, as the saying is? What sort of private teaching can stand fast and not be washed away by such a torrent of praise and blame, swept and borne along in whatever direction it may flow? He will call the same things noble and shameful that they do, practice whatever they practice, be as they are.

Quite necessarily, Socrates, he said.   d

Nor have we yet even stated the greatest necessity, I replied.

What is it? he said.

What these educators and sophists add by deeds if they do not persuade by words. Or do you not know that they punish those who do not obey with loss of civil rights and fines and death?

Yes, certainly, he said.

Then what other sophist or what private words do you think can prevail against them?

None, I think, he replied.   e

No, I replied. On the contrary, it is quite unreasonable even to try. For there neither is, nor has been, nor can ever be a different sort of character relative to virtue running contrary to the education they provide—humanly speaking, my friend, though as the proverb has it, we must leave out of account the divine. For rest assured: you will not be mistaken in saying that in such established constitutions as this, whatever is preserved or has   493a become what it ought is preserved by divine apportionment.

I very much agree, he said.

Then agree still further on this, I replied:

What?

Among those who teach for private pay, whom they therefore call sophists and regard as rivals, each teaches and calls wisdom nothing except these opinions of the multitude formed when they gather together. It is as though one kept a great strong beast and studied its moods and desires, and   b how to approach and handle it, and when and why it becomes most savage or gentle, and what sounds it is accustomed to make in either case, and again which sounds uttered by another will soothe or make it angry. Having once learned all this by spending time in the beast's company, he would call it wisdom, organize it as if he thought it an art and turn to the teaching of it. Though in truth knowing nothing at all about which opinions and desires are noble or shameful, good or evil, just or unjust, he would apply all

c   these names to the opinions of the great beast, calling what pleases it good and what angers it evil, with no other account to offer. On the contrary, things necessary he would call noble and just, never having seen the nature of the necessary and the good and how great the difference really is between them;[5] nor can he show it to another. Do you not think such a person would make a remarkably strange educator?

I do indeed, he said.

d   Do you think, then, there is any difference between him and someone who believes that wisdom, whether in painting or music or politics, consists in recognizing the mood and pleasures of a large and varied crowd? Because if someone has intercourse with them and exhibits poetry or any other craftsmanship or service to a city, he makes the multitude his own master beyond what is necessary, and the so-called Necessity of Diomedes[6] will make him do the things of which they approve. But that those things are also good and noble in very truth—have you ever yet heard anyone render an account of this which was not ridiculous?

e   I think not, he replied, nor that I ever shall.

Then with all this in mind, please recollect: the beautiful itself, as distinct from the many beautiful things, each thing by itself as distinct from the many particular things—is it possible that a multitude should admit or believe it to exist?

494a   Hardly, he said.

So it is impossible for a multitude to love wisdom, I replied.

Yes.

And those who pursue philosophy are therefore necessarily censured by them?

Necessarily.

---

5. What is necessary cannot be avoided because it is unforeseen; it is unforeseen because it is not understood; it is not understood because the sophist must conform to the opinions of the beast (492d).

6. Diomedes bound Odysseus and drove him with blows from the flat of his sword.

And by all those private persons who have intercourse with the crowd and desire to please it.

Clearly.

Given this situation, do you see any salvation for a philosophical nature, so that it may abide in its practice and carry through to its end? Reflect on what has been said: we agreed that quickness to learn and memory and courage and high-mindedness belong to this nature.

b

Yes.

Now, this sort of person is first in everything from childhood up, especially if his body is comparable to his soul?[7]

Certainly, he said.

When he becomes older, I suppose, his relatives and fellow citizens will wish to use him for their own purposes.

Of course.

They will fawn on him with requests and honors, anticipating the power that will be his and flattering it in advance.

c

So it likes to happen, at any rate, he said.

What do you think he will do in such circumstances? I replied. Especially if he belongs to a great city and is wealthy and well born in it, as well as handsome and tall. Won't he be filled with an impossible hope, believing himself competent to manage the affairs of Greeks and barbarians alike, exalting himself to a great height, filled with pretense and empty pride without intelligence?

d

Yes, he said.

Then suppose someone came to a person in this condition and gently spoke the truth: that intelligence is not in him, but he needs it, and that it cannot be possessed unless he slaves for the possession of it. Do you think it will be easy for him to listen, in the midst of these great evils?

Far from it, he said.

But then, I replied, if through excellence of nature and kinship to rea-

e

---

7. It is often supposed that the passage which follows offers a portrait of the young Alcibiades. Cf. *Alcibiades* I 103a ff.

soning, one man could somehow become aware, and bent and drawn toward philosophy, what do we suppose those who think that his useful companionship is being destroyed will do? Will they not say everything, do anything, to prevent him from being persuaded, and use private plots and
public prosecutions to forestall anyone who tries to persuade him?

495a   Necessarily, he replied.

Is it possible that such a person will love wisdom?

Of course not.

You see, then, I replied, that we were not mistaken in saying that the very
parts of the philosophical nature, when they arise amid evil nurture, are in
a way responsible for a falling away from the practice of philosophy; and so
too such so-called goods as wealth and all provision of the sort.

No, we were not mistaken, he replied. It was rightly said.

b   Such and so great, then, dear friend, I said, is the destruction and corruption of the best nature in respect to the most noble practice—and rare
enough in any case, we claim. It is from among these men that those who
work the greatest evils to cities and private persons arise—and the greatest
goods, when the stream happens to set in that direction. A petty nature
never does any great thing to either.

Very true, he replied.

THE BALD-HEADED TINKER (495C-496A)

c   Thus then those to whom philosophy most properly belongs fall away, leaving her desolate and unwed, while they themselves live a life neither proper
nor true. Like an orphan bereft of kinsmen, she is shamed by other unworthy suitors who rush in and fasten upon her a reproach of the sort you describe: that some who consort with her are worthless, and the majority worthy of many evils.

In fact these things are said, he answered.

d   Yes, and reasonably said, I replied. For other little people see that the
ground is vacant but full of fine names and pretensions, and just as those
who escape from prison are glad to seek sanctuary in temples, so those who

are cleverest at their own little arts skip from those arts into philosophy. For the prestige attaching to philosophy, even thus practiced, nevertheless remains more imposing than that of other arts. Many desire it even though their natures are imperfect, their souls warped and disfigured by the drudgery of their vulgar occupations even as their bodies are broken by their arts and public crafts—isn't that inevitable?

Yes, he said.

To look at them, I replied, they don't differ at all from a little bald-headed tinker newly released from jail, who has gotten hold of some money, taken a bath, gotten a new cloak, and is ready to become a bridegroom—intending to marry his master's daughter in her poverty and abandonment.

Not very different, he said.

What sort of offspring are such parents likely to beget? Base and worthless?

Inevitably.

Then what sort of thoughts and judgments may we say those unequal to education will beget when they unworthily approach and have intercourse with philosophy? Will not their offspring truly deserve to be called sophisms, and contain nothing legitimate or possessed of genuine wisdom?

Most certainly, he said.

THE SAVING REMNANT (496A–497A)

But a tiny remnant among those worthy of intercourse with philosophy is left, Adeimantus, I replied. Perhaps a noble and well-bred character caught by exile, who naturally abides in philosophy for lack of those influences which corrupt, or when a great soul grows up in a small city and disdains and scorns its affairs; or perhaps some few, naturally talented, might come to it from another art they justly despise. There may also be the bridle which checks our friend Theages: everything else prepared Theages to fall away from philosophy, but his sickliness of body restrains him and holds him back from political affairs. My own case is hardly worth mentioning,

e

496a

b

c

the Divine Sign:[8] for it has surely come to few or none before me. Those who once become members of this small band, and taste how sweet and blessed is the possession, and have also sufficiently observed the madness of the multitude, realize that there is scarcely anyone in public affairs who is

d   not unsound, nor any ally with whom one might go to the aid of what is just and still survive. He is like a man fallen among wild beasts, unwilling to join in wrongdoing, and being but one, unable to oppose the savagery of all. Before he could benefit his city or his friends he would be destroyed, worthless to himself and to others. Reflecting on all this, he keeps quiet and does what is his own, like a traveler taking shelter behind a wall from a storm of wind-tossed dust and hail. Seeing the others filled with anomie,

e   lawlessness, he is content if he can somehow live clear of injustice and unholy deeds while this life lasts, and takes his departure with noble hope, serene and content at his leaving.

Why really, he replied, it is no small achievement.

497a   Yet not the greatest either, I said, because he did not meet with a suitable constitution. For there his own growth would be fostered and he will preserve the commonwealth, along with what is his own.

THAT A PHILOSOPHICAL RULER IS POSSIBLE (497A–502C)

I think it has fairly been told why there is prejudice against philosophy, and why the prejudice is unjust—unless you have something more to add.

No, I have nothing more to say about it, he replied. But among present-day constitutions, which do you claim is suitable?

b   Not a one of them, I said. On the contrary, that is exactly what I am complaining about: not a single city as now constituted is worthy of a philosophical nature. That is why that nature is twisted and altered. As foreign seed sown in alien soil is like to be overmastered and vanish into the native growth, so also this kind does not now receive its own power, but is

c   cast out into an alien character. But if ever it gets the best constitution, then

8. See *Apology* 31d, *Euthyphro* 3b, *Phaedrus* 242b, *Theaetetus* 151a.

even as it is itself best, it will at that point make clear that it really is divine, and the others in nature and practice merely human. Clearly then, you are next going to ask what this constitution is.

No, he replied. I wasn't going to ask that, but whether it is this constitution we have described in founding the city or another.

In other respects, I replied, it is this. But there is also the exact thing we mentioned before: that there must always be some element present in the city which holds the same account of the constitution that you as lawgiver held in giving its laws.

Yes, that was said, he replied.

But not sufficiently made clear, I said, for fear of topics[9] which require, as your objections show, a long and difficult proof. Indeed, the hardest part still remains.

What is that?

How a city can deal with philosophy and not be destroyed. For all great things are dangerous, and, as the proverb has it, excellent things really are hard.

That is evident, he said. Nevertheless, please carry the demonstration through to the end.

If I do not, I replied, it will not be for want of trying, but for lack of ability. "You're here, and you'll witness my effort." Consider how eagerly and even rashly I mean to claim that a city must deal with this pursuit, the opposite of now.

How so?

As things stand now, I replied, those who touch philosophy at all are young men just past childhood, in the interval before setting up a household and beginning to earn their own living. Just when they approach the hardest part of it, they quit—and yet, they are made out to be most accomplished in philosophy. By the hardest part I mean what has to do with reasoning. Later on, if invited by others who engage in philosophical conver-

d

e

498a

9. The reference is to the discussion of the status of women and children (V 449b ff.) and to the
   possibility of realizing the perfect city. (471c ff.)

sation, they think it a great thing if they consent even to become hearers, because they suppose philosophy should be engaged in only as a hobby. With few exceptions, as they approach old age, their light is quenched more thoroughly than the Sun of Heraclitus, inasmuch as it is not again rekindled.

b

How should it be, then? he said.

Exactly the opposite. As boys and young men they should deal with education and philosophy in a way suited to their youth, and while growing into manhood take very good care of their bodies as a support to philosophy. As age advances and the soul begins to reach maturity, they should intensify exercise of the body; when strength abates and they are beyond political and military service, they should at that point be allowed to graze unfettered and do nothing but philosophy except as a hobby, if they are to live happily and, in dying, add a fitting apportionment in the other world to the life they have lived here.

c

Truly, you seem much in earnest, Socrates. Though I suppose most of your hearers are even more earnest in their opposition. They do not at all intend to be persuaded—beginning with Thrasymachus.

Don't pick a fight between me and Thrasymachus when we have just become friends, I replied—not that we were enemies before. For we will spare no effort until we either convince him and the others, or accomplish something useful in respect to that life when they are born again and meet with such arguments as these.[10]

d

You mention a short time! he said.

Why, no time at all compared to the whole of it, I said. Still, it is no wonder that most people are not persuaded of what is being said. They never hear what's now so clear,[11] but plenty of rhyming jingles intentionally

e

10. Adam remarks: "It is from casual allusions like the present, made in all seriousness, that we can best understand how profound and practical was Plato's belief in immortality. The seed sown here may bear its fruit in another life, so that the educator need not despair."

11. Plato here imitates the jingling style of Gorgias and other rhetoricians of his school, in a manner not easily reproduced in English. Shorey gives, "For of the thing here spoken they have never beheld a token." M. Chambry's French does rather better: "car elle n'a jamais vu exécutée

made like each other instead of occurring spontaneously, as just happened. But a man whose meter is measured by virtue, and made like it so far as possible in word and deed, and who holds power in a city of the same sort— this they have never yet seen, neither once nor many times. Or do you think so?

Not at all.

499a

Nor again, my friend, have they sufficiently become hearers of free and noble arguments which intensely and in every way seek the truth for the sake of knowing, with scant welcome to that eristical cleverness which tends toward nothing but opinion and disputation both in law courts and private conversations.

No, he said.

For these reasons, I replied, and foreseeing this, we then said under compulsion of the truth and despite our fears, that neither a city nor a constitution, nor equally again a man, will ever become perfect until some necessity derived from fortune[12] constrains philosophers, few and uncorrupted and now called useless, to be concerned for their city whether they wish it or not, and the city to obey them. Or else that a genuine love of genuine philosophy, derived from some divine inspiration, should chance to occur among the sons of present-day potentates and kings, or their fathers. It is reasonable to suppose, I claim, that either or both are possible. Otherwise, we would justly be ridiculed for expressing the equivalent of a vain wish.

b

c

Yes.

If then some necessity has arisen in the limitlessness of time past, or exists even now in some barbarian land far beyond our view, or again in time to come, for those preeminent in philosophy to be concerned for a city, we are ready to contend in argument that the constitution we have described has come to be, or is, or will come to be, when this Muse becomes mistress of a city. For it is not impossible, nor do we speak of impossibilities. But we do agree it is difficult.

d

---

l'idée qui est à présent discutée." It has been suggested that the butt of this was Isocrates, but the remark applies generally to Gorgias and those like Isocrates who imitated him.

12. See IX 592a. Fortune, of course, includes misfortune.

I think so, he said.

Will you say again that most people do not agree, I replied?

Perhaps, he said.

e   Don't be so hard on them, my friend, I replied. They will surely hold a different opinion if you point out who it is you say are philosophers—not in a spirit of controversy but of conciliation, to remove their prejudice against the love of learning. Define the philosophical nature and its pursuits as you did just now so that they will not believe you mean the people they

500a   think. Or even if they do regard philosophers that way, do you deny that they will then change their opinion and answer differently? Do you think people are harsh with those who are not harsh, jealous of those who are not jealous but ungrudging and gentle? I will anticipate you by saying I believe that so harsh a nature occurs in some few, but not many.

b   I heartily agree, he said.

Do you also agree that the harshness of the multitude toward philosophy is due to outsiders bursting in like boisterous revelers where they do not belong? Abusive, quarrelsome, ever fond of spiteful gossip about people, they act in ways least suited to philosophy.

Certainly, he said.

c   For surely, Adeimantus, no one who truly has his understanding fixed on things which are has leisure to look downward to the affairs of men, and to fight with them, filled with jealousy and bitterness. He looks rather to things which are well ordered and ever the same, and sees that they neither do nor suffer injustice at each other's hands, but hold all things in beauty and order according to reason. These he imitates, and makes himself like them in the highest degree possible. Or do you think there is any device by which one can admire what he has intercourse with but not imitate it?

Impossible, he said.

d   Then the philosopher in his intercourse with the divine order becomes himself well ordered and divine, so far as it is possible for a man. Still, there is much scope for slander everywhere.

Yes.

Suppose then, I said, that a necessity arose for him, instead of molding only himself, to practice putting what he sees in that world yonder into the characters of men in private and in public life. Do you think he will be a bad craftsman of temperance and justice, and civic virtue as a whole?

Surely not, he replied.

But if the multitude realizes that we are telling the truth about him, will they still then be angry at philosophers, and doubt us when we say that a city will never be happy unless artists sketch it using the divine pattern and standard?

e

They will not be angry, he replied, if they are aware of it. But what kind of sketch do you mean?

501a

They would take both a city and the characters of men, I replied, and first clean them like a tablet—which is not easy. Still, you know that they would immediately differ from the others in this: they would refuse to touch a city or private person, or to draft laws, before receiving a clean tablet or cleaning it themselves.

Yes, and rightly, he said.

Then do you think, after this, they would trace the figure of the constitution?

Of course.

Next, I suppose, they would constantly look in each of two directions as the work proceeds: to what is by nature just and beautiful and temperate and all such as that; and again, to that which they are introducing among men—combining and mixing the human image from man's various pursuits, but founding their inference on what Homer called, when it comes to be present among men, the form and image of god.

b

Right, he said.

I suppose they would erase and redraw, over and again, until so far as they could they had constructed a human character as dear to god as possible.

c

The picture would at any rate be very beautiful, he said.

Will we then at all persuade those whom you said were poised to attack us? I replied. They were angry before because we gave the city over to the sort of man we praised as an artist of constitutions. Hearing this now, will they be more gentle?

Much more gentle, he replied, if they have good sense.

d   Yes, because what can they dispute? That philosophers are lovers of being and truth?

Surely not, he said.

Or that their nature, which we have described, is akin to what is best?

Not that either.

Well, will not this sort of nature, if it meets with its own proper pursuits, be completely good and philosophical, if indeed any other is? Or will they claim rather those whom we have excluded?

e   Surely not.

Then will they still be angry if we say that, until the philosophical kind belonging to a city comes to power, there will be no surcease from evils either for city or citizens, nor will the constitution which we imagine in discourse ever achieve completion in fact?

Perhaps less angry, he said.

May we say that, instead of less angry, I replied, they will become completely gentle and persuaded, so that if nothing else they will agree for very shame?

502a   Certainly, he said.

Then let us assume that they have been persuaded, I said. Will anyone dispute that children of kings or potentates might happen to be born with philosophical natures?

No, he said.

But if so born, can anyone say they must necessarily be corrupted? We will concede that it is difficult for them to be preserved. But that not even one among all of them might be saved in all of time—could anyone argue that?

Hardly.

b   But surely, I replied, even one is enough to accomplish all that now seems incredible, if his city can be persuaded to obey.

Yes, one is enough, he said.

Because if a ruler gives the laws and practices we have described, I replied, it is surely not impossible for citizens to be willing to act that way.

Not at all.

Again, is there anything surprising and impossible if others judge as we do?

I think not, he replied.

Again, we have sufficiently explained in what went before, I suppose, that if indeed possible, it is surely best.

Yes.

So now it follows for us concerning lawgiving, it seems, that what we described is best if it can be realized, and though difficult not, however, impossible.

Yes, it follows, he said.

ADVANCED EDUCATION: THE LONGER WAY (502C–504D)

Then since this conclusion has with difficulty been achieved, it next remains to tell how, and from what studies and practices, the saviors of the constitution will come to be present, and at what age each takes up each study.

Yes, he said.

I got nothing by my cleverness, I replied, in passing over earlier the difficulty involved in the possession of wives and the begetting of children and the establishment of rulers, knowing that the complete truth would give offense and be difficult. For now comes the duty of discussing them nonetheless. The matter of wives and children is settled, but that of the rulers must be pursued as though from the beginning. We were saying, if you recall, that they must prove lovers of their city, tested in the midst of pleasures and pains, and prove not to throw over their conviction among toils or fears or any change of fortune. One incapable of this must be rejected. But one who passes through it everywhere without taint, like gold tried in fire, must be assigned to rule and given honors in life and after death as prizes of the con-

c

d

e

503a

test. Something like this was said earlier, when the argument hurried by with covered face, fearful of stirring up what is now before us.

b   Very true, he said. I remember.

I shrink from saying what is now so boldly hazarded, my friend, but let us now venture to say it: philosophers must be established as Guardians in the strictest sense.

Yes, he said.

Bear in mind then that you will likely have very few of them; for they must have the nature we have described, but the parts belonging to it will seldom consent to grow together into one, but mostly be scattered.

c   How do you mean? he said.

Quickness to learn, memory, incisiveness, acuity, and everything that follows on these—you know that youthful spirits and high intelligence often refuse to combine with a willingness to live orderly lives accompanied by quiet and stability. Instead, people like this are carried by their acuteness in any chance direction and stability utterly escapes them.

True, he said.

d   On the other hand, the firm and stable characters which one might prefer to rely on, steadfast against fear in war and hard to move, act the same way again toward learning. It is as though they were torpid—hard to move, slow to learn and filled with sleep and yawning—when something like this takes hard work.

That's so, he said.

But we claimed that one must have a fair and goodly share of both, or be given no share of education in the most exact sense, nor of honor or rule.

Rightly, he replied.

Now, you think it will be rare?

Of course.

e   Then they must be tested in the toils and fears and pleasures of which we spoke, and still further, we can now state what we then passed over, that they must also be exercised in many studies to see whether they can indeed bear up under the highest and most important studies, or whether they in fact fail of courage, like those who play the coward in other tests.

It surely suits to consider matters this way, he said. But what do you   504a
mean by the highest and most important studies?

You no doubt recall, I replied, that we distinguished three forms of soul,
and were drawing conclusions about what justice and temperance and
courage and wisdom would each be.

If I did not, he said, I would not deserve to hear what remains.

And you recall what we said before of them?

Which was?

We said, surely, that the best possible view of them would require an-   b
other longer way,[13] which would become evident in the traveling of it,
though it would be possible to add proofs consistent with and consequent
on things already stated.[14] You said that sufficed, and thus then what was
said lacked exactitude, as it appeared to me, but it would be for you to say if
it satisfied you.

Why yes, measurably, he said. And so it surely also appeared to the others.

But my friend, I replied, a measure of such things as this which in any   c
way falls short of what really is is hardly a measure: for nothing imperfect is
a measure of anything. But people sometimes think it suffices, and that
there is no further need to inquire.

Yes, he said. Many people are so affected through laziness.

The affection least needed for a Guardian of a city and its laws, I replied.

No doubt, he replied. Such a person must go round the longer way, and   d
work no less hard at learning than at bodily exercise.[15] Otherwise, as we
were just now saying, he will never attain to the goal of the greatest and
most important study, which most especially belongs to him.

13. At IV 435d. The account of justice, temperance, courage, and wisdom in Book IV was founded
    on the composite nature of the tripartite soul. Socrates now suggests need for a metaphysical
    account of the virtues founded on the nature of the Good. The soul in its ultimate nature is
    perhaps not composite (X 611b).
14. Because the Good will not be defined but only alluded to in an image, justice will not be de-
    fined. The argument of the *Republic* is not demonstrative but dialectical, resting on premises
    the respondent agrees that he knows rather than on proof.
15. The "longer way" is here seen to include advanced education in the sciences and dialectic.

THE GOOD IS NOT KNOWLEDGE OR PLEASURE (504D–506D)

Not the greatest, surely? he said. Is anything greater than justice and the other virtues we have explained?

There is indeed, I replied, and we must not contemplate a mere rough outline of those virtues, as we are now doing, without proceeding to the completely finished work. Is it not ridiculous to strain every nerve to get the most pure and accurate knowledge of other things of little worth, but not to demand greatest accuracy in matters of greatest importance?

Yes, he said. But do you think anyone will let you off without asking what the greatest and most important study is, what you say it is about?

Of course, I replied. Go ahead and ask. You've certainly heard it often enough. Either you do not now realize that, or you intend to make trouble by raising objections. I think it is the latter. For you have often heard that the greatest and most important study is the Idea of the Good, by which just things and the rest become useful and beneficial. And you pretty well now know that I intend to mention it, and to say in addition that we do not sufficiently know it. But if we do not know it, then however well we may know other things without it, you know we gain no benefit, even as we gain no benefit if we possess anything without the Good. Or do you think there is profit in any possession, if it is not Good? Or in understanding all other things without the Good, but understanding nothing beautiful and good?

I certainly do not, he said.

Furthermore, you also know that most people think the Good is pleasure, though the cleverer sort think it is knowledge.

Of course.

Yes, and those who believe the latter, my friend, cannot show what kind of knowledge, but are compelled in the end to say knowledge of the Good.

And quite ridiculously, he said.

Of course, I replied. How should it not be so, if they blame us because we do not know the Good, and again, speak as if they thought we knew it. For they say it is knowledge of good, supposing that we do after all understand what they mean when they utter the word "good."

Very true, he said.

What about those who define the Good as pleasure? Are they any less filled with wandering than the others? Are they not compelled also to agree that there are bad pleasures?

Yes, certainly.

It follows then, I suppose, that they agree that the same things are good and bad. Not so?

Certainly.   d

Then evidently there are many great disputes about it?

Of course.

But then, is it not evident that though many people would choose what seems just and beautiful, even if it is not really so, they nevertheless do and possess and judge these things? But it is not enough to possess things which merely seem good; instead, they seek what really is good. Here, at this point, all disdain the seeming.

Yes, he said.

This then is what every soul pursues and for the sake of which it acts   e
in everything, dimly divining that it is something but perplexed and unable sufficiently to grasp what it is, or to attain to the sort of steadfast belief she has about other things—thereby also missing any benefit those
other things might have. Shall the best men in the city, in whose hands
we are placing everything, be left in the dark about such and so great a
matter?

Surely not, he said.   506a

At any rate, I said, I suppose that if it is not known in what way just and
beautiful things are good, someone ignorant of this would be far from possessing a worthy guardian of themselves. My guess is that no one will sufficiently know anything before he sufficiently knows this.

An excellent guess, he said.

Now, our constitution will have been perfectly ordered, if the sort of
guardian who knows these things oversees it?

Necessarily, he said. But what about you, Socrates? Do you claim the   b
Good is knowledge, or pleasure? Or something else besides?

What a man! I replied. You have shown all along that what seemed so to the others would not suffice for you.

No, Socrates, he said, because it does not appear just in me to try to state the judgments of others but not my own, after spending so much time worrying about it.

c   Well, but do you think it just to speak of what one does not know as if he thought he knew? I replied.

Certainly not as if he thought he knew, he said, but nevertheless as one who is willing to say what he thinks, given that he thinks it.

Are you not aware, I said, that all opinions without knowledge are flawed? The best of them are blind. Or do you think those who judge something truly without thought differ at all from blind men traveling the right road?

No, he said.

d   Would you then contemplate flawed things, halt and blind, when it is possible to hear bright and beautiful things from others?

For heaven's sake, Socrates, Glaucon replied, don't stop as if you were at an end. Oblige us. As you explained about justice and temperance and the rest, please also explain about the Good.

THE SUN AND THE IDEA OF THE GOOD (506D–509C)

In fact, I will be very glad to oblige, my friend, I replied. But I fear I will not be able to, that in my eagerness I will only invite ridicule for my clumsiness. For the present, my friends, let us dismiss what the Good is in itself—for

e   that appears to me a larger task than to arrive, according to the present line of attack, at what now seems true to me. What appears to be both offspring of the Good and most like it, I am willing to tell, if it pleases you.[16] If not, let it go.

Please speak, he said. You will pay your debt another time for the explanation you owe of the father.

16. Plural. Socrates is addressing the group.

I might wish, I said, that I were able to pay the debt and allow you to receive the principal, rather than, as now, only the interest.[17] But at any rate accept the interest and offspring of the Good itself. Take care, however, that I do not in some way mislead you against my will, and render a false account of the offspring.

507a

We will take care as best we can, he said. Only speak.

Yes, I said, once we've come to agreement. Recollect what was said before and at this point has often been said elsewhere.

What is that? he replied.

b

We say there are many beautiful things and many good things, and so on, I replied, and we distinguish them in discourse.

Yes, we do.

And again, there is beautiful itself, and good itself, and so for everything which we formerly assumed to be many. But now we turn and assume one single Idea of each, supposing that it is one, and in each case we call it what is.

That's so.

And some things are visible but not intelligible, we say, but the Ideas again are intelligible but not visible.

Certainly.

Then by what of ourselves do we see things seen?

c

By sight, he said.

Then also we hear things heard by hearing, I replied, and everything sensible by the other senses?

Of course.

Then have you ever realized, I replied, with what extraordinary lavishness the craftsman of the senses has wrought the power to see and to be seen?[18]

Why, no, he said.

Consider this: do hearing and sound need in addition another kind in respect to hearing and being heard, such that if a third thing is not present, the one will not hear, the other not be heard?

17. *tokos.* An untranslatable pun: the Greek word means both interest and offspring.
18. Lavish because sight is unique in requiring an additional valuable element, namely light.

d   No, he said, they need nothing in addition.

Nor I suppose are there many other senses—in order not to say none—that need in addition anything of this sort.[19] Can you mention any?

I cannot, he replied.

But don't you realize that sight and the visible need something in addition?

How so?

Sight may be in eyes, surely, and he who has it may try to use it; and color may be present in objects; but if a third kind of thing proper and peculiar to this very thing is not present in addition, you know that sight will see nothing and the colors will be invisible.

e   What is it you mean? he said.

Why, what you call light, I replied.[20]

True, he said.

So it is by no small idea that the sensation of seeing and the power of being seen are yoked together by a yoke more valuable than that yoking the rest, if indeed light is not itself without value.

508a   But surely, it is far from being without value, he said.

Now, which among the gods in heaven[21] do you hold responsible as master of this—whose light causes vision to see what is most beautiful, and things seen to be seen?

Just what you and other people say, he replied: it is clear you are asking about the Sun.

19. It may be objected that sound requires a third thing, namely, air, as Plato himself acknowledged (*Timaeus* 67b–c). But unlike sight and the light of the eyes, hearing is passive, a stroke (πληγή) through the ears by air on brain and blood, reaching the soul; if sound is a stroke of air, air is not "a third thing."

20. If sound is produced by particles striking the ear, it may be treated as an extension of touch, and therefore not analogous to light. The disanalogy becomes more evident if we correct for anachronism. We conceive light as rays impinging on the eye, a passive receptor, as sound waves impinge upon the ears. Plato thought of the eye as active, the visual image being the product of rays issuing from things seen and meeting with rays issuing from the eye which sees them. Cf. *Timaeus* 45b–d, 58c, 67b, 80a.

21. The stars are gods—that is, immortal living animals. *Laws* 821b, 899b, 950d; *Epinomis* 985b, 988d; *Apology* 26d. Cf. *Cratylus* 397d.

Now, vision is dependent upon this god in the following way:

How?

Vision is not the Sun—neither itself nor that in which it comes to be present, which we call the eye.

No.

Yes, but I suppose the eye is the most sunlike of the organs of sensation?[22]

By far.

Then too, the power which it has is dispensed by the Sun, and possessed as a kind of overflow?

Of course.

Then again, the Sun is not vision, but, as cause of vision, is seen by vision itself?

That's so, he said.

This then, I replied, you may say is what I meant as the offspring of the Good, which the Good generated in analogy to itself: that as the Good stands to thought and things known in the intelligible place, so the Sun stands to vision and things seen in the visible place.

How do you mean? he said. Please explain further.

You know that eyes, I replied, when one no longer turns them toward those things whose colors are overspread by the light of day, but by moonlight or starlight, become dull and appear nearly blind, as if pure vision were not present.

Indeed, he said.

Yes, but I suppose when the Sun illuminates their object, they see clearly, and vision proves to be present in these same eyes.

Of course.

So also then conceive what belongs to the soul: when it is fixed upon what truth and reality illuminate, it conceives and knows it, and proves to possess thought. But when it is fixed upon what is mixed with darkness,

22. Because the eye emits rays—the light in the eyes.

upon what comes to be and passes away, it judges and becomes dull and changes opinions back and forth, and seems not to possess thought.

Yes.

e   This then, which provides truth to things known and gives to the knower the power of knowing, you must say is the Idea of the Good. As cause of knowledge and of truth, you must understand it as being known. But beautiful as knowledge and truth both are, you will rightly believe it is other and still more beautiful than they. Even as there it is right to regard
509a   light and vision as Sun-like, but wrong to believe them the Sun, so also here it is right to regard knowledge and truth as Good-like, but wrong to believe either of them the Good. Instead, the possession of the Good is still more to be valued.[23]

You mean a matchless beauty, he said, if it provides knowledge and truth, but is itself beyond them in beauty. For you surely don't mean it is pleasure.

Don't blaspheme, I replied. But examine the image of it still further in this way:

b   How?

I suppose you will say that the Sun provides not only the power of being seen to things seen, but also of becoming and growth and nurture, though it is not itself becoming.

Of course.

And say also for things known, then, not only that intelligibility is present by agency of the Good, but reality and being is also present to them by it, though the Good is not being, but even beyond being, surpassing it in respect to dignity and power.

c   And Glaucon was quite amused: By Apollo![24] he said, Divine superiority!

It is your own fault, I replied, for making me say what I think about it.

23. The passage offers a series of ratios, explicable in terms of proportionality: the Good is to the Sun as truth is to light, as Ideas are to objects of sight, as knowledge is to vision, as thought is to sight, as mind is to eye.
24. Apollo, god of music and poetry, is also god of the Sun.

THE DIVIDED LINE (509C–511E)

Yes, and don't stop unless for good reason, he said, but go through the like-ness about the Sun again to see if you are leaving something out.

Why, I left out a great deal, I said.

Don't omit even a little, he said.

I think I'm actually omitting a lot, I replied. Nevertheless, as far as possi-ble at present, I won't willingly do so.

Please don't, he said.

Conceive then, I replied, that as I say, there are these two, the one king over the intelligible kind and place, the other again over the visible—I don't say "heaven," so that you won't think I'm playing on the name.[25] But you have then these two forms, visible and intelligible?

Yes.

Then take a line divided, as it were, into two unequal sections, one rep-resenting the visible kind, the other the intelligible. Divide each of the two sections again in the same ratio. By reason of their clarity and obscureness relative to each other, you will have, as one distinct section in the visible, images. By images I mean, first, shadows, next, reflections in water and in things so constituted as to be close-grained and smooth and shiny, and everything of the sort, if you understand.

Why, I do understand.

Put the other section then as that of which this is an image, namely, the animals around us, and all plants that grow and the whole kind of artifacts.

Yes, he said.

Would you also say, I replied, that in respect to truth and untruth, it is divided so that as the opinable[26] is to the knowable, so what is made like is to that which it is made like?

I will indeed, he said.

d

e

510a

b

25. The *Cratylus* (396b–c) suggests that the word for heaven, *ouranos,* is etymologically connected with the verb *horan,* to see, from which *to horaton,* the visible, is derived.

26. The judgeable or opinable now substitutes for the visible, with consequent breadth of applica-tion.

Consider then again how the section of the intelligible is to be divided: In what way?

In one section of it, soul is compelled to inquire from hypotheses, using as images the things which before were imitated, and proceeding not to a first principle but to a conclusion. In the other section, again, it goes from hypothesis to unhypothetical first principle,[27] and, without those things which that other section used as images, it makes its inquiry by forms by themselves through themselves.

I don't sufficiently understand what you mean, he said.

c   Try again then, I replied. You will learn more easily when the following is said by way of introduction. I suppose you know that those who trouble themselves about geometry and calculations and such things assume or hypothesize the odd and the even, the figures and three forms of angle, and in respect to each inquiry other things sister to these, as if they knew them. They suppose they do know them, making them "hypotheses" indeed, things laid down, and they do not think fit to render any further account of
d   them either to themselves or others, supposing them evident to all. They start from these and then go through what remains, ending agreeably[28] at the conclusion for which they set in motion their inquiry.

Of course, he said. I do know that.

Then you also know that they use visible forms and fashion arguments about them, thinking not about them but about the things they are like, making arguments for the sake of the square itself and the diagonal itself,
e   instead of what they draw. And so in other cases. They use as images the very things they construct and draw, of which there are also shadows and images in water, seeking to see those things themselves which one cannot see otherwise than by the understanding.

511a   True, he said.

This form is intelligible, I said, though soul is compelled to use hypotheses in the investigation of it, not proceeding to a first principle, be-

27. The Idea of the Good, VII 532a ff.

28. Agreement would seem to involve implication and not mere compatibility: the conclusion cannot be false if the premises are true.

cause it is unable to climb higher than its hypotheses; but using as images the very things from which images were made by things below them, these, as opposed to those, have been adjudged and valued as clear.

I understand, he said: you mean what falls under geometry and its sister arts.

Then by the other section of the intelligible, understand me to mean what reason itself grasps through the power of dialectic, making the hypotheses not first principles but really hypotheses, things laid down as steppingstones and starting points, in order to proceed to what is unhypothetical, the first principle of the All. Once having grasped it, soul again in turn takes hold of what it contains and in this way descends to a conclusion, making use of nothing that is sensible, but of forms by themselves, through themselves, in respect to themselves; and it ends in forms.

I understand, he said, though not sufficiently—I think you describe an immense task. But you wish to distinguish what is contemplated by the knowledge of dialectic whose object is what is and is intelligible, as more clear than what is contemplated by the so-called arts,[29] for which the hypotheses are first principles. Those who contemplate them are compelled to contemplate them by understanding, not perception, and because they do not go back to a first principle in their inquiry but proceed from hypotheses, you think they do not possess thought about them, even though they are intelligible with a first principle. I think you call the possession of geometers and people of that sort understanding, not thought, supposing that understanding is something intermediate between opinion and thought.

You've understood me most satisfactorily, I replied. Apply these four affections arising in the soul to the four divisions of the line: Thought to the highest, Understanding to the second, give Belief the third, and Imagination the last. Arrange them in a proportion, so that as their objects have a share of truth, so also they have a share of clarity.

I understand, and I agree to arrange them as you say, he replied.

29. That is, the mathematical arts, to be described in Book VII as part of advanced education.

Divided Line

States of Mind	Objects
Intelligible or Knowable World A. Thought or Knowledge Dialectic: rises from hypotheses to unhypothetical first principle. Uses no images. Begins with forms, moves through forms, ends in forms.	Object of Dialectic: what is and is intelligible: unhypothetical first principle (form of the Good), all other forms including mathematical forms.
B. Understanding Travels downward from hypotheses to a conclusion, not a first principle. Concerned with geometry and calculation and in general the arts. Treats its hypotheses as self-evident and does not render an account of them. Uses as images contents of C, which have images of their own in D.	Objects of the arts: fully intelligible only when seen in connection with first principle.
Visible or Opinable World C. Belief	All animals, plants and artifacts. That of which D is an image.
D. Imagination	Shadows, reflections in water and in mirrors.

Book VII

Next then, I said, concerning education and the lack of it, compare our 514a
own nature to a situation like this: Picture people as dwelling in a cavernous
underground chamber, with an entrance opening upward to the light, and
a long passageway running down the whole length of the cave. They have
been there since childhood, legs and necks fettered so they cannot move:
they see only what is in front of them, unable to turn their heads because of
the bonds. But light reaches them from a fire burning some distance behind b
and above them. Between the fire and the prisoners, picture a track a bit
higher up, and a little wall built along it like the screens in front of the per-
formers at puppet shows, above which they show the puppets.

I see it, he said.

See also then people carrying all sorts of artificial objects alongside this 515a
little wall, statues of men and other animals, made of wood and stone and
all sorts of things. Some of the carriers are talking, it is likely, others silent.

A strange image, he said, and strange prisoners.

Like ourselves, I replied. For first, do you think such prisoners see anything of themselves or one another except the shadows cast by the fire on the wall of the cave in front of them?

Why, how could they, he said, if they had been compelled to hold their heads motionless throughout life?

b   What about the objects being carried along. Isn't it the same?

Of course.

Then if they were able to converse with one another, don't you think they would acknowledge as things which are, the things that they saw?[1]

Necessarily.

What if the prison also had an echo from the wall opposite. Whenever some one of those passing gave utterance, do you think they would believe anything except the passing shadow spoke?

Emphatically not, he said.

c   Such prisoners, then, I replied, would not acknowledge as true anything except shadows of artificial objects.

Quite necessarily, he said.

Consider then, I replied, what release and healing from the bonds of un-wisdom would consist in, if it by nature occurred to them in this way: whenever one of them was released, and suddenly compelled to stand up-right and turn his head and walk and look upward to the light, he would feel pain in doing all this, and because his eyes were dazzled, he would be

d   unable to discern those things yonder whose shadows he had seen before. What do you suppose he would say, if someone told him that what he had seen before was foolishness, but that now, being somewhat nearer to what is and turned toward more real objects, he would see more correctly? Espe-cially if, after being shown each of the things which are passing, he was compelled by questioning to answer what it is? Don't you suppose he would

1. Shorey comments: "As we use the word tree of the trees we see, though the reality is the idea of a tree, so they would speak of the shadows as the world, though the real reference unknown to them would be to the objects that cause the shadows, and back of the objects to the things of the 'real' world of which they are copies. The general meaning, which is quite certain, is that they would suppose the shadows to be the realities. . . . They suppose that the names refer to the passing shadows, but (as we know) they really apply to the objects. Ideas and particulars are homonymous."

be perplexed and at a loss, and believe the things he saw before more true than those pointed out to him now?

Yes, he said.

Then suppose he were also compelled to look toward the light itself. It   e
would hurt his eyes, and he would turn away in order to escape to the things he was able to see, and acknowledge them as really more clear than what was being shown him.

That's so, he said.

But if someone forcibly dragged him from there up the rugged steep ascent, I replied, and did not let go until he had hauled him into the light of the sun, wouldn't he suffer and be distressed as he was dragged along? And when he came to the light, his eyes would be so filled with its brightness that he   516a
would be unable to see even one among the things now claimed to be true?

No, he said, at least not immediately.

Then I suppose he would have to become accustomed to it, if he is going to see the things above. It would be easiest first to look at shadows, next, at images in water of men and other things, and afterward at the things themselves; after this, it would be easier to contemplate things in the heaven and   b
the heaven itself by night, and gaze at the light of the stars and the moon, than at the sun and its light by day.

Of course.

Finally then, I suppose, the sun. Not appearances of it in water or in alien seats: he would be able to look at it alone by itself in its own place, and contemplate it as it is.

Necessarily, he said.

After this, he would at that point infer of it that it is this which produces the seasons and the years and governs everything in the visible place, and is in some manner cause of all the things they used to see.

It is clear, he said, that he would arrive next at this conclusion along with   c
that.

Suppose he were to recall his first dwelling place, and the wisdom there, and his fellow prisoners then. Wouldn't he think himself happy in the change, and pity them?

Indeed.

d Suppose they had honors and prizes for those who most acutely discern and best remember the shadows that pass—which of them usually comes before, and after, and at the same time—and from this was then best able to guess what was coming next. Do you think he would want what they have, and envy them their honors and positions of power? Or would he feel, as Homer has it, that he would much prefer to be the slave of a landless man and suffer anything at all, rather than believe those things and live that life?[2]

e Yes, he said, I think he would suffer anything rather than accept that life.

Consider this too, I replied. If such a man went down again and sat upon the same seat,[3] would not his eyes be filled with darkness, coming suddenly from the sun?

Yes, indeed, he said.

Suppose then he had to compete again in judging those shadows with people who had always been prisoners, while his vision was dim, before his eyes settled down—and it would take some little time to get used to the darkness. Wouldn't he be laughed at? Wouldn't it be said of him that he had journeyed upward only to return with his eyes ruined, that it wasn't worth it even to try to go up? And if they were able somehow to lay hands on the man trying to release them and lead them up, and kill him, they would kill him.[4]

Certainly, he said.

517a

THE CAVE APPLIED TO THE SUN AND THE LINE (517A–518B)

This image, my dear Glaucon, I replied, must be applied as a whole to what b was said before, likening the seat which appears through sight to the prison

---

2. *Odyssey* XI 489–490. Achilles visits the place of the dead and declares that he would rather be the servant of a landless man on earth than king of the flickering shades of the dead. By implication, the prisoners chained in the cave suffer a living death.

3. *thakon:* seat, but also privy seat. Plato is sometimes careless of the neo-Victorian sensibilities of his translators.

4. An allusion to the trial and death of Socrates.

dwelling, and the light of the fire in it to the power of the sun. If you assume that the ascent upward and the vision of things above is the upward journey of the soul to the intelligible place, you will not mistake my surmise, since you desire to hear it. God alone knows whether it happens to be true, but these appearances appear thus to me. In the intelligible place, the Idea of the Good is seen finally and with difficulty, but once seen, it must be inferred that it is the cause of all things right and beautiful. In the visible place it gives birth to Light and to the Sun, the Lord of Light; in the intelligible place it is itself Lord, and provides intelligence and truth. It must also be inferred that whoever intends to act wisely in public or private must see it.

So far as I am able, he said, I concur.

Come then, I replied, and concur also in this: do not be surprised that those who arrive here refuse to take part in the affairs of men; rather, their souls ever press on to spend their time above. For it is surely likely to be so, if the foregoing image once again applies.

Yes, he said.

Then do you think it at all surprising, I replied, if someone who has come from contemplation of divine things to the evils of human life is awkward, and appears quite ridiculous when, with vision still dim and before becoming sufficiently accustomed to the present darkness, he is compelled, in law courts or elsewhere, to contend about the shadows of what is just, or about images of the things of which they are shadows, and to dispute about how they are understood by those who have never seen justice itself?

It would not at all be surprising, he said.

But a reasonable man might remember, I replied, that eyes become disturbed in two ways and for two reasons: by shifting from light to darkness, and from darkness to light. He would acknowledge that this same thing also happens with soul, and whenever he saw it disturbed and unable to see something, he would not thoughtlessly laugh, but inquire whether it had been blinded by unaccustomed darkness after coming from a brighter life, or whether in passing from greater ignorance to a brighter life it had been dazzled by yet more light; and thus he would count one soul happy in its experience and its life, but pity the other, and if he wished to laugh at it, his laughter would be less ridiculous than laughter at a soul come down from the light above.

A very fair statement, he said.

EDUCATION AND VIRTUE (518B–519D)

c   If this is true, I said, we must acknowledge that education is not what it is said to be by some, who profess to be able to put knowledge into a soul where it is not present, as though putting sight into blind eyes.

They do claim that, he said.

The present account signifies, I replied, that this power is present in the soul of each person, along with the instrument by which each person un-
d   derstands. It is as if an eye could not turn from darkness to what is bright except in company with the whole body. Just so, this instrument must be converted from what becomes by turning in company with the whole soul until it has become capable of being lifted up to contemplate what is, and the brightest of what is. But this, we say, is the Good. Not so?

Yes.

Then there would be an art whose object is to effect this very thing, this conversion, I replied, to turn the soul around in the easiest and most effective way. Not to put sight into it, for we may suppose it already has it, but to contrive that it not be turned to look in the wrong direction, but where it should.

It seems so, he said.

The other virtues commonly said to belong to the soul are not far re-
e   moved from things of the body—for they are afterward produced by habits and practices where they were not really present before—but the virtue of intelligence assuredly happens to be something more divine, it seems: it never loses its power, but becomes useful and beneficial or useless and harm-
519a   ful because of the way it is turned. Or have you never noticed, among those said to be bad but wise, how shrewd is the vision of their petty souls and how keenly it sees the things toward which it is turned? There's nothing the

matter with their vision, but it is compelled to the service of evil, so that the more keenly it sees, the more evils it works.

Of course, he replied.

And yet, I replied, if such a nature were pruned from childhood up— b
cleared, as it were, of those leaden weights, akin to becoming, which are attached to it by gluttony and greedy pleasures of that kind and bend the vision of the soul downward—if, freed from these, it were turned round at last to things which are true, then this same thing belonging to these same people would see things yonder most keenly, even as the objects toward which it is now turned.

Yes, likely enough, he said.

But isn't it also likely, I replied, and even necessary from what has been said, that a city cannot ever sufficiently be governed by those who are uneducated and without experience of truth, nor again by those allowed to c
pass their whole time in education? Not the one, because they have no single target in life at which to aim in every action, public and private; not the other, because they'll be unwilling to act, believing they've been transported to the Isles of the Blessed while still alive.

True, he said.

Then it is our own task as founders, I replied, to compel the best natures to attain to the knowledge which we formerly described as most important: to see the Good and rise upward in that ascent. And when they have as- d
cended and sufficiently seen, not to allow to them what is now allowed.

What is that?

To abide there, I replied, and refuse to go back down again among the prisoners and share their labors and honors, whether of lesser or more serious worth.

THE DUTY TO GOVERN (519D–521B)

Then we'll do them an injustice? he said. We'll cause them to live a worse life when they're capable of better?

You again forget, my friend, I replied, that it is not a concern of law that e

some one class in a city should do and fare surpassingly well, but to contrive
520a   that this should come to be present in the city as a whole, harmoniously
uniting citizens by persuasion and necessity, causing them to share with
each other the benefit each is capable of providing to the community at
large. Law produces such men in a city not in order to allow them to turn in
any direction they each may wish, but in order that it may use them to bind
the city together.

True, he said. I did forget.

Consider further, Glaucon, I said, that we will not do an injustice to the
philosophers who arise among us; we will speak justly to them in requiring
them to care for and guard the rest. For we shall say that people of their sort
b   born in other cities reasonably do not share their labors; for they grew up on
their own in spite of the constitution in each city, and it is right that as self-
sustaining and indebted for nurture to no one, they should not be quick to
make payment for being nurtured. But as for you, we will say, we bred you
for yourselves and for the rest of the city, as kings and leaders in the hive.
c   You are better and more perfectly educated than the rest, and more able to
have a share of both ways of life. You must go down then, each in his turn,
to dwell with the others and become accustomed to see in the darkness. For
once used to it, you will see immeasurably better than those there, and you
will know each of the images for what it is, and of what it is an image,[5]
through having seen the truth of things beautiful and just and good. And in
this way you will govern our city wide awake instead of in a dream, as most
cities are now governed, where people fight over shadows and quarrel about
d   office, supposing it a great good. The truth is surely this: that city is necessarily best and most free of faction in which those least eager to rule shall
rule, and the city governed oppositely gains the opposite.

Of course, he said.

Then do you suppose those we have nurtured, when they hear this, will
disobey and refuse to take their turn in sharing the labors of the city, but
dwell most of the time with one another in what is pure?

---

5. These images evidently include both the shadows on the wall of the cave and the objects, imitations of things outside, which cast those shadows.

Impossible, he said. For we require just things of just men. Still, each of   e
them will assuredly enter upon office as a necessity, the opposite of those
who rule in each city now.

That's so, my friend, I replied. It is possible to have a well-governed city
only if you find a life better than ruling for those who are to rule. For in it   521a
only will the really rich rule—rich not in gold but in the wealth required for
happiness, namely, a good and reasonable life. But if beggars starved of
good things in their private lives enter on the public business, thinking
there to seize the Good, it is impossible. When office comes to be fought
over, this inner war destroys them and the rest of the city.

Very true, he said.   b

Can you suggest any life which scorns political office, I replied, except
that of genuine philosophy?

I most certainly cannot, he replied.

But it is those who are not in love with office who must go to it; otherwise, rivals will fight.

Of course.

Then who will you compel to guardianship of the city, except those who
are wisest about the things through which a city is best governed, and have
other honors and a better life than the political life?

No one else at all, he said.

HOW GUARDIANS ARE LED UPWARD TO THE LIGHT (521C–522D)

Would you then have us at this point consider how such people as this will   c
come to be present and how to lead them upward to the light, as some are
said to have ascended from the Underworld to the gods?

How could I not wish it? he said.

This then, it seems, is no mere flip of an oystershell,[6] but a conversion of
soul from a day which is like night to genuine day, an ascent to what is real
which we say is true philosophy.

6. The reference is to a children's game: the shell was black on one side, white on the other, indi-
cating randomness of result, the flip of a coin.

Of course.

Then we must examine which studies have this power?

d   Certainly.

What study, Glaucon, would draw a soul from what becomes to what is? It occurs to me even as I speak: didn't we say that while young they must become athletes of war?

Yes.

So the study we seek must have this in addition:

What?

It must not be useless to soldiers.

Certainly, he said, if that's possible.

e   In what went before we educated them in gymnastic and in music and literature.

Yes, he said.

And gymnastic, I take it, is wholly devoted to what comes to be and perishes: for it presides over bodily growth and decay.

It appears so.

522a   So this is not the study we seek.

No.

But perhaps instead music, as we've previously explained it?

Hardly, he said. That was the counterpart of gymnastic, if you recall. It educated the Guardians by habit, not knowledge, imparting a kind of tunefulness by mode and gracefulness by rhythm, and certain other dispositions akin to these in the content of the verse, whether fictional or true. But there was no study in it leading to a good of the sort you are now seeking.

b   You remind me most exactly, I replied: for really, it contained nothing of this sort. And yet, dear Glaucon, what does? For the arts all doubtless seem base and vulgar.

Of course. But what other study is still left, apart from music and gymnastic and the arts?

Come, I replied. If we cannot grasp anything outside them, let us grasp something that stretches through them all.

c   Such as?

Such as that common thing which every art and branch of understanding and knowledge makes use of—indeed, among the first things everyone has to learn.

What's that? he said.

That little matter of distinguishing one[7] and two and three, I replied. I mean, in brief, number and calculation. Isn't it true that every art and branch of knowledge is required to become a partaker of them?

Very much so, he said.

Including the art of war? I said.

Necessarily, he said.   d

On the stage, at any rate, Palamedes constantly makes Agamemnon look utterly ridiculous as a general. Haven't you noticed that Palamedes claims he discovered number and marshaled the ranks for the army at Troy and counted the ships and everything else, as though he thought they'd never been counted before? Agamemnon, since he didn't know how to count, it seems, didn't even know how many feet he had. And yet, what sort of a general is that, do you think?

A strange one, he said, if true.

QUALIFICATION BY OPPOSITES AND THE EXISTENCE
OF IDEAS (522E-524D)

Then shall we assume it a necessary study for a soldier to be able to calculate   e
and count? I replied.

Yes, especially if he is to understand anything at all about ordering in ranks—or even if he is to be human.

Then do you conceive this study as I do? I said.

How is that?

Very likely it is among the studies we seek which by nature lead toward   523a
thought. Yet though it draws the mind toward reality, no one uses it rightly.

---

7. One, in apposition with two and three. Used as a noun, the expression has no opposite, as distinct from the adjectival use, whose opposite is "many."

How do you mean? he said.

I'll try to make clear what I think, I replied. I distinguish in my own mind between what leads where we say and what does not. Become my coadjutor and assent or deny, so that we may see more clearly if it is as I suspect.

Show me, he said.

b   Very well, I replied. You will observe that some among our perceptions do not summon thought to inquiry, supposing them adequately judged by perception; others demand in every case that thought inquire, supposing that perception produces nothing healthy or sound.

Clearly you mean things appearing at a distance, and in scene painting.

You don't quite get what I mean, I replied.

Well, what do you mean? he said.

c   Those which do not summon thought, I replied, do not at the same time pass over into an opposite perception.[8] But I assume that those which summon thought do so, when the perception no more makes clear this than the opposite, whether it is projected from near at hand or far off. You'll know more clearly what I mean from this. Here, we say, are three fingers, the smallest, the second and the middle.

Of course, he said.

Understand me then to claim that they are seen near at hand. But consider this about them:

What?

d   Each of them appears equally a finger, and in this there is no difference, whether seen in the middle or at the end, whether black or white, thick or thin, and so on. For in all these cases, the mind or soul of most people is not compelled to inquire of thought what a finger is. For sight nowhere signifies to it that the finger is at the same time the opposite of a finger.

Of course not, he said.

Then such a thing as this likely does not summon or arouse thought, I replied.

8. The word *aisthesis* may mean perception or sensation or, more generally, awareness. The contrary judgments which perception provides are attributed to opinion in V 479a–e.

No.

What about their size? Does sight sufficiently see the largeness and the smallness of them? Does it make no difference to it if one of them is situated in the middle or on the end? And so similarly for touch—thickness and thinness, softness and hardness? And the other senses—aren't they also deficient in making such things as this clear? Or does each of them act like this: first, the sense ordered to the hard is required also to be ordered to the soft, and announces to the soul that it supposes it is perceiving both hard and soft as the same thing?[9]

That's so, he said.

Then in such cases again, I replied, the soul is necessarily perplexed as to what perception signifies to her by "hard," since perception says that the same thing is also soft; and what perception of the light and heavy means by "light" and "heavy," whether it signifies that the heavy is light and the light is heavy.

In fact, he said, these messages to the soul are strange, and need investigation.

So it is likely in these circumstances, I replied, that soul first summons calculation and thought to consider whether each of the things reported is one or two.

Of course.

If they appear to be two, each of the two appears different and one?

Yes.

So if each of two is one but both are two, the soul will conceive the two as separate; for if inseparable, it would surely conceive not two but one.

Right.

But surely sight saw large and small, we say, not separated but mixed together. Not so?

Yes.

For the clarification of this, thought was compelled to see great and small, not mixed together but separated, in the opposite way from sight?

9. Or "perceiving the same thing as both hard and soft."

True.

From this it first occurs to us to ask what the large is, and again, what the small is?[10]

To be sure.

And thus then we called the one intelligible, the other visible.

d   Quite rightly, he said.

This then is what I was trying to say just now, that some things summon the understanding, others do not. What affects perception in opposite ways at the same time I distinguish as summoning it; what does not does not awaken thought.[11]

At this point I understand, and it seems so to me too.

ARITHMETIC (524D–526C)

Then of which sort do number and the one seem to be?

I don't know, he said.

e   Why, reckon it up from what has already been said. If one were sufficiently seen alone by itself or grasped by any other perception, as we said of the finger, it would not draw the soul to reality. But if some result of opposition is always seen with it at the same time, so that it appears no more one than the opposite, there would then at that point be need for judgment, and soul would be compelled to inward perplexity and inquiry, stirring up reflection within itself and asking what one itself is. In this way, study of one would be among the things which lead and convert the soul to the contemplation of what is.

---

10. Or "What largeness is, and again, what smallness is."

11. This should be distinguished, as Plato suggests at 523b, from 602cff., where sense error and the illusions of perspective involve qualification by opposites. Sense error implies, at least by itself, not that forms exist but only that we sometimes misapprehend particulars, a kind of misapprehension to be dispelled by counting, weighing, and measuring. What is at issue in 602cff. may be the difference between imagination and belief. It is plainly not the difference between opinion and knowledge. The argument from opposites turns on the fact that particulars are and do not merely seem qualified by opposites. Measurement will only confirm the appearance that my third finger is both large and small (cf. 523b).

But surely sight of it does involve this, and in no small degree, he said: 525a
for we do see the same thing at the same time as one and as unlimited in
multitude.

Then since one, I replied, the whole of number is also affected this same
way?

Of course.

Moreover, calculation and arithmetic are wholly concerned with number.

Indeed.

Yes, but they appear to lead toward truth. b

Remarkably so.

So they would be among the studies we are seeking, it seems. For a soldier must learn them to marshal his troops in ranks, a philosopher because
he must rise above becoming in order to grasp reality, or never become
skilled in the calculations of reason.

That's so, he said.

But our Guardian, as it happens, is both soldier and philosopher.

Of course.

Then it would be suitable to prescribe this study by law, and persuade
those who are to have a share of the most important affairs in the city to go
to calculation and engage in it, not as mere amateurs, but until they arrive c
at contemplation in thought by itself of the nature of the numbers, not for
the sake of buying or selling as if they were studying to be merchants or
shopkeepers, but for the sake of war and the easiest conversion of the soul
itself from becoming to truth and reality.

Excellent, he said.

Again, I replied, since we have mentioned the study of calculation, it d
now also occurs to me how subtle it is, and how useful to us in what we
wish, if one pursues it for the sake of knowledge, not commerce.

How so? he said.

We were just saying how emphatically it leads the soul upward and compels it to discuss the numbers themselves, refusing to accept it if someone
converses by putting forward numbers which have visible or tangible bod-

e   ies.[12] For you surely know that if someone undertakes to divide one itself in speech, those who are skilled in these matters laugh and won't allow it. On the contrary, if you break it up, they multiply it, taking care that one should never appear not one, but many parts.

Very true, he said.

526a   Then Glaucon, suppose someone should ask them, "What kind of numbers are you discussing, my friends, in which each one is such as you think fit to claim it is, completely equal to every other, not differing in the slightest and having within itself no part at all?" What do you suppose they would answer?

This, I suppose, that they are speaking of those things which admit of being conceived in thought alone, and cannot be dealt with otherwise at all.

You see then, my friend, I replied, that this study really happens to be necessary for us, since it appears to compel soul to use thought by itself for purposes of truth by itself?

b   Yes, he said, and it does so quite emphatically.

But did you ever notice this? Natural calculators are naturally quick in pretty nearly every study, and slower folk, if educated and trained in calculation, nevertheless become quicker than they were before even if they gain no other benefit, and all improve?

That's so, he said.

c   Again, you'll not easily find many studies which require more work to learn and practice than this, I think.

No.

Then for all these reasons, the study of calculation must not be neglected: those best in their natures must be educated in it.

I agree, he replied.

12. The Greek word for number, *arithmos,* is ambiguous between that by which we count, and that which is counted or countable—the number 7 and the seven books on the table. Thus it makes sense, in Greek, to speak of visible or tangible numbers—that is, things numerable.

GEOMETRY (526C–527C)

Very well, let this one thing be settled for us, I said. But second, let us inquire whether what is continuous with it at all concerns us.

What's that? Do you mean geometry? he said.

Exactly, I replied.

Clearly we're concerned with as much of it as is relevant to warfare, he said. For in pitching camps and occupying positions and concentrating and deploying an army, and all other formations both in battle itself and on the march, someone skilled in geometry is superior to what he would be if he were not.

But still, I said, even a small part of geometry and calculation suffices for that sort of thing. We must consider whether proceeding to the major and more advanced part of geometry tends at all to make it easier to behold the Idea of the Good. Everything tends there, we claim, in so far as it compels soul to be turned round to that place in which the happiest of what is exists, which soul must in every way behold.

You're right, he said.

If geometry compels contemplation of reality, it concerns us, but if of becoming, it does not.

So we claim.

No one with even a little experience of geometry, I replied, will dispute that this knowledge is quite opposite to the language used by those who deal with it.

How so? he said.

Their language is surely both ludicrous and necessary. They speak as if they thought they were doing something, as if all their words were for the sake of action. They talk about "squaring" and "applying" and "adding," and use words like that. But the whole study, surely, is undertaken for the sake of knowledge.

Most certainly, he said.

Then this must still further be agreed:

What?

It is knowledge of what always is, not of what sometimes comes to be and passes away.

Readily granted, he said. Geometry is knowledge of what always is.

So it would draw a soul toward truth, my friend, and be productive of philosophical understanding, by directing upward what we now wrong-fully direct downward.

Yes, in the highest possible degree, he said.

c So in precisely that degree, I replied, we must require that those in our beautiful city shall not in any way neglect geometry. And in fact, even its in-cidental value is not slight.

Which is? he asked.

There is what you just mentioned about warfare, I replied. And espe-cially for the better reception of all studies, we know there is an immeasur-able difference between having grasped geometry and not.

Most emphatically, he said.

May we then put this as a second study for the young?

Yes, he said.

SOLID GEOMETRY (527D–528E)

d Then shall we put astronomy third? What do you think?

I think so, he said. Having better awareness of seasons and months and years is important for farming and sailing, but no less for military com-mand.

I'm amused, I replied. You seem afraid the multitude will think you're re-quiring useless studies. It is not at all trivial, though it is hard to believe, that

e there is an organ in the soul of every man which is purified and rekindled in these studies when it has been destroyed and blinded by other pursuits, an organ more worth saving than ten thousand eyes; for truth is seen by it alone. Those who concur in this cannot but suppose you speak well. Those who have been quite unaware of it will naturally believe you talk nonsense,

528a for they see no other benefit worth mentioning in these pursuits. So con-sider right here to whom you're speaking. Or do you perhaps speak to neither but instead discuss what is of utmost importance to yourself, though you'd surely not begrudge someone else if he could at all profit from it?

That, he said. I choose to speak, and ask and answer questions, mostly for my own sake.

Then retrace your steps, I replied. For we were wrong just now in what we took up next in order to geometry.

How so? he said.

After plane geometry, I replied, we took solids already in circular motion, before taking them alone by themselves. But surely it is right to take the third dimension next in order after the second, and this, I suppose, concerns the dimension of cubics and what has a share of depth.

Yes, he said. But Socrates, it seems these things have not yet been discovered.[13]

For two reasons, I replied. They are not strongly pursued because no city holds them in honor, difficult as they are, and those who pursue them need a director, without whom they will not make discoveries. First, he is hard to find, and next, even if found, those who pursue these inquiries would be too proud to obey him as things now stand. But if a whole city held these studies in honor and joined in supervision, they would be persuaded, and continuous and sustained inquiry would then bring how it is to light. Although even now, despised by the public, hampered by those who pursue it and yet can render no account of its usefulness, it nevertheless grows despite all, by sheer force of its charm, and it would not be surprising if it at last became clear.

Surely it has surpassing charm, he said. But tell me more clearly what you meant just now. You assumed, I think, that geometry deals with the plane.

Yes, I replied.

And then at first, astronomy was next, he said, but afterward you took it back.

13. The development of solid geometry, and specifically equations of the third degree, was primarily the work of Theaetetus in the Academy, long after the dramatic date of the *Republic*.

Yes, I said, for in my haste to explain everything, I made the less speed. The study of the dimension of depth, or solids, is next in order. I passed over it because the state of the inquiry is ridiculous, so I spoke of astronomy, after geometry, as motion of solids.

e   That's right, he said.

ASTRONOMY (528E–530C)

Let's put astronomy as a fourth study, then, I replied, supposing that what is now being passed over can be assumed to exist, if a city will pursue it.

Reasonably enough, he replied. And instead of the vulgar praise of astronomy for which you just rebuked me, Socrates, I will praise it now in the

529a   way you seek: for I think it is clear to everyone that it compels a soul[14] to look upward, and leads from here to yonder.

Clear perhaps to everyone but me, I replied. For I don't think so.

Why? he said.

Because those who try to lead us upward to philosophy now handle it in such a way as to cause the soul to look downward.

What do you mean? he said.

I think you perhaps have too generous a conception of what it is to study

b   things above, I replied. If someone learned something by craning his neck and looking up at the decorations on the ceiling, very likely you'd think he contemplated them by thought, not his eyes. Well, maybe you're right, and I'm being foolish. For I cannot acknowledge that any other study causes a soul to look upward except that study which concerns what is and is invisible. If someone undertakes to learn something from sensible things, whether by looking up with mouth open or down with mouth shut, I would deny he

c   ever learns at all, because there is no knowledge of such things as this. His soul is looking down, not up, even if he pursues his studies by land or by sea, floating on his back.

I deserve that, he said. You're right to criticize me. But why then did you

14. Here as often elsewhere, soul = mind.

say that astronomy, if it is to be of benefit for what we intend to study, must be studied contrary to the way people do now?

For this reason, I replied. These intricate traceries in the heavens, since they have been embroidered in a visible place, are believed to be most beautiful and most exact among things visible. Yet they fall far short of things which are genuine and true, namely, movements in respect to which the real speed and the real slowness are moved relative to each other, in true and genuine number and in all true figures, and, being moved, move the things within them; which indeed can be grasped by reason and understanding, not by sight. Do you disagree?

Not at all, he said.

We must use the embroideries of heaven, I said, as standards and examples for the study of those things, just as if one had happened on diagrams drawn by Daedalus or some other craftsman or painter, wrought with surpassing care. Anyone experienced in geometry would believe, on seeing such things, that even though most beautifully produced, it would be ridiculous to inquire into them seriously, in the expectation that they hold within themselves the truth of equals or doubles or of any other ratio.

How could it not be ridiculous? he said.

Then don't you suppose, I replied, that a real astronomer will be affected the same way in viewing the motions of the stars? He will acknowledge that such works are organized with superlative beauty, and that they and the things in them are thus organized by the craftsman of the heavens. But the ratio of night to day, and of these to month, and month to year, and of the other stars to these and to each other—don't you suppose he will believe it absurd for a man to suppose them always the same, that they do not vary even though they have body and are visible, and seek to grasp the truth of them?

So it seems to me, at any rate, he said, as I listen to you now.

As in geometry, so also in astronomy, we will proceed by using problems. We will let what is in the heavens alone, if we intend really to have a share of astronomy, and from being useless render useful the intelligence naturally in the soul.

d

e

530a

b

c   The task you set is many times more difficult than astronomy as it is now pursued.

Yes, I suppose it is, I said. And we will assign other such tasks, if we are to be of any benefit as legislators. Can you think of any other suitable studies?

No, I can't, not on the spur of the moment, he said.

HARMONICS (530C–531C)

Motion, I replied, provides not one but many forms, I think. Perhaps it takes a wise man to state them all, but two at least are evident even to us.

d   What are they, then?

There is in addition to astronomy, I replied, its counterpart.

What is that?

Very likely as eyes are fixed on astronomy, I said, so also ears are fixed on motion of attunement,[15] and these are sister sciences to each other, as the Pythagoreans say.[16] And we agree, Glaucon, do we not?

Yes, he said.

e   Then since the task is great, I replied, we will learn by inquiring of them what they have to say about these subjects, and whether there is anything to add. And through all this, we will watch out for our own concern.

Which is?

That those we are educating shall never undertake to learn anything which is imperfect, and which does not gain the place yonder to which all must attain, as we were saying just now about astronomy. Aren't you aware

531a   that people act somewhat the same way about attunement? They vainly measure audible consonances and tones against each other, in useless labor like the astronomers.

Yes, he said, absurdly enough. They talk about something they call least intervals, and lay their ears along their instruments as though they were try-ing to overhear the conversation next door. Some claim they can still hear a

15. That is, the motion of air in various velocities, accounting for proportional differences of pitch. Cf. III 397b, 398d–e, *Timaeus* 67b, 80a ff.

16. Exhibited in the Music of the Spheres, X 617b ff.

tone in between, and that this is the smallest interval by which to measure; others argue that the sounds are at that point the same. Both set their ears ahead of their minds.

You mean those good folk who persecute and torture the strings, I said, and rack them on the pegs? Not to draw the image out too far—blows struck by the plectrum, accusations and denials and bluster from the strings—I'll set aside the image and deny I mean those people, but rather those others we were just now saying we would question about attunement. They do the same thing as those in astronomy: they seek numbers in these audible consonances, but they do not ascend to problems, to examining what numbers are consonant and what are not, and in each case, why.

You describe a task not human but divine, he said.

But useful for inquiry into the beautiful and good, I replied—and useless if otherwise pursued.

Very likely, he said.

DIALECTIC (531C–535A)

Yes, I replied, and I suppose that if the investigation of everything we have discussed has arrived at their communion and kinship with one another, and they are reckoned together by their near relation to one another, then our concern for them is relevant to what we wish, and not work done in vain. Otherwise, it is in vain.

I guess so, he said. But it is an immense task you describe, Socrates.

You mean it is merely a prelude, I replied. Don't we know that all this is a preamble to the law itself, a prelude to the song we must learn? For you surely don't think people skilled in this are dialecticians?

Most certainly not, he said, unless perhaps a very few of those I've met.

But further, I said, do you think that anyone who cannot render and receive an account will ever know anything of what we claim must be known?

No again, he said.

Well, Glaucon, I said, is this at last the very law which dialectic fulfills,

b

c

d

e

532a

the song which it performs? Being intelligible, the power of vision, which we said undertakes to look at the animals by themselves, and at the stars by themselves and finally at the Sun itself, would imitate it. So also, when one undertakes by dialectical conversation, without any of the senses, to begin to make his way through reason to what each thing is by itself, and does not give over until he grasps by thought itself what the Good is by itself, he reaches the end of the intelligible, even as, before, the power of vision reached the end of the visible.

b   Certainly, he said.

Well then, don't you call this journey dialectic?

Of course.

Yes, I replied. It is release from bondage and conversion from shadows to images and the light, and ascent out of the cave into the sunlight—and there, even still, inability to look at animals and plants and the light of the sun, but only at divine[17] appearances in water and shadows of things which are, though not shadows of images cast by that different sort of light which is itself a shadow compared to the Sun. This whole business of the arts we have described has this power to lead what is noblest in soul upward to the vision of what is best among things which are, even as before what was clearest in body led upward to the vision of what is brightest in the bodily and visible place.

d   I accept this, he said. And yet, I think it is very hard to accept, though in another way hard to reject. Nevertheless—because it must not only be heard now but often repeated hereafter—let us assume that these things are as now told and proceed to the melody itself, and explain it as we explained the prelude. State then what character the power of dialectic has and ac-

e   cording to what forms it is divided, and again, what its methods are. For at this point they would lead, it seems, to where upon arrival there would be, as it were, a stopping place on the way and an end of the journey.

533a   You will no longer be able to follow, my dear Glaucon, I replied—

17. The appearances of things outside the cave are divine because they are images of divine agency, as opposed to the shadows within the cave, cast by images which are products of human crafts-manship and a fire which is an image of the Sun.

though not for any unwillingness on my part—you would not then see an image of what I mean, but the very truth itself, at least as it appears to me, though whether it really is that way or not, I cannot yet worthily affirm. But it must be strongly maintained that something of this sort is there for the seeing. Not so?

Of course.

And also that the power of dialectic would alone reveal it to someone experienced in what we have just now described. It is possible in no other way.

This too, he said, is worth affirming.

At any rate, I replied, no one will dispute us and claim that any other   b
method of inquiry undertakes to grasp in every case what each thing by itself is. On the contrary: the other arts are all directed either to the beliefs and desires of men, or to generation and combination, or to the service of things which grow and are put together. And we see that the remaining arts—geometry and the studies which follow on it, which we said grasp something of what is—merely dream about reality. They cannot see with   c
waking vision so long as they make use of hypotheses and leave them undisturbed, unable to render an account of them. For with a starting point which one does not know, and a conclusion and intermediate premises woven together from what one does not know—by what device can this sort of agreement and implication ever become knowledge?

None, he replied.

Dialectic, I rejoined, is the only method of inquiry which proceeds in this way: it does away with hypotheses[18] and proceeds to the starting point   d
and the first principle itself in order to make its results secure. Finding that the eye of the soul is really sunk in a slough of barbarous mud, dialectic gently draws and leads it upward, using as assistants and helpers the arts we have described—which we often through force of habit call branches of knowledge, though they need another name, in that they are more clear

18. There is a standing dispute as to whether doing away with hypotheses means merely doing away with their hypothetical character or altering their content. Both, surely: for example, the mathematician will define number as a plurality of units, a definition the dialectician will not accept.

than opinion but more obscure than knowledge. In what went before we marked this off as understanding; but when an inquiry of such great magnitude lies before us, the dispute, I think, is not about a name.

e   Of course not, he said.[19]

Then as before, I replied, it suffices to call the first portion knowledge, 534a   the second understanding, the third belief, and the fourth imagination. The latter two together are opinion, the former two, thought. And opinion is concerned with becoming, thought with being. And being is to becoming as thought is to opinion, and thought is to opinion as knowledge is to belief, and understanding to imagination. But let us dismiss the proportionality of that to which they are directed, Glaucon, and the twofold division of each of the two, opinable and intelligible, so that we do not get involved in discussions many times as long as those we've had.

b   Why, I agree with you about the others, he said, in so far as I am able to follow.

And do you also call a dialectician one who accepts a reasoned account of the nature and reality of each thing? Will you deny that insofar as one cannot render a reasoned account to himself and to another, he in that degree cannot be said to have intelligence about it?

How could I deny it, he replied?

c   Then so in like manner about the Good. Whoever cannot distinguish the Idea of the Good by reason and set it apart from all other things, and, as though in battle, fight his way through all refutations in his eagerness to argue not according to opinion but according to reality, and proceed in all this without tripping up in argument—you will claim that someone like that knows neither the Good itself nor any other good. Rather, if in some way he grasps a deficient image of it, he does so by opinion, not knowledge,

19. The translation omits a sentence (533e) which is certainly corrupt, athetized by Adam and Shorey as an interpolation, and not printed either by Aldus or Stephanus, who had access to many older manuscripts now lost. Davies and Vaughn give: "You are quite right, said he: we only want a name which when applied to a mental state shall indicate clearly what phenomena it describes."

and sleeps and dreams away his present life. Before ever he awakens here, he will go to the place of the dead and fall asleep completely.

Yes, he replied. I shall emphatically assert all of this.   d

Moreover, these children of yours whom you are raising and educating in discourse—if ever you should raise them in fact, you would not, I think, allow them to be rulers in the city and to control matters of utmost importance, while being, as it were, irrational quantities?

Of course not, he said.

Then you will provide by law that they should instead receive this education, from which they will be able to ask and answer questions with utmost knowledge?

I will so provide, he said, in company with you.   e

Do you think then, I said, that dialectic is set like a copingstone over the subjects of study, and that no other study higher than it would rightly be put above it, but at this point the subjects of study have an end?

Yes, he said.   535a

THE PROGRAM OF STUDIES (535A–541B)

The issue of distribution remains, I replied: to whom we shall give these studies, and in what way.

Clearly, he said.

Do you recall then what sort of people we picked in the previous selection of rulers?

Of course, he replied.

Then do you suppose, I replied, that those same natures are to be selected in other matters? For the most steadfast and courageous are to be chosen, and so far as possible the most handsome. And we must seek in addition not only nobility and strength of character, but they must also have the gifts of nature conducive to this sort of education.   b

What sort do you distinguish?

Acuteness in studies, dear friend, I said, and no difficulty in learning.

Souls shrink from hard study even more than from hard physical exercise, because the labor is more properly their own and not shared with the body.

True, he said.

c   We must also then seek memory and persistence, and in everything, love of work. How else do you suppose anyone will consent to bodily toil, and also complete so much study and learning?

No one will, he replied, unless possessed of great natural ability.

At any rate, the present error, I replied, and the dishonor which has fallen on philosophy that I mentioned before, is because people do not worthily lay hold of her: for she must be grasped not by illegitimate but by rightful sons.

How do you mean? he said.

d   First, I said, whoever intends to lay hold of her must not limp in his love of work, half fond of it, half not. This occurs when someone loves exercise and hunting and all bodily exertion, but does not love learning, is neither fond of listening nor capable of inquiry, but in all this hates work. He also limps if the opposite obtains.

Very true, he said.

e   So also, I replied, we shall assume that a soul is in the same way also crippled relative to truth, if it hates voluntary falsehood and cannot bear it itself and is greatly angered when others speak falsely, but complacently accepts involuntary falsehood and is not distressed when convicted of being ignorant, but cheerfully wallows in ignorance like a wild boar.

536a   Certainly, he said.

And relative to temperance and courage and high-mindedness, I replied, and all the parts of virtue, it is especially necessary to distinguish the illegitimate from the rightful child. For when anyone, private person or city, does not know how to tell them apart, they act at random, and make use unawares of illegitimate cripples, some as friends, some as rulers.

That's so, he said.

b   Then we must pay careful attention to everything of this sort, I replied, since if we educate men sound of limb and sound of mind, and bring them to this great study and this great exercise, justice herself will not find fault with us, and we shall preserve the city and the constitution. But if we lead people of a different kind to it, we'll do the exact opposite, and pour down upon philosophy a still greater flood of ridicule.

A shameful thing indeed, he replied.

Of course, I said. But it seems I'm at the moment being ridiculous myself.

In what way? he said.   c

I forgot we were playing, I replied, and spoke rather tendentiously. For as I was speaking I glanced toward philosophy, and when I saw her subjected to unmerited insult, I became angry, I think, and as it were lost my temper at those responsible, and said what I said too vehemently.

Certainly not too vehemently for me as a hearer, he said.

But for me as a speaker, I replied. Still, here is something we must not overlook: in our earlier selection we picked old men, but here that won't do. We must not let Solon persuade us that an old man is capable of learning   d
many things, any more than he is capable of running a race. Great and many labors all belong to the young.

Necessarily, he said.

Then the study of calculation and geometry, and all the propaedeutic studies required as preliminary to dialectic, should be introduced in childhood—though not in the shape of instruction imposed as compulsory learning.

Why not?   e

Because, I replied, there is no subject which a free man should learn slavishly. Constrained bodily labor makes the body no worse, but nothing learned under constraint abides in the soul.

True, he said.

Then don't raise children in their studies by constraint, my friend, I   537a
replied, but let their learning come as play, so that you may also be better able to discern what task each is naturally fitted for.

What you say makes sense, he said.

Now, do you remember, I replied, that we said the children should be taken to war on horseback as spectators, and where it is safe, brought in close and given a taste of blood like young pups?

Yes, I remember, he said.

Those who in all this constantly show themselves most apt for physical labor and study and danger, I said, are to be enrolled among a select number.

b   At what age?

As soon as they are released from the necessary physical exercises, I replied. For during this time, whether it lasts two years or three, it is impossible to do anything else: weariness and sleep are enemies of study. At the same time too, how they each show themselves at physical exercise is one of their tests and not the least important.

Of course, he said.

c   After this time, then, I replied, those selected from among the twenty-year-olds will receive greater honors than the rest. The disconnected studies they pursued as children in the course of their education must now be brought together into a synoptic vision of the kinship of those studies to each other and to the nature of what is.

Only this sort of learning, at any rate, he said, firmly abides in those in whom it comes to be present.

Yes, I replied, and it is a most important test of a dialectical nature or the lack of it; for the dialectician, and only he, is capable of synoptic vision.

I agree, he replied.

d   Then it will be necessary, I replied, for you to observe who among them is especially steadfast in learning, and in war and other lawful duties. These in turn, when they pass their thirtieth year, you must select from among those previously selected and promote to greater honors still, testing them by the power of dialectic to determine who is able to dispense with eyes and the other senses and to proceed to being itself in the company of truth. And here then, my friend, is a task requiring great watchfulness.

Why, especially? he replied.

Don't you realize, I replied, how great is the evil which now occurs in   e
philosophical conversation?

How so? he replied.

It surely fills people with lawlessness, I said.

Yes, it does, he said.

Do you think it is at all surprising that they are so affected? I said. Don't
you sympathize?

In what way, especially? he said.

It is as though a supposititious child was raised in the midst of great   538a
wealth and a great and powerful family, and surrounded by many flatterers,
I replied.[20] Imagine then that when he once became a man, he became
aware that he was not the child of his alleged parents, yet could not find his
real mother and father. Can you guess how he would be disposed toward his
flatterers and his presumed parents in that time in which he did not know
of his adoption, and after he knew? Would you like to hear my guess?

Please, he said.

My guess is that he would be more likely to honor his father and mother   b
and the rest of his putative kindred than his flatterers: less likely to see them
lack for anything, less likely to speak or act toward them with any disrespect, less likely to disobey them in important matters than the flatterers, in
the time when he did not know the truth.

Naturally, he said.

But when on the other hand he became aware of what is, my guess is that
his honor and regard would diminish for them but increase for his flatterers; he would be much more likely to heed them than before; at that point   c
he would live according to their ways and openly associate with them. He
wouldn't care at all about his former father and the rest of his putative relatives, unless his natural disposition was remarkably good.

All that you say is such as might occur, he said. But how does the comparison bear on those who deal with arguments?

20. What follows is the background story of the *Oedipus Rex.*

As follows. We possess from childhood, I take it, certain convictions about things just and beautiful. We have been raised in them as though by parents, obeying and honoring them.

Yes.

d   Again, other pursuits opposed to these possess pleasures which flatter our soul and draw it to themselves, but they fail to persuade people of good character, who honor their ancestral heritage and are loyal to it.

That's so.

Now, when a man of this sort passes to the question of what the beautiful is, I replied, and answers what he heard from the lawgiver, the argument refutes him—and often and everywhere refutes him—until his opinion is overturned, and he supposes this thing or that is no more beautiful than

e   ugly; and so similarly for just and good and what before he especially held in honor. After this, what do you suppose he will do in the matter of honor and respect for authority?

Necessarily, he said, he will not still equally honor or obey.

Given that he does not believe that they are his own, or honor them as he did before, I replied, and that he cannot discover what is true, is it likely that he will attach himself to any other kind of life than that of a flatterer?[21]

539a   It is not, he said.

Then I suppose, from being law abiding, he will seem to have become lawless.

Necessarily.

This then is the likely condition of those who grasp philosophical arguments in this way, I said. As I was just saying, it deserves a great deal of sympathy.

Yes, even pity, he said.

Then in order that this pity may not arise for your thirty-year-olds, every precaution must be taken in introducing them to philosophical arguments.

Yes, he replied.

21. Shorey, citing 442a–b and *Laws* 633e, translates, "any other way of life than that which flatters his desires."

Isn't one main precaution not letting them taste philosophical argu-   b
ments while young? I suppose you're aware that youngsters, when they first
get a taste of philosophical arguments, treat them as a game and always use
them merely to contradict. They imitate those who refute them, and refute
others, delighting like puppies in tugging at anyone who comes near them
and tearing them apart in words.

Yes, it's quite remarkable, he said.

When they have been refuted by many people and refuted many people   c
themselves, they quickly fall into extreme disbelief of all that they believed
before. And from this they bring discredit among other people on themselves and the whole of philosophy.

Very true, he said.

An older person will refuse to take part in such madness, I replied. He
will imitate those who proceed to philosophical conversation in order to examine the truth, instead of playing at childish contradictions. He will be
more reasonable, and cause his pursuit to be more valued instead of less.

Rightly, he said.   d

What was said before about all this was meant as a precaution: that anyone allowed to take part in these arguments must be orderly and steadfast in
nature—not, as now, any chance person who happens along, however un-
fit?

Certainly, he said.

Does it suffice then for participation in philosophical arguments to persist in them strenuously and do nothing else, as with the corresponding
bodily exercises, but for twice as many years?

Do you mean six years, or four? he said.   e

It doesn't matter, I said. Put it at five. After this, they must go back down
again into the cave, and be compelled to govern both in military matters
and the other offices suitable for young men, so that they may not be inferior to the rest in experience. And here once again, they must be put to the
test, to see whether they will stand fast when pulled in all different direc-   540a
tions or whether they will give way.

How much time do you allow for that? he replied.

Fifteen years, I replied. On reaching the age of fifty, those who have survived and distinguished themselves in all action and every kind of knowledge must be led at last to the end: they must be compelled to lift up the in-
b ner light of the soul to gaze on what by itself provides light to all, and when they have seen the Good itself, to use that, each in his turn, as a standard and example for the right ordering of city and private citizens, and of themselves for the remainder of their lives. For the most part, they will devote their time to philosophy, but when their turns come, they will labor in political affairs and each govern for the sake of the city—considering it something not noble but necessary. Each generation ever in this way educating the next to take its place as Guardians of the city, they will at length depart
c to dwell in the Isles of the Blest. The city will make public memorials and sacrifices for them as to divinities, if the Pythian Oracle concurs, but if not, as to happy and godlike men.

You've portrayed the rulers as though you were a sculptor, Socrates—magnificently.

And the female rulers too, Glaucon, I replied. For you mustn't suppose that what I've said applies to men more than women, in so far as they are sufficient in natural abilities.

Rightly, he said, since they are to share all equally with men, as we described.

d Well then, I said. You agree that what we have said about the city and its constitution is not a mere vain wish? Though difficult, it is in a way possible, and possible in no other way than described. When those who are truly philosophers, one or more, become masters in their city, and despise existing honors, believing them servile and worthless, but count what is right and the honors derived from it of utmost importance, and the just as high-
e est and most necessary—they will by this then serve their own city and cause it to flourish, thoroughly setting in order its affairs.

How? he said.

541a They will send everyone in the city older than the age of ten to the country, I replied, and remove the children from the habits they at present get from their parents. Instead, they will rear them in their own ways and laws which are as we have explained. And thus they will most quickly and easily establish such a city and constitution as we have described, and make it happy and in highest degree beneficial to the people among whom it may come to exist.

Quite so, he said. I think you've well told how it would arise, Socrates— if ever it does arise.

Then at this point, I said, the arguments about this city and the man who is like it suffice for us? For it is also surely clear of what sort we shall say he must be.   b

Yes, he said. And to answer your question, I think it is at an end.

Book VIII

543a   Very well. So it is agreed, Glaucon, that if a city is to be preeminently well
founded, there will be community of women, community of children and
all education, and, similarly, common pursuits in war and in peace. And
those who have become best in philosophy and warfare will be kings among
them.

Yes, he said.

b   We further agreed that when rulers are once established, they will lead
their soldiers and settle them in quarters of the kind we described, common
to all, with nothing private to any. Besides these dwellings, if you recall, we
further agreed what sort of property they will have.

Yes, he said. I certainly recall that we thought they must possess nothing
at all of what other people now do. As guardians and warriors, they should
c   receive yearly subsistence as pay from the others for their guardianship, to
care for themselves and the rest of the city.

That's right, I said. But come, since we're finished here, let us remember
where we digressed so that we may travel the same path again.

Not difficult, he said. You were speaking pretty much as you are now, as

if your account of the city were complete. You were saying that you assumed that such a city as you then described and the man who is like it are   d
good, even though, it seems, you could tell of a still more excellent city and   544a
man.[1] But if this city is right, the others then, you claimed, are wrong. Of
the remaining constitutions, you said, as I recall, that there are four forms
worth considering, to observe their defects and those again of the men who
are like them, so that by once observing them all and reaching agreement
about the best and worst men, we might inquire whether the best is most
happy and the worst most miserable, or whether it is otherwise. And when
I asked what four constitutions you meant, at that point Polemarchus and   b
Adeimantus interrupted, and so you then took up the argument which has
brought us to this point.

You remember very accurately, I said.

Again then, like a wrestler, take the same hold. Try to give me the same
answer you were about to give before.

If I can, I replied.

Please, he replied. I surely want to hear what four constitutions you
meant.

No difficulty there, I replied. For there are some which also have definite   c
names, which most people praise—your Cretan and Spartan constitutions.
Second and second in praise is Oligarchy, so called, a constitution dense
with teeming evils. Next comes its opponent and successor, Democracy,
and then noble Tyranny, surpassing all the rest as fourth and last disease of
a city. Or do you have any other kind of constitution which is also assumed
to be clearly distinct in form? No doubt hereditary monarchies and pur-   d
chased kingships and other constitutions of the sort are somehow intermediate; you find them no less among barbarians than among Greeks.

Yes, he said. At any rate there are many strange reports.

Now, I replied, you know that there must also be as many forms of character among men as there are constitutions? Or do you think that constitu-

---

1. A reference to "the longer way," IV 435d, VI 504b–d, and a city based on knowledge of the
   Good rather than right habit, described in V 472b–VII.

e tions are born of oak or rock, rather than the dispositions of men in cities, which as it were incline the scales and draw other things after them?

From nowhere but this, he said.

Then if there are five kinds of city, there would also be five fixed dispositions of soul among private citizens.

Certainly.

But we have already described the man who is like aristocracy, whom we rightly claim is good and just.

545a   Yes.

Then we must next proceed to his inferiors: to the competitive and ambitious man who corresponds to the established Spartan constitution, and again, the oligarchic, the democratic, and the tyrannical man, in order to observe the most unjust man and set him over against the most just, and so complete our inquiry into how unmixed justice stands to unmixed injustice in respect to the happiness and misery of the possessor. We may in this way be persuaded by Thrasymachus to pursue either injustice or justice by the argument now coming to light.

b   We must most certainly do this, he said.

Now, we began by examining the character of constitutions before those of private citizens, for we thought constitutions were more clear. So now then, we must first consider the ambitious constitution—I can't think of another name in common use for it. Call it either timocracy or timarchy.

c   And we will consider in addition this sort of man. Next, oligarchy and oligarchic man, and afterward we will look to democracy and view the democratic man. Fourth, we will come to the city ruled by tyranny and observe it, and then look into a tyrannical soul, and try to become sufficient judges of the issue we have set for ourselves.

Yes, our view and judgment will in this way accord with reason, he said.

TRANSITION FROM ARISTOCRACY TO TIMOCRACY (545C–547C)

Come then, I replied, let us try to tell how timocracy might come to be from aristocracy. Or is it simply this: that every constitutional change de-

rives from the ruling class itself when faction arises within it? If it is of one   d
mind, even if it is very small, the constitution cannot be moved.

Yes, that's so.

How then, Glaucon, will our city be moved, I said, and in what way will
the Guardians and rulers become divided against each other and themselves? Would you have us, like Homer, invoke the Muses to tell us "How   e
first Strife befell?" and claim that though they speak in a lofty tragic style, as
if in earnest, they are in fact only playing and teasing us as though we were
children?

How?   546a

As follows:[2] "Difficult it is for a city so founded to be moved. But since
all that comes to be admits destruction, not even this kind of foundation
will abide for all time, but will suffer dissolution. Its dissolution is this: not
only for plants in the earth but also for animals upon it, there comes fertility and barrenness of soul and bodies, when the revolutions for each complete the circumferences of their circles, short for the short-lived, oppositely   b
for the opposite. As for your own kind of propitious birth and barrenness,
wise though the leaders of the city whom you have educated may be, they
will not the more by calculation combined with perception hit upon them,
but miss, and sometimes will beget children when they ought not. For a divine creature, there is a period encompassed by a number which is perfect;
for a human creature, by the first number in which root and square in-
creases, comprehending three intervals and four limits, of elements that are   c
like and unlike and admit increase and diminution, they make all things
appear mutually agreeable and rational one with another. Of which the ratio of four to three, in lowest terms, joined or wedded to five, produces two
attunements when thrice increased: the one equal an equal number of

2. The Greek here is of extreme difficulty. It is unlikely that it was clear even to Plato's original au-
dience, and by Cicero's time it had become a proverbial riddle. The translation follows Adam
and T. L. Heath. The Muses speak with intentional obscurity, concealing what are perhaps
fairly simple mathematical conceptions in high-flown language. Cornford was no doubt right
to suggest that "the serious idea behind this seemingly fanciful passage is the affinity and corre-
spondence of macrocosm and microcosm and the embodiment of mathematical principles in
both."

times, so many times one hundred; the other equal to the former in side, but oblong, consisting on one side of a hundred squares of rational diameters of five diminished by one each or, if of irrational diameters, by two, and

d   on the other side, of one hundred cubes of three. This sum is a geometrical number, and lord of better and worse births. When your Guardians are ignorant of it, they join bridegrooms and brides out of due season, and children will be neither well endowed nor fortunate. Their predecessors will establish the best of them in office, but they are nevertheless unequal to it, and when in their turn they enter on the powers of their fathers, they will

e   begin as Guardians to neglect us, the Muses, believing first music of less importance than they ought, and second, gymnastic; whence our young people will forget us. In consequence, rulers will be established who lack the Guardian's ability to test the kinds among you, Hesiod's races of gold and

547a   silver and bronze and iron. When iron is alloyed with silver, bronze with gold, they will generate unlikeness and irregularity and lack of attunement, which, where it occurs, always produces enmity and war. Such, we must say, is the lineage of faction and party strife, wherever it may occur."

Yes, he replied, we'll say this answer is correct.

Necessarily, I replied. After all, they're Muses.[3]

b   What do they say next? he answered.

That when faction and party strife arose, I replied, each of two kinds were pulled apart: the races of iron and bronze toward moneymaking and the possession of houses and land and silver and gold; but the other two races again, the races of gold and silver, because they are by nature not poor but rich, led souls toward virtue and the ancient order of things. Straining violently against each other, they agreed on a mean, distributing to themselves land and houses for private ownership, while reducing to slavery

c   those whom they before guarded as free men and friends and supporters; they now hold them as serfs and servants, while they themselves are concerned for war and their own protection.

---

3. A wry comment. According to Hesiod, the Muses know how to tell the truth, and some things which are not the truth.

I agree. This is where the change begins, he said.

Then this constitution would be a kind of mean between aristocracy and oligarchy? I replied.

Of course.

TIMOCRACY (547C–548D)

Then that is how it will change. But once changed, how will it be governed? Or is it evident, because it is a mean, that in some things it will imitate the earlier constitution and in others oligarchy, but that it will also have some-   d
thing peculiar to itself?

Yes, he said.

In honoring its rulers, in abstention of the military class from farming and practical arts and other ways of making money, in establishing common meals and concern for physical training and the exercises of war—in all such things it will imitate the previous constitution?

Yes.

Yes, but in its fear of placing wise men in office, because men of the sort   e
it possesses are no longer single-minded and straightforward but mixed, in its inclination toward spirited and simpler men whose natural bent is toward war rather than peace, in its holding in honor the tricks and devices of   548a
war and in its incessant waging of war—these for the most part will be peculiar to itself?

Yes.

Such people will desire money, as in oligarchies, I said. They will value silver and gold surreptitiously but without restraint, because they also have private storerooms where they can conceal their treasures, and again, sheltered houses, literally little nests, in which they can spend money on women and any other extravagances they please.

Very true, he said.   b

Again, they will be avaricious. Because they value money and cannot possess it openly; but they will be prodigal with other people's money, due to appetite. They will enjoy their pleasures in secret, like children escaping from their father, the Law, because they have been educated not by persuasion but by force, through neglect of the genuine Muse who is accompanied by reasoning and philosophy and through honoring gymnastic at the expense of music.

c   You certainly describe a constitution mixed from good and evil, he said.

It is indeed mixed, I replied. But because it is governed by the spirited part alone, one thing is most conspicuous in it, namely, competitive ambition.

Yes, very much so, he replied.

So this constitution will have come to be in this way and be of this sort, I replied. Of course, we are merely sketching in words the outline of a con-
d   stitution, without constructing it in detail, since it suffices even from a sketch to discern the most just and most unjust man; it would be an impracticable task to explain at length every constitution and every character without leaving anything out.

Quite right, he said.

THE TIMOCRAT (548D–550C)

Then what man corresponds to this constitution? Of what sort is he, and how does he arise?

I suppose in competitiveness he comes close to Glaucon here, said Adeimantus.

e   Yes, perhaps, I replied. But not, I think, in this:
What?

He must be more self-willed and lacking in culture, I replied, yet fond of it, and fond of listening, though no orator. Such a man would be harsh with
549a   slaves instead of feeling disdain as well-educated people do, but he will be gentle with free men and very obedient to his rulers; ambitious and emulous of command, he will not claim office on the basis of his ability to speak or anything like that, but on the basis of deeds of warfare and what concerns it, and he is fond of exercise and hunting.

Yes, this character belongs to that constitution, he said.

Such a man when young will disdain money, I replied, but welcome it   b
the more as he grows older, because he has a share of the moneymaking nature and is not pure and unmixed in the matter of virtue, due to lack of the
best guardian.

What guardian is that? asked Adeimantus.

Reason mixed with the arts of the Muses, I replied. This alone, when it
once comes to be present, dwells in him who has it as savior of virtue
through the whole of life.

Well put, he said.

Such then is the youthful timocrat, I replied, and like that sort of city.

Of course.   c

He comes to be somewhat as follows, I said. Sometimes he is the young
son of a good father dwelling in an ill-governed city, a father who avoids
honors and offices and litigation and all such distraction, willing to be at a
disadvantage so as not to have trouble.

And the son? he said.

Well to begin with, I replied, he hears his mother complain that her hus- d
band is not one of the rulers and she is therefore at a disadvantage among
the other women; and next, she sees he does not care much about money
and does not fight and squabble in private lawsuits or public assembly, but
is indifferent to all that sort of thing, and she perceives that he is constantly
absorbed in his own thoughts, without much regard for herself or disregard
either—for all these reasons she is angry, and tells the boy his father is not
much of a man and too easygoing, and other things of the sort women like
to nag about.

Yes, said Adeimantus, there are plenty of these feminine complaints.   e

Then you know, I replied, that even the household servants of such families, though they seem well intentioned, sometimes surreptitiously say the
same sorts of thing to the sons; and if they see the father not suing someone
who owes him money or has done some other wrong, they urge the son
when he becomes a man to punish all such folk and be a better man than his 550a
father. And when he is out of the house he sees and hears other things of the
same sort: those who do what is their own in the city are called foolish and

of little account, while those who do not do what is their own are honored and praised. So the young man sees and hears all this, and at the same time hears his father's conversation and views his practices at closer range than others do, and he is pulled both ways. His father waters the growth of the rational part in his soul, the others the appetitive and spirited parts. Because his nature is not that of a bad man but he is mixed up in bad company, he is drawn by both of them and reaches a compromise: he gives over the government within himself to the middle element of competitiveness and spirit, and becomes an arrogant and ambitious man, a lover of honor.

I think you have exactly explained how he is produced, he said.

So we have the second constitution, I replied, and the second man.

Yes, he said.

TRANSITION FROM TIMOCRACY TO OLIGARCHY (550C–551B)

Then next, as Aeschylus has it, shall we tell of "another man matched with another city"? Or instead take the city first, according to our hypothesis?

The latter, surely, he said.

The next constitution, as I suppose, would be oligarchy.

What kind of government do you mean by oligarchy? he asked.

That constitution based on a property qualification, I replied, in which the rich rule, and the poor have no share of office.

I see, he replied.

Then shall we tell how timarchy first changes to oligarchy?

Yes.

Surely it is clear even to a blind man how it changes, I replied.

How so?

That storehouse full of private gold which each man has, I said, destroys this sort of constitution. For they first find ways to spend their money, and subvert the laws to do it; they and their wives both disobey.

Likely enough, he said.

Next I suppose, one man watches another and emulates him, and they make the majority like themselves.

Likely enough.

From there, I said, they press on in the pursuit of money. To the degree they believe it more valuable, they count virtue less valuable. Or is not virtue opposed to wealth in such a way that, when each of the two is placed on the scale, the balance ever inclines, as it were, in the opposite direction?

Indeed, he said.

So when wealth and the wealthy are valued in a city, virtue and good men are less valued.

Clearly.   551a

But what is valued is practiced; what is not valued is neglected.

True.

So instead of competitive and ambitious men, they end up becoming covetous lovers of gain; they praise and admire the rich man and put him in office, but despise the poor.

Of course.

So at that point they enact a law which is the defining mark of an oli-   b
garchical constitution: they prescribe a sum of money, greater where more oligarchical, less where less, and announce that no one shall hold office whose estate does not meet the prescribed sum. They accomplish this by force of arms or they establish this sort of constitution even before that, by putting in fear. Not so?

Of course it is so.

So that is pretty much how oligarchy is established.

THE OLIGARCHICAL CONSTITUTION (551B–553A)

Yes, he said. But what is the character of its constitution, and what sorts of defects do we say it has?

First, I said, there is the very thing which defines it. Suppose someone   c
made ships' pilots on the basis of a property qualification, and would not accept a poor man even if he were the better pilot.

Evil is the voyage they would sail, he replied.

The same also for any other kind of rule?

I think so.

Except a city? I asked. Or a city too?

Most especially a city, he said, inasmuch as the rule is both most difficult and most important.

So this would be an immense defect in oligarchy.

d   So it appears.

Really? Is this defect then smaller:

What?

That this sort of city is by necessity not one but two, the city of the rich and the city of the poor, dwelling in the same place and ever plotting against each other.

It certainly is no smaller, he said.

But surely this is not good: they are no doubt unable to wage war because they are compelled either to arm the majority, and fear them more than their enemies, or not to use them and appear in actual battle as oli-

e   garchs indeed—rulers of few. At the same time, they refuse to pay taxes because they love money.

No, it is not good.

Really? Do you think it right for the same people in this sort of constitution at the same time to meddle in farming and business and war? We criticized that before.

552a   It is by no means right.

Consider then whether this constitution is the first to admit the gravest of all evils.

Which is?

Letting a man sell all that he owns, and allowing the things which are his own to be possessed by another; and once having sold, to continue to dwell in the city without being part of it, neither businessman nor craftsman, horseman nor hoplite, but carried on the rolls as a pauper without means.

b   Yes, this city is the first to allow this, he said.

Now, that sort of thing is not forbidden in oligarchies? For otherwise, some would not be excessively rich, others utterly destitute.

You're right.

But reflect on this: when such a man was still rich and spent his money, was he then of any greater benefit to the city in respect to what we were just now discussing? Or did he seem to be among its rulers, when in truth he was neither ruler nor servant, but a mere consumer?

That, he said. He seemed a ruler, but he was nothing but a consumer.

Would you have us then say of him, I replied, that even as a drone comes to be present in a comb as a plague to the hive, so also this sort of man comes to be present as a drone in his house, as a plague to the city?

Most certainly, Socrates, he said.

Now, Adeimantus, the god has made all flying drones stingless, but some which go on foot are stingless and some have terrible stings. From the stingless come those who end up as beggars in old age. From those with stings come all who have been properly declared criminals.

Very true, he said.

So it is clear that in a city where you see beggars, I replied, there surely also lie concealed, somewhere in the place, thieves and cutpurses and temple robbers, craftsmen of all such evils.

Yes, he said.

Now, do you not see beggars in oligarchical cities?

Yes, he said, almost everybody outside of the rulers.

Are we not then to suppose, I said, that there are also many criminals among them possessed of stings, whom the rulers are concerned to contain by force?

Yes, he said.

Then shall we say they are there through lack of education and evil nurture, and an evil condition of the constitution?

Yes.

Such then would be the oligarchical city and so many the evils it contains—maybe even more.

Yes, pretty much so, he said.

THE OLIGARCH (553A–555B)

We are finished, then, I replied, with the constitution which people call oligarchy because of its property qualification for rulers. Let us next examine the man who is like it: how he comes to be, and what he is when he has come to be.

Certainly, he said.

Now, the change from timocratic to oligarchic man is mainly as follows: How?

When the timocrat's son is born, the child first emulates his father and follows in his footsteps. Next, he sees him suddenly dashed against the city like a ship against rocks, spilling out what belongs to him, and his very self. Perhaps his father was a general or held some other high office, and was thrown into court and hurt by lying informers, and killed or exiled or disenfranchised, his whole estate confiscated.

It is possible, he said.

Yes, but in seeing this, and suffering it and losing his inheritance, my friend, the son I think is frightened, and straightway thrusts ambition and the spirited part headlong from the throne within his own soul. Brought low by poverty, he turns greedily to moneymaking, and little by little, by scrimping and saving and hard work, he accumulates wealth. Don't you suppose such a man then seats the appetitive and avaricious part on that same throne and makes it a Great King within himself, crowned, armored, and girt with sword?[4]

Yes, he said.

But the rational and spirited parts, I suppose, are reduced to slavery and made to squat on the ground on either side beneath the throne. He allows the one to reflect on and consider nothing except how to make more money from less; he allows the other to admire and value nothing except wealth and wealthy men, to be ambitious for no other single thing except possession of money and what conduces to its possession.

b

c

d

4. The Great King of Persia was an absolute monarch.

There is no other change so quick and strong as that from youthful ambition to avarice, he said.

This then is the oligarchical man? I replied.   e

The change which produced him, at any rate, is from a man like the constitution from which oligarchy derived.

Then let us inquire whether he will be like it.

Yes.   554a

First then, he will be like it in attaching utmost importance to money?

Of course.

And further, in being parsimonious and hardworking, satisfying only his necessary desires and refusing other expenditures, while enslaving other desires as vain?

Certainly.

A sordid fellow, I replied, bent on making a profit from everything, an acquisitive man—but the multitude actually praises him. Will he not be like the oligarchical constitution?

So it seems to me, he said: money at any rate is especially valued by that   b
city and this sort of man.

I expect such a man pays no attention to education, I replied.

I think not, he said. For otherwise, he would not have appointed a blind leader for his chorus and especially value him.[5]

Well put, I replied. But consider this: may we not say that dronelike desires come to be present in him through lack of education—some desires beggarly, some criminal and forcibly contained by his other concerns?

Yes, he said.   c

Do you know where to look to see their criminality? I said.

Where? he said.

To the guardianship of orphans, and anyplace else where there is ample opportunity to do injustice and get away with it.

True.

Now, isn't it clear from this that in his other dealings, where seeming to   d

5. Plutus, the God of Wealth, is blind. Cf. *Laws* I 631c.

be just gives him a good reputation, such a man forcibly holds back other evil desires present in him by a kind of constrained decency—not persuading them that "better not," not taming them by reason but by necessity and fear, trembling for the rest of his estate?

Yes, of course, he said.

But surely, my friend, I replied, when other people's money is to be spent, you will find present in most of them desires akin to the drone.

Very much so, he replied.

Nor would such a man be free from inward faction. He is not one but two, though for the most part his better desires master the worse.

e   That's so.

For this reason then, I suppose, he presents a more seemly appearance than most, but true virtue, which derives from unanimity and attunement of soul, quite escapes him.

I think so.

555a   Again, the parsimonious man as private citizen in a city is an inferior competitor for any victory or other honorable distinction. He refuses to spend money for the sake of a good reputation and such contests as those, fearing to awaken his spendthrift desires and summon them. In oligarchical manner, as allies to his ambition; he fights with but few of his own forces, and for the most part he is beaten—and rich.

Yes, he said.

Have we then any further doubt, I replied, that the parsimonious money maker corresponds by resemblance to the city ruled by oligarchy?

b   None at all, he said.

TRANSITION FROM OLIGARCHY TO DEMOCRACY (555B–557A)

We must next then, as it seems, examine democracy: how it comes to be, and having come to be, what sort of character it has, in order that we may in turn know the character of this sort of man and stand him alongside the rest for judgment.

We would proceed consistently, at any rate, he said.

Now, I replied, does the constitution change from oligarchy to democracy in some such way as this: through insatiable desire for what is set before it as good, namely, the need to become as rich as possible?

How so?

Because, I think, those who rule in it due to their great wealth refuse to   c
restrain by law the young men who become intemperate, or to prevent them from spending and wasting what is their own, in order that they may become richer and more honored still by lending money on the property of such people and buying them out.

Yes, certainly.

At this point, then, it is clearly impossible to value wealth in a city and at the same time adequately possess temperance in its citizens? One or the other is inevitably neglected.

Yes, that's fairly clear, he said.   d

In oligarchies, then, disregard and encouragement of licentiousness sometimes compel people of a not ignoble nature to become poor.

Yes.

Yet there they sit in the city, I suppose, armed with stings and weapons, some reduced to need by debt, some disenfranchised, others both, hating and plotting against those who acquired what was theirs and against the others, longing for revolution.

That's so.   e

But the money makers keep their eyes to the ground and don't even seem to see them, and if ever any of those who remain submits to it, they wound him by inserting the sting of their money. They harvest as offspring and interest many times the parent sum, and produce more drones and beggars in the city.

Yes, many more, he said.   556a

And when this sort of evil flares up in it, I replied, they refuse to quench the flames by restraining a man from disposing of his property in whatever way he likes, or again, to do away with such things by using a different law.

What law?

The next best: it compels citizens to be concerned for virtue. For if it were required that contracts voluntarily entered on are entered mainly at one's own risk, the pursuit of money would be less shameless in the city, and

b fewer evils of the sort we just now described would grow up in it.

Many fewer, he replied.

But as it is, I said, and for all such reasons as these, the rulers reduce those ruled in the city to this condition. As for themselves and their own families—are not their young spoiled with luxury and laziness both physical and mental, too soft to bear up against pleasures and pains and idleness?

Of course.

c But they themselves neglect everything except making money, and count virtue no more important than the paupers do.

Of course not.

Given this situation, what happens when rulers and ruled are thrown together on a journey, or some other common enterprise—perhaps a religious festival or a campaign, or when they become fellow sailors or soldiers,

d or observe each other in actual battle? There the poor are not looked down upon by the rich, but often a poor man, lean and sunburned, is posted in battle beside a rich man, pale and encumbered with quantities of flesh, and sees him full of breathlessness and perplexity. Don't you suppose he thinks, "These people are rich because of our own cowardice," and when they meet together in private, one advises another, "These men are ours; they are nothing"?

e I know very well that they do so, he said.

Then just as an unhealthy body needs but a small shock from outside to bring on sickness, and sometimes is set against itself by itself even without that, so too a city in this same condition needs but slight provocation when one side brings in external allies from an oligarchical city, or the other side from a democracy. The city is sick and wars on itself; and sometimes it is set against itself even without outside help.

557a Yes, emphatically.

Democracy then, I think, arises when the poor triumph, put some of the rest to death, exile others, and give the remainder an equal share of civic rights and offices. And for the most part, offices in it are assigned by lot.

Yes, he said. This is the establishment of democracy, whether it comes through force of arms or whether the others withdraw out of fear.

THE DEMOCRATIC CONSTITUTION (557A–558C)

Then what is the character of their life? I replied. And again, of what sort is this constitution? For it is clear that this sort of man will turn out to be a democratic man.

Yes, he said.   b

First then, they are free, and the city is full of freedom and frankness and liberty to do in it whatever one wishes.

Yes, at least so it is said, he replied.

And where there is liberty, clearly each person privately arranges his own life to suit himself.

Yes.

Then especially in this constitution, I suppose, there will be present all   c
sorts and conditions of men.

Of course.

It is perhaps the most beautiful of constitutions, I said. Like a cloak of many colors decked out with every hue, this city is thus also decorated with every character and would appear very beautiful. And no doubt the majority of people judge it to be very beautiful, I continued, as women and children do when they see variety.

Yes, he said.

And it is also convenient to search in it for a constitution, my friend, I   d
replied.

How so?

Because, it contains all kinds of constitutions, because of liberty. Anyone who wishes to establish a city, as we were doing just now, need only enter a democratic city and pick out the kind of constitution that suits him, as though he had arrived at a bazaar of constitutions, and in this way found his city.

At any rate, he would not be at a loss for examples, he said.   e

In this city, I said, there is no necessity to rule, even if one is competent to rule, nor again to be ruled if you do not wish it, nor to go to war when they make war nor to make peace when the rest do unless you want peace. Again, if some law forbids you to hold office or be a judge, you hold office nonetheless, and serve as a judge if the fit is upon you. Is not this a divinely sweet and pleasant way of life—for the time being?

Yes, perhaps for that moment, he said.

And is there not charm in the gentle presence of some of those who have been convicted of crime? Did you never yet see anyone in this sort of constitution who has been sentenced to death or exile, and nonetheless stays on and wanders to and fro in the midst of things—as though no one noticed, or ever saw him slinking around like a hero's ghost?

Yes, he said.

And the forbearance, the utter absence of any petty concern for trifles, the contempt for what we solemnly claimed when we were founding the city—that unless someone is of an extraordinary nature, he would never become a good man unless he were educated among beautiful things straight from childhood, and practiced all such pursuits. How grandly the city tramples all this under foot without a thought for any practices a man has engaged in before entering politics, honoring him if only he claims to be well disposed toward the multitude.

Noble forbearance indeed, he said.

These things then, and others akin to them, belong to democracy, I said. It is, it seems, a pleasant constitution, anarchical and varied, distributing a kind of equality to equal and unequal alike.

What you say is well known, he said.

NECESSARY AND UNNECESSARY DESIRES (558C–559D)

Consider then what this sort of man is in private, I replied. Or must we first consider, as we did with the constitution, how he comes to be?

Yes, he said.

Well, is it not thus? I expect that a son of our parsimonious and oligarchical man would be raised by his father in his father's habits?

Of course.

So he forcibly governs the spendthrift pleasures within himself, which do not make money. So they are not called necessary.

Clearly, he said.

Would you have us then first distinguish necessary and unnecessary desires, I replied, so that we may not carry on our discussion in the dark?

Yes, he replied.

Desires we are not able to get rid of would rightly be called necessary, and also those whose satisfaction is beneficial to us? For our nature necessarily seeks both of these, does it not?

Yes.

So we rightly say they are necessary.

Yes.

What about desires which could be got rid of if one practiced from youth, and whose presence does no good and sometimes the opposite? Would we not properly call them all unnecessary?

Yes.

Shall we then choose an example of each, in order to grasp them in outline?

We must do so.

Then desire to eat in the amount required for health and good condition, and to eat plain bread and meat, would be necessary?

I think so.

Yes, and desire for bread is surely necessary in both respects: it is beneficial, and if it ceases one cannot live.

Yes.

Desire for meat is necessary if it somehow provides a benefit relative to good condition.

Of course.

What about desire beyond this, and for other kinds of food? Desire ca-

d

e

559a

b

pable of being disciplined and educated from youth, which for the most part can be got rid of, and which is harmful to the body and harmful to the soul relative to wisdom and being temperate—would such desire not rightly be called unnecessary?

c   Yes, very rightly.

Let us then also say that such desires are spendthrift, while those others are profitable because useful.

Certainly.

Shall we also say the same about sexual desires and the rest?

Yes.

Now, when we called a man a drone just now, we meant that he teemed with pleasures and desires of this sort and was ruled by unnecessary desires. The man ruled by necessary desires is parsimonious and oligarchical?

d   Certainly.

THE DEMOCRAT (559D–562A)

Again then, I replied, let us tell how democratic man comes to be from oligarchic man. For the most part, at least, it appears to me to happen this way:

How?

When a young man reared as we just described, parsimoniously and without education, once tastes the honey of the drones, and associates with wild and clever creatures capable of providing all kinds of pleasures in every kind of way, there, you may surely suppose, is the beginning of a change in him from inner oligarchy to democracy.

e   Quite necessarily, he said.

Now, as the city changed when an external alliance aided one of its parties, like to like, so also the young man changes when external desires, like and kindred in form, in turn come to the aid of one of the desires he already has.

Indeed.

And if an alliance derived from his father, I suppose, or perhaps other relatives who admonish and reproach him, lends contrary support to his inner oligarchy, there then arises faction and counterfaction and a battle within him against himself.

Of course.

And sometimes, I suppose, the democratic faction gives way to the oligarchic, and some desires are destroyed, others exiled, and a kind of shame comes to be present in the soul of the young man, and order is again restored.

Yes, sometimes, he said.

But sometimes again, I suppose, other desires akin to those exiled are secretly nursed through the father's ignorance of education, and become many and strong.

Yes, he said, so things like to happen, at any rate.

b

Then they drag him back to the same associations, and by secret intercourse beget a multitude.

Of course.

In the end then, I suppose, they seize the citadel of the young man's soul, perceiving it empty of learning and noble practices and true words, which indeed are best watchmen and guardians in the understandings of men dear to the gods.

Very true.

c

Instead, I suppose, false and deceptive words and opinions rush to occupy the same place in such a person.

Emphatically so, he said.

So back he goes again to the Lotus Eaters and dwells with them openly, and if any support for the parsimonious element in his soul arrives from his relatives, the deceptive words of the Lotus Eaters slam shut the gates of the royal fortress within him. They refuse entrance to the allies, refuse to admit as emissaries the wise words of elder friends in private station, and they prevail in their fight. They call shame the height of foolishness and thrust it out a dishonored fugitive; they call temperance cowardice and drag it through

d

the mire and expel it; they teach that moderate and seemly expenditure is boorish and unworthy of a free man; and they combine with a multitude of useless desires to drive it into exile.

e

Yes.

But no doubt when they have emptied and purified the soul of him whom they possess and initiated him into even greater mysteries, they next in torchlit procession, accompanied by a great chorus, lead back insolence and anarchy and shamelessness and waste, crowned, hymned, and called by endearing little names; insolence they call good breeding, anarchy freedom, 561a waste magnificence, shamelessness courage. Isn't it in some such way as this, I continued, that while young, he changes from being reared in the satisfaction of necessary desires to the liberation and release of unnecessary and useless pleasures?

Yes, he replied, quite obviously.

In subsequent life then, I expect, such a person would spend no more money and toil and time on necessary than on unnecessary pleasures. If he is lucky and not driven beyond bounds by Bacchic frenzy, if the tumult b within him somewhat subsides as he grows older and he accepts back parts of what was exiled and does not give himself up wholly to what entered afterward; then he passes his life with pleasures established in a kind of equality, and constantly gives over the government of himself, as it were by the luck of the draw, to whichever happens along until it is satisfied, and then to another, despising none but nourishing all equally.

Of course.

And if anyone says that some pleasures belong to excellent and good desires, others to bad desires, and that some should be served and honored, c others chastised and enslaved, he does not accept it as a true account, I continued, nor admit it into the guard tower of his soul. Rather, in all this he shakes his head and claims they are all alike and to be valued equally.

That's very much his condition and how he acts, he said.

So he in this way lives out his life day by day, I replied, delighting in the desire that happens along. Now he gets drunk and abandons himself to the d sound of the flute, next he drinks water and diets, but then again he exercises; sometimes he is lazy and neglectful of everything, but then spends his time as though in philosophy. Often he goes into politics, and leaps to his feet and says and does whatever occurs to him; occasionally he envies military men and is carried in that direction, or envies businessmen and is carried again toward that. There is neither order nor necessity present to his life, but he calls this life pleasant and free and blessed, and holds to it through everything.

You have described the life of a man governed by complete equality, he replied.[6]

e

Yes, I replied, and I expect he's filled with an extreme plurality of all kinds of characters, beautiful and many-colored. As with that city whose life many men and women would envy, so with this man, for he contains within himself most multitudinous examples of constitutions and characters.

Yes, that's so, he said.

Well then, do we rank this sort of man a counterpart of democracy, and suppose he would rightly be called democratic?

562a

Yes, he said.

TRANSITION FROM DEMOCRACY TO TYRANNY (562A–566D)

It remains then for us to describe the finest constitution of all, I said, and the finest man—tyranny and the tyrant.

Quite so, he said.

Come then, dear friend, how does tyranny come to be? Because it is pretty clear that it changes from democracy.

Yes.

Does not tyranny arise from democracy in somewhat the same way that democracy arose from oligarchy?

How so?

b

6. Adam translates, "to whom all laws are equal," and remarks, "Equal laws (isonomy) was the proud claim of democracy. The democratic man practises what he preaches—by impartially ignoring every law."

What was put forward as good, I replied, through which oligarchy was established, was excessive wealth, was it not?

Yes.

The insatiability of wealth, the neglect of other things for moneymaking, also destroyed it?

True, he said.

Well, insatiable desire for what democracy defines as good overthrows it too?

What do you say it defines as good?

Freedom, I said. For surely in a democratically governed city you would hear that this is its finest possession, and for this reason, only this city is fit to dwell in for those by nature free.

c   Yes, this statement is surely often made, he said.

Then here is what I was just now about to say, I replied: insatiable desire for freedom and neglect of other things alters this constitution and prepares the demand for tyranny.

How so? he said.

d   I expect that when a democratically governed city, thirsty for freedom, meets with evil cupbearers as leaders and drinks too deeply of its own unmixed wine, then, unless the rulers are very gentle and provide much freedom, it accuses them of being blood-stained oligarchs and punishes them.

Yes, he said, they do this.

It treats with contempt, as willing slaves, as nothing, those who obey the rulers, I said, but it praises and honors in public and private rulers who rule like subjects, and subjects who are like rulers. In such a city as this, does not freedom necessarily extend to everything?

e   Of course.

Yes, and it even steals into private houses, my friend, I replied. In the end, the very beasts are imbued with anarchy.

How do you mean? he replied.

For example, I said, father is accustomed to become like child and to fear his sons, son to become like father, and neither respect nor fear his parents, so that he may be free indeed. Resident alien becomes the equal of citizen, citizen of resident alien, and foreigner likewise.

Yes, it happens that way, he said.

It does. And other little things happen too, I replied. In such circumstances, teachers fear and timidly flatter pupils, pupils despise teachers and so too their tutors. In general, the young copy their elders and compete with them in words and deeds, while the old stoop to the level of the young, full of witty jests and pleasantries; they imitate the young, lest they seem to be disagreeable or despotic.

Of course, he said.

b

Yes, my friend, I replied, and the extremity of freedom for the multitude in this sort of city is reached when chattel slaves of both sexes are no less free than their purchasers. I almost forgot to mention how great the freedom and equality of rights is among women toward men and men toward women.

Well, as Aeschylus has it, he said, "Shall we say what now comes to our lips?"

c

Of course, I said, and I mean to do so. Someone who has not experienced it would not believe how much more free even domestic animals are here than elsewhere. Dogs literally become like their mistresses, as the proverb has it, and even horses and asses are accustomed to travel with much freedom and dignity, jostling anyone they meet in the streets if he doesn't get out of the way. And everything else is thus full of freedom.

You're telling me my dream, he said. For I often experience the same thing myself when traveling to the country.

d

To sum up then, I replied, when all these things are taken together, you realize how touchy it makes the souls of the citizens, so that if anyone proffers any kind of servitude whatever, they are angry and will not abide it. For in the end, you doubtless know that they do not even give thought to the laws, written or unwritten, in order not to have any master anywhere.

I know it very well, he said.

e

This then, my friend, I replied, is the fine and sprightly government from which tyranny is bred, I think.

Sprightly indeed, he said. But what comes next?

The same disease which arose in oligarchy and destroyed it, I replied, arises here and in this, stronger and more virulent because of the prevailing

liberty, and it enslaves democracy. And really, excess likes to provoke a corresponding change in the opposite direction—in seasons, in plants and
bodies, and most especially in constitutions.

564a   Probably, he said.

For too much freedom, in private citizens and in city, seems to change to
nothing else except too much slavery.

Yes.

Then it is probable, I said, that tyranny is established from no other constitution than democracy, the most savage and extreme slavery, I suppose,
from the height of freedom.

That is reasonable, he said.

But I don't think you asked about this, I replied, but rather what disease
grows up the same in oligarchy and democracy, and enslaves it.

b   True, he said.

It is that class of lazy and spendthrift men I was mentioning, I said. The
bravest among them lead, the more unmanly follow. We likened them to
drones, some with stings, others stingless.

Yes, and rightly, he said.

Both cause disturbance when present in any constitution, I said; they are
like phlegm and bile in the body. Which is also why the good physician and

c   the lawgiver of a city, no less than a wise beekeeper, must take care in advance specifically to prevent their presence. But if they do come to be present, he must cut them out, cells and all, as quickly as possible.

Yes, most emphatically, he replied.

To grasp more distinctly what we mean, I replied, let us look at it this
way:

How?

d   Let us in discourse divide the democratically governed city into three
parts—as is actually the case. One such part, the class of drones, surely
grows up in it, no less than in oligarchical government, through liberty.

That's so.

Yes, but it is much more shrewd and bitter in this city than in that.

Why?

There, the class of drones was not held in honor but kept out of office; it was without exercise and did not become strong. But in a democracy it is surely with few exceptions the prevailing element, and what is most shrewd and bitter in it speaks and acts, while the rest sit near the speaker's platform and hum and buzz and allow no speech to the contrary, so everything under this sort of constitution with few exceptions is managed by this element.

Yes indeed, he replied.   e

Another class of this sort is always separated off from the multitude.

What is it?

Where all are engaged in making money, those who are by nature most orderly for the most part become richest.

Probably.

This is the most plentiful supply of honey for the drones, I suppose, and it is easiest to steal from that source.

Of course, he said. Who would want to steal honey from those who have only a little?

Such rich folk as these are called, I suppose, a pasture for drones.

Pretty much so, he said.

The people would be a third class, those who work with their hands and   565a take no part in public affairs and have few possessions, but the most numerous and determinative element in a democracy whenever they are assembled.

Yes, he said. But they often refuse to do it, unless they get a share of honey.

Well, they always do get a share, I replied, in so far as the leaders are able to take away the substance of those who have it and distribute it to the people, keeping most of it themselves.

Yes, he replied, the people do get a share that way.   b

But those from whom it is taken are compelled to defend themselves, I suppose, by speeches in public and doing whatever else they can?

Of course.

So they get accused by the rest of plotting against the people and being oligarchs, even if they have no desire for revolution.

Of course.

c   In the end then, when they see the people undertaking to wrong them, not willingly but in ignorance and deceived by false accusers, then at that point, whether they wish it or not, they truly become oligarchs—not willingly, but the drone also implants this evil by its sting.

Quite so.

So there are impeachments and judgments and trials one of another.

Yes.

The people are always accustomed to put forward some one man as their special champion, and nourish him and make him grow great?

Yes.

d   This then is clear, I replied. When a tyrant grows, he sprouts from the root of popular leadership and from nowhere else.

Very clear.

What is the origin of the change from popular leader to tyrant? Clearly, when the popular leader begins to act like the story told at the shrine of Lycaean Zeus in Arcadia.

What story? he said.

Namely, that anyone who once tastes of the entrails of a human being, a single piece minced up in the flesh of other sacrificial victims, inevitably becomes a werewolf. Haven't you heard the tale?

e   I have.

In the same way, if someone is leader of a people and has gained control of a mob that obeys him implicitly, he will not scruple to shed kindred blood. With unjust accusations of the usual sort, and stained with blood, he will drag a man into court and blot out his life. With unhallowed tongue,
566a   with the taste of kinsman's murder in his mouth, he will banish and slay, while hinting at abolition of debts and redistribution of land. Is it not fated that such a man should necessarily be destroyed by his enemies, or become a tyrant and change from man to wolf?

Quite necessarily, he said.

So he raises a faction against those who have substantive estates, I said.

Yes.

Now, if he is driven into exile, and forcibly returns despite his enemies, he comes back a full and finished tyrant?

Clearly.

But if they are unable to exile him or kill him by slandering him to the city, they plot in secret to assassinate him?

So at any rate it likes to happen, he said.

All who reach this point next discover the much-urged plea of the tyrant: to ask the people for a bodyguard, in order that their protector may be safe among them.

Indeed, he said.

So they provide it, I suppose, afraid for him and confident in themselves.

Yes.

When a man of wealth sees this, and is accused with his wealth of hating the people, then, my friend, as the oracle given to Croesus had it, he "flees to the River Hermus, many-pebbled; he does not stay, and is not ashamed to be a coward."

No, he said. He would hardly have a chance to feel shame twice.

I suppose if caught, I replied, he is put to death.

Inevitably.

But as for that popular leader himself, it is clear that he does not "lie stretched out mightily in his might."[7] On the contrary, having overthrown many others, he now stands in the chariot of state as driver, a finished tyrant instead of a popular leader.

It will come to that, he said.

THE TYRANT (566D–569C)

Shall we then describe the happiness of the man, and that of the city in which this sort of creature arises? I replied.

By all means, he said.

Well at first, in the early days, I said, he has a smile and a greeting for

7. Like Hector's charioteer, *Iliad* XVI 776.

everyone he meets. He denies that he is a tyrant, and makes many promises both in public and private. He frees the people from debts and distributes land to them and to those around himself, and he pretends to be gracious and gentle to all.

Necessarily, he said.

Yes, but when he has come to terms with some of his external enemies, I think, and destroyed others, and things are quiet with them, first he begins constantly to stir up wars, in order that the people may need a leader.

Yes, very likely.

567a   And also so that, by becoming poor through paying taxes, they may be compelled to devote themselves to their day-to-day existence, and plot against him the less?

Clearly.

And also, should he suspect any of having free thoughts and not submitting to his rule, I suppose he would find a pretext to destroy them by betraying them to the enemy? For all these reasons, a tyrant always necessarily stirs up war?

Yes.

In doing this, he is the more readily hated by the citizens?

b   Of course.

Then too, some among those who helped establish him in power speak frankly to him and to each other, and criticize what is happening—and they happen to be the bravest.

Very likely.

Then the tyrant must get rid of them all if he intends to rule, until no one worth anything is left, friend or foe.

Clearly.

c   So he must keep a sharp eye out to see who is brave, who is high minded, who is wise, who is rich. And thus his happiness consists in this, that he is necessarily an enemy to all of them whether he wishes it or not, and must plot against them until he has purged the city of them.

A fine purgation indeed, he said.

Yes, I replied, the opposite of medical purgation, which removes the worst and leaves the best. He does exactly the opposite.

As it seems he must, he said, if indeed he is to rule.

So he is bound by a blessed necessity, I said, which requires him either to   d
dwell in the company of a multitude of inferiors and be hated by them, or
not to live at all.

Such is the necessity, he replied.

The more he is hated by the citizens for so acting, the larger and more
trustworthy the guard he will need?

Of course.

Then who is trustworthy? And where will they come from?

Many will come of their own accord, he said—and come flying, if he
pays them.

Drones, by the Dog! I replied. I think you mean all sorts of foreign
drones.

True, he said. I think so.   e

But would he refuse the home-grown kind?

How do you mean?

Depriving citizens of their slaves, setting them free and making them his
own guards?

Of course, he said. Since they would surely be the most trustworthy people he has.

What a blessed thing you say it is to be a tyrant, I replied, if such are the
friends and trusty men he has to rely on, after destroying those he had before.

But surely, that is the sort he has got, he said.   568a

These companions no doubt admire him, I said, and these new citizens
will associate with him, but decent folk will hate and shun him.

Why would they not?

It is not for nothing, I replied, that tragedy is in general thought to be
wise, and Euripides surpassingly so in it.

Why?

Because of his utterance, so very characteristic of his reflective understanding, that "tyrants are wise by converse with the wise." He meant, clearly, that those with whom the tyrant associates are the wise.

b   Yes, he said, and he eulogizes the tyrant as "equal to a god," and he and other poets say much else to the same effect.

Accordingly, I said, because the tragic poets are wise, they will forgive us, and all whose government is close to ours, if we do not admit them to our constitution because they sing the praises of tyranny.

I think they will forgive us, at least the more clever among them.

c   But I expect they will go to other cities, gather the crowds, hire fine big persuasive voices and drag the constitutions into democracy and tyranny.

Yes.

They will receive pay for this and be honored in addition—primarily by tyrants, as is reasonable, but also by democracies. But the higher they rise in the ascending scale of constitutions, the more their reputation will fail, as though unable to proceed for lack of breath.

d   Of course.

But we digress, I said. Let us speak again of that armed camp of the tyrant—beautiful, multitudinous, varied in kind, and never the same—and tell how it derives its support.

Clearly, he said, if there is money in the temples of the city, he will spend it as long as it lasts, along with the property of those he destroys, requiring the people to pay fewer taxes.

e   But when that runs out?

Clearly, he said, he will support himself from his patrimony, himself and his drinking partners and his companions and mistresses.

I see, I replied: because the people who gave birth to the tyrant will support him and his companions.

Quite necessarily, he said.

How do you mean? I said. Suppose the people resent it and say it is not right for a son in the prime of life to be supported by his father, but on the contrary, father by son—that the people did not beget and establish him in

569a   order that, when he became great, they would then be slaves of their own slaves and support him and their own slaves along with other rabble, but rather in order that, when he became their leader, they would be freed from the rich men in the city and the so-called gentlemen. And now they bid him and his companions to depart the city, like a father driving a son from his house along with a crowd of drunken companions.

At that point, by Zeus, he replied, they will learn at their peril what he is, and what sort of creature they have given birth to and welcomed and nourished—and that it is weaker driving out stronger.

How do you mean? I replied. Will the tyrant dare use force against his b
own father, and strike him if he disobeys?

Yes, he said—once he has disarmed him.

You mean the tyrant is a parricide, I replied—harsh nurse to old age. At this point it would be tyranny open and avowed, it seems. The people, as the saying goes, have fled the smoke of servitude to free men only to fall into the fire of mastership by slaves. Instead of their former excessive and unseasonable freedom, they have entangled themselves in the harshest and most bitter kind of slavery, that of slavery to slaves.

Yes, he said. These things happen so. c

Really? I said. Will anyone disagree if we claim that we have sufficiently explained the change from democracy to tyranny, and what sort of thing tyranny is when it has come to be?

We have done so quite sufficiently, he said.

Book IX

LAWLESS DESIRES (571A–572B)

571a   It remains to consider the tyrannical man himself, I replied: how he develops from democratic man, and once having come to be, of what sort he is, and his manner of life, whether wretched or blessed.

Yes, that remains, he said.

Then do you know what I still want? I replied.

What?

I don't think we have sufficiently distinguished what sorts of desires there are, and how many. But lacking this, the inquiry will be the more unclear.

b   Well, it's not too late, he replied.

No. Consider what I wish to examine. It is this: among unnecessary pleasures and desires, some seem lawless; very likely they are present in everyone, but in some people they are disciplined by the laws and by better desires in company with reason, and they can either be completely got rid of, or left few and weak. But in other people they are stronger and more numerous.

c   What desires do you mean? he said.

296

Those roused in sleep, I replied, when the rest of the soul slumbers—the rational and gentle and ruling element of the person. But the wild and beastlike element, flown with food or drink, leaps up and shakes off sleep and undertakes to go forth and fulfill its own character. You know that in such circumstances it dares everything, supposing itself loosed from all shame and released from all wisdom. For it does not shrink from attempt-   d ing sexual intercourse with a mother, as it supposes, and anyone else among men, gods, or beasts; or from committing any murder; and it abstains from no food. In a word, it falls short of no extremity of madness or shameless-ness.

Very true, he said.

But when a person is self-possessed and healthy and temperate, I sup-pose, and goes to sleep after awakening his own rational part and feeding it with excellent reasoning and inquiries, he arrives at self-awareness and self-understanding, giving neither excess nor deficiency to the appetitive part, so that it may be lulled to rest, and not by its pleasure or pain provoke dis-   572a turbance in what is best, but allows it to inquire alone by itself and to desire something in singleness and purity, and to perceive what it does not know, whether past or present or to come. He also tames the spirited element in like manner: he does not go to his sleep with spirit roused, or moved to anger against anyone. Having thus quieted these two forms but stirred and moved the third, in which intelligence is present, he thus goes to his rest, and as you know, in such circumstance he most especially touches the truth, and the visions which appear in his dreams are then least lawless.

Quite so, he said.   b

Well, we have been carried too far past our point. What we meant to ob-serve is this, namely, that there is in each of us a form of desire which is ter-rible and wild and unlawful, however decent some of us may seem to be, and this then becomes evident in sleep. Consider whether you think there's anything in what I say. Do you agree?

Why, yes, I do.

THE LIFE OF THE TYRANT (572B–576B)

c Then recollect what sort of person we claimed the democratic man to be. He was raised from youth by a parsimonious father, who valued only the acquisitive desires and despised those which are unnecessary but exist for the sake of entertainment and play. Not so?

Yes.

But by associating with cleverer men filled with the lawless desires we just described, the democrat is moved to their form of life and every kind of insolence, and hates his father's parsimony. But since he has a better nature than those who corrupt him, he is drawn in both directions and establishes

d a mean intermediate between the two characters. Then, moderately enjoying each, as he supposes, he lives a life neither lawless nor unfree, having become a democrat after being an oligarch.

This was and is our judgment about this sort of person, he said.

Assume then again, I replied, that such a man, become older, has then a young son raised in his own habits of life.

I assume it.

Assume also that the same things which happened to his father happen to him. He is led into every kind of lawlessness, which is called complete

e freedom by those who seduce him. His father and the rest of his kin support his intermediate desires, but the others support the opposite. When those terrible wizards and tyrant-makers despair of controlling the young man otherwise, they contrive to implant in him an Eros, an overmastering passion, as leader of those idle desires which divide his means among them-

573a selves—a monstrous winged drone. Do you think an Eros is aught else, among such desires as these?

Only that, he replied.

Then when the other desires buzz around him, full of incense and myrrh, wreathed in wine and the pleasures released in the midst of such companionship, they nourish the drone and cause its utmost increase, and plant in it the goad and sting of longing. At that point this leader of the soul

b is stung to frenzy, with madness for its bodyguard, and if it can lay hold of any judgments or desires accounted good in the man and still capable of shame, it kills them and pushes them away, until it has purged him of temperance, and filled him with madness imported from without.

You perfectly describe the origin of the tyrannical man, he said.

Isn't it for some such reason as this, I replied, that Eros is long said to be a tyrant?

Very likely, he said.

Doesn't a drunken man also have something of a tyrannical cast of mind, my friend? I said.

He does.

And again, the disturbed madman tries and hopes to be able to rule not only men, but gods as well?

Yes, he said.

A man becomes in the strict sense tyrannical, my friend, I replied, when either by nature or practices or both he has become drunken and erotic and choleric.

Quite so.

Such then, it seems, his origin, and this the man. But what is his way of life?

As the joke has it, he said, you tell me.

So I will, I said. For next there are festivals among them, I suppose, and feasts and meretricious revelry and everything of the sort, if a tyrannical master passion dwells within and governs everything belonging to the soul.

Necessarily, he said.

Then many other terrible desires besides shoot up each day and night, requiring many things?

Yes.

If there is any income, it is quickly spent?

Certainly.

Next then comes borrowing, and curtailing of estate?

Of course.

When all is gone, the close-packed, vehement desires nested within the man necessarily cry out? He and his companions are driven by other desires as by goads, and surpassingly by Eros itself, leading all the rest as captain of their guard, to rage in frenzy and to consider who has something they can take by fraud or force?

574a   Yes, he said.

He must necessarily get money from somewhere, or be encompassed by suffering and torment?

Yes.

Now, just as the pleasures which prevail in him overreach and outdo his original pleasures and take what belongs to them, so also he himself, though younger, sees fit to overreach his father and mother: if he has spent his own portion, he helps himself and takes his parents' property.

Why, what else? he said.

b   Should they not allow it, he will first try to steal from his parents and defraud them?

Certainly.

And when he can't, he will next take by force?

I think so, he said.

If the old man and woman resist and fight, my friend, would he take care to refrain from acting the tyrant?

I don't feel altogether cheerful about the parents of such a man, he replied.

c   Really, Adeimantus? You think that for the sake of a dear new love and an unnecessary mistress, he would strike the mother long dear to him, and necessary as related by ties of blood? Or that for the sake of a dear boy in the bloom of youth, an unnecessary companion, he would strike his aged father, necessary as related by ties of blood and the oldest of his friends? Or beat his parents and cause them to be enslaved by those others he brought into the same house?

Yes indeed, he replied.

How blessed it seems to bear a tyrant son, I replied.

Very, he said.

d   What happens when the possessions of mother and father fail such a man, with the swarm of pleasures still gathered great within him? He first breaks into someone's house, or strips the cloak off somebody abroad late at night, and next cleans out a temple? And in all of this, new opinions just released from slavery, in company with that Eros whose bodyguards they are, overmaster opinions about things noble and shameful held since childhood and long accounted right. Formerly, when he was himself still democratically governed from within by laws and his father, these opinions were loosed only in sleep. But under the tyranny of Eros, he has always become while awake what he sometimes was in dream. He will abstain from no murder however terrible, from no food, from no deed. The Eros within him lives in all anarchy and lawlessness, because it is by itself sole ruler. It will lead him who has it, as it leads a city, to dare all that will nourish it and the crowd of appetites around it, some introduced from without by evil communications, some released and set free from within by similar dispositions within himself. Isn't this the life of such a man?

It is, he said.

If there are only a few such men in a city, I replied, and the majority is sane, these men will go abroad to serve as bodyguards to some other tyrant, or as paid mercenaries if there is a war somewhere. But in time of peace and quiet, they do many small evils in the city itself.

What evils do you mean?

Stealing, for example, and burglary, purse cutting, highway robbery, temple theft, kidnapping. Sometimes, if they have speaking ability, they are paid informers and bear false witness and take bribes.

Small evils indeed, he said—if such men are few.

Yes, I replied, little evils—small compared to great. The sum of them for a city doesn't even come close, as the saying is, in wickedness and misery compared to the tyrant. For when such men become numerous in a city, and they and others who follow them become aware of their own number, they then, assisted by the folly of the people, beget the tyrant—that man who contains within himself the greatest and most immense tyrant in his soul.

d   Very probably, he said. For he'd be most tyrannical.

Now if the people yield voluntarily, well and good. But if the city resists, then even as previously he chastised his mother and father, so now again he will chastise his fatherland if he can, introducing new companions and by their agency reducing his fatherland—or his long beloved motherland, as the Cretans say—to slavery. And he will hold and keep it. This would be the goal of such a man's desire.

e   Exactly this, he replied.

Here is how they are in private, before they rule, I replied: first, they associate with flatterers ready for any service, or if they need something from someone, they get down on their knees and do not scruple to assume every posture of intimacy; but once they get what they want, they act like strangers.

576a   Very much so.

So in the whole of their life, they never live as friends to any one, but always as masters of someone or slaves of someone else. A tyrannical nature always leaves freedom and true friendship untasted.

Certainly.

Wouldn't we be right to call such men faithless?

Of course.

And further, if we were right before about what justice is, to call them as unjust as it is possible to be?

b   But surely we were right, he replied.

Then let us sum up the worst man, I replied. He is one who, while awake, is of such stuff as we described in dreams.

Yes.

This then is what those most tyrannical by nature become, should they achieve sole rule. And the longer they dwell in tyranny, the more they become this way.

Necessarily, said Glaucon, taking up the argument.

Comparison of Just and Unjust Lives in Respect to Happiness (576b–592b)

THE ANALOGY OF SOUL AND STATE RECALLED (576B–577B)

Then whoever proves most wicked will also prove most miserable? And whoever acts the tyrant for the longest time becomes especially and for the longest time most miserable? But no doubt the multitude holds many different opinions.   c

That, at any rate, is surely so, he said.

Now, I replied, the tyrannical man corresponds to the tyrannical city, and the democratic man to the democratic city, and so for the rest?

Surely.

Then as city is to city in virtue and happiness, so also man is to man?

Of course.   d

How then is the city ruled by a tyrant related in virtue to a royal city of the sort we first described?

Completely opposite, he said. The one is best, the other worst.

I won't ask which of the two you mean, I said, because it is obvious. But do you judge similarly in respect to happiness and misery, or otherwise? Let us not be dazzled by looking only at the tyrant, who is but one man, nor at some few of those around him. We must enter into and view the whole city, and thus declare an opinion after sinking down into it and examining it all.

A fair suggestion, he said. And it is clear to everyone that a city ruled by a tyrant can scarcely be more wretched, nor more happy if ruled by a king.   e

Now, would I be right also to suggest the same about the corresponding men? I replied. They are properly judged only by him who is able by understanding to sink down into the character of a man and see through it, not viewing it from the outside like a child dazzled by the external appearance which tyrants assume, but able to see right through it. Should we not all do well to hearken to one who is able to judge because he has dwelt in the same place and witnessed the tyrant's behavior in his own home and how he behaves toward its members, in circumstances in which the tyrant is seen stripped of his theatrical garb, and again, how he behaves in the dangers of   b public life? We might bid one who has seen all this to declare how the tyrant stands to the others in happiness and misery.

You're quite right to suggest this, he said.

Would you then have us pretend that we are among those able to judge, I replied, and that at this point we have met such men, in order to have someone who can answer what we ask?

Of course.

FIRST CONTEST: FREEDOM, WEALTH, AND SECURITY (577C–580A)

c   Come then, I said, and consider: bearing in mind the likeness of the city and the man, examine them point by point and state how each of the two is affected.

How do you mean? he said.

First, to speak of the city, I replied, will you say the city ruled by a tyrant is free or enslaved?

As utterly enslaved as it is possible to be, he said.

Yet surely you see masters and free men in it.

I see a little something of that, he said. But on the whole, the most decent element in it is dishonorably and wretchedly enslaved.

d   If then man is like city, I said, isn't the same order also necessarily present in him? His soul teems with slavery and lack of freedom. The elements of it which were most decent are enslaved, while a small part, the most worthless and insane, rules as master?

Necessarily, he said.

Will you say that such a soul is enslaved, or free?

Enslaved, surely.

Again, the city enslaved and ruled by a tyrant least does what it wishes?

Of course.

e   And so, speaking of soul as a whole, the soul ruled by a tyrant will least do what it wishes. It will constantly be dragged about by force and stung to frenzy, full of disturbance and remorse.

Of course.

Is the city ruled by a tyrant necessarily rich or impoverished?

Impoverished.

So a tyrannical soul is necessarily ever needy and insatiable. 578a

True, he replied.

Then doesn't such a city and such a man necessarily teem with fear?

Yes, very much so.

Would you expect to find more weeping and lamentation, grief and pain, in any other city?

Not at all.

Nor in any other man? Do you believe such things more frequent in anyone except this tyrannical man, driven mad by passions and desires?

How could they be? he said.

Then as you look to all this and other things of the same sort, I suppose b you judge it most wretched among cities.

And rightly, he said.

Yes, very much so, I replied. But again, what do you say about the tyrannical man when you look to these same things?

That he is by far the most wretched among the others, he said.

In this you are mistaken, I replied.

How so? he said.

I don't think such a person is quite there yet, I said.

Who is, then? he said.

There's a man you'll perhaps think is more wretched still.

Who is it?

The tyrannical man who does not live out his life as a private citizen, I c replied, but is unlucky, and by some misfortune is provided means to become a tyrant.

I infer from what was said before that you're right, he said.

Yes, I replied. But still, one mustn't assume such things, but examine them carefully by such argument as this. For the inquiry concerns what is of utmost importance, namely, a good or evil life.

Quite right, he replied.

Consider then whether there perhaps is something in what I say. For I think we must conceive of it by inquiring from this:

d   From what?

From every single private citizen in our cities who is rich and owns many slaves. For they have this point of resemblance to tyrants: rule over many, though no doubt the multitude of the tyrant's slaves is greater.

Yes.

Now, you know that this person is confident, and unafraid of his servants?

What would he have to fear?

Nothing, I said. But do you understand the reason?

Yes: because the whole city would come to the aid of any one of its citizens.

e   Excellent, I replied. But suppose a god lifted one man with fifty slaves or more out of the city, and put him and his wife and children, along with the rest of his estate and his slaves, in a deserted place where no free man could help him. What sort of fear, and how great, do you think he would feel for himself and his wife and children, lest they be destroyed by his servants?

I think he would be in utter terror, he replied.

579a   Then at that point he would be compelled to fawn on some of his own slaves, and promise many things, and free them much against his will. He would turn out to be a flatterer of servants.

Inevitably, he said, or he would be destroyed.

What if the god surrounded him with a multitude of neighbors who refused to tolerate it if one person should think fit to be master of another, I replied, but if anyone anywhere did such a thing, punish him with extreme penalties?

b   I think he would be still worse off in every respect, he said. He would be surrounded by watchful enemies on all sides.

Well, isn't the tyrant in just such a prison, if he is by nature as we've described, and filled with multiple fears and passions of every kind? His is a greedy and inquisitive soul, and yet, alone among those in the city, he cannot travel anywhere abroad or attend the festivals which other free men desire to see. He lives for the most part secluded in his house like a woman, envying other citizens if they go abroad and see something good.

Most assuredly, he said.   c

Then greater by such evils as these is the harvest reaped by a man ill constituted within himself—the tyrannical man whom you just now judged to be most wretched because he did not live out his life as a private citizen, but was compelled by some misfortune to become a tyrant and, himself ungoverned, to undertake the government of others. It is as if an invalid, sick of body and incontinent, were compelled to pass his life not in retirement but competing and contending against other bodies.

Your likeness is most exact and true, Socrates, he said.   d

Then, my dear Glaucon, I replied, his condition is completely wretched, and the tyrant lives still worse than the man you judged to live most badly.

Agreed, he said.

So in actual truth, even if no one thinks so, the real tyrant is really a slave. He dwells in abject servility, a flatterer of the worst sorts of men. He finds   e
no satisfaction for his desires, but proves to be in most need of the greatest number of things, poor in very truth, if one knows how to view his soul as a whole. He teems with fear throughout his life, full of convulsions and pangs, if indeed he resembles the disposition of the city he rules. But he does resemble it, doesn't he?

Yes, very much so, he said   580a

Then shall we also assign in addition to the fellow what we were saying before? He necessarily is, and is becoming still more so by reason of his rule, envious, faithless, unjust, friendless, unholy, a host and nurse to every kind of vice. As a result of all this, he is especially unfortunate, and makes those around him the same.

No one with good sense will contradict you, he said.

THE JUDGMENT OF GLAUCON (580A – C)

b   Come then, I said. At this point, like a final judge, you too must so declare:
who in your opinion is first in happiness, and who is second? Judge the five
in order: king, timocrat, oligarch, democrat, and tyrant.

Why, the decision is easy, he said. I judge them like choruses in the order
of their entrance, in respect to virtue and vice and happiness and unhappi-
ness.

c   Then shall we hire a herald? I replied. Or shall I myself proclaim that the
son of Ariston judges the best and most just man most happy, and he is
most kingly and king over himself. The most evil and most unjust man is
most miserable, and again, he is not only most tyrannical, but especially
also tyrant over himself and his city.

Let it be so proclaimed, he said.

Then I pronounce in addition, I said, that this is so whether or not it escapes the notice of all men and gods.

Yes, he said.

SECOND CONTEST: PLEASURE AND THE DISTINCTION BETWEEN
THREE PARTS OF THE SOUL (580C–583A)

Very well then, I said. This would be one proof. But consider this second
proof, and see if you think there is anything in it:

d   What is it?

Since, even as a city is divided into three forms or parts, so also the soul
of each individual is trebly divided, I replied, it will also admit, I think, a
further proof.

What is it?

This. Since there are three forms, it appears to me there are also three
kinds of pleasure proper and peculiar to each, and so too desires and ruling
principles.

How do you mean? he said.

One part of the soul, we say, is what a man learns by. Another, that by

which he is angry. As for the third, we have no single name proper and peculiar to it because it is multiform, but we named it after what is biggest and   e
strongest in it: we call it appetitive, because of the intensity of its desires for
food and drink and sex and all else that follows on these; yes, and money
loving too, because it is by money that such desires are especially satisfied.

Yes, he said.   581a

Now, if we further say that its pleasure and liking is for gain, we would
best sum up the account under one main heading, so that we would be clear
whenever we speak of this part of the soul. We rightly call it money loving
or gain loving?

I think so, at any rate, he said.

Again, don't we say that the spirited element is always directed as a whole
toward mastery and victory and good repute?

Yes.   b

Then it would be appropriate to call it competitive and ambitious?

Very appropriate.

Moreover, as to what we learn by, it is clear to everyone that it always and
in everything strains after knowledge of the truth as it is, and is least concerned among the forms with money and reputation?

Yes.

Then it would accord with its character to call it a lover of learning and
wisdom?

Of course.

Now, it rules in the souls of some men, I replied, but in other men, one
of the two other elements, whichever may occur?

That's so, he said.   c

For this reason, then, we also say there are three primary kinds among
men: philosophical, competitive, and gain loving?

Quite so.

And three forms of pleasure, one underlying each of these?

Of course.

You know then, I replied, that if you ask these three men, each in his
turn, which among these lives is most pleasant, each will especially praise

his own. The businessman will say that compared to profit, the pleasure of honor or learning is of no value, except if something belonging to it makes money.

d   True, he said.

What about the ambitious man, the lover of honor? I replied. Doesn't he believe that the pleasure derived from money is in some sense vulgar, and again that the pleasure derived from learning is mere smoke and nonsense, except as learning brings honor?

That's so, he said.

e   And the lover of wisdom? I replied. How do we suppose he will regard other pleasures, compared to the pleasure of knowing the truth as it is, and being always in its presence while he learns? Aren't those other pleasures far removed from real pleasure? He will call them really necessary, because he would have no use for them if they were not necessary?

Without question, he said.

Now, when the pleasures of each form and the life itself are in dispute, I said, not compared to what is more noble and shameful in living nor to better and worse, but to what is more pleasant in itself and free from pain, how might we know which of these men speaks most truly?

582a   I can't really tell, he said.

But consider this. By what should a thing be judged, if it is to be judged well? Is it not by experience and intelligence and reason? Could one have a better standard of judgment than these?

Hardly, he said.

Consider then which of these three men is most experienced in all the pleasures we mentioned. Do you think the lover of gain is more experienced in the pleasure derived from knowing, studying the truth as it is, or the philosopher more experienced in the pleasure derived from gain?

b   There's a big difference, he said. For the philosopher has necessarily tasted those other pleasures starting from childhood. But it is not necessary for the lover of gain to taste the pleasure of studying the nature of things which are, and to discover how sweet it is or to gain experience in it—and not easy either, even if he were eager to do so.

So the philosopher, I replied, is much superior to the lover of gain in his experience of both kinds of pleasures.

Yes, very much so.   c

How does he stand compared to the lover of honor? Is he less experienced in the pleasure derived from honor than the other is in the pleasure derived from thought?

Why, honor follows for all of them, he said, if they actually achieve what they are each after. In fact the wealthy are honored by the multitude, and so are the courageous and the wise; so they all experience the sort of pleasure derived from being honored. But it is impossible for anyone but the philosopher to have tasted the sort of pleasure which derives from the vision of what is.

Then as far as experience goes, I said, he is in the best position among   d
these men to judge.

Yes.

Moreover, his experience alone will have been accompanied by wisdom.

Of course.

Again, the instrument through which it is necessary to judge is not the instrument of the lover of gain or even the lover of honor, but of the philosopher.

How so?

We were saying it is necessary to judge through reasoning. Not so?

Yes.

But reasoning is the philosopher's special instrument.

Of course.

Now, if what is judged were judged by wealth and gain, what the lover of   e
gain praises and blames would necessarily be most true.

Yes.

But if judged by honor and victory and courage, would it not be what the competitive and ambitious man praises and blames?

Clearly.

But since it is to be decided by experience and wisdom and reason?

Necessarily, he said, it must be what the lover of wisdom and lover of reason praises as most true and real.

583a   So of these three kinds of pleasure, the most pleasant would belong to
this part of the soul by which we learn, and life is most pleasant in him
among us in whom this rules.

How could it be otherwise? he said. At any rate, the wise man when he
praises his own life speaks with authority.

What does the judge say is the second life and the second kind of pleasure? I said.

Clearly the pleasure of the warrior and lover of honor; for it is nearer the
first than the pleasure of the money maker.

Then the lover of gain, it seems, is last.

Of course, he replied.

THIRD CONTEST: REAL AND UNREAL PLEASURES (583B–587B)

b   These two arguments thus then follow sequentially and in order, and twice
the just man has vanquished the unjust. But in Olympic manner, a third for
Zeus Savior, Olympian Zeus. Consider that the pleasure of the others, except that of the wise, is not wholly true nor pure, but a kind of shadow
painting, as I think I've heard some wise man describe it. Here is the most
important and decisive of falls.

Yes, but how do you mean?

c   I'll find out, I said, if you will answer as I inquire.

Please ask, he said.

Tell me then, I replied. We say that pain is the opposite of positive enjoyment?

Indeed.

There is also such a thing as neither enjoying nor being in pain?

Of course.

It is a mean intermediate between both those two, a kind of quietness of
soul concerning them? Do you agree?

Yes, he replied.

You recall what people say when they're sick? I replied.

What?

How nothing is more pleasant than being healthy, though they didn't realize it before they got sick.

I do recall, he said.   d

Then too, you hear people in great pain saying that nothing is more pleasant than surcease from suffering?

Yes.

And I suppose you're also aware that in many other such circumstances, people in pain sing the praises of cessation of pain, supposing that sort of quietness most pleasant, rather than positive enjoyment.

Yes, he said, quietness no doubt then becomes pleasant and welcome.

And therefore when enjoyment stops, I said, the quietness of pleasure   e
will be painful?

Perhaps, he said.

So quietness, which we just now said is intermediate between pain and pleasure, will sometimes be both pain and pleasure.

So it seems.

Is it possible for what is neither of two to become both?

I think not.

Again, pleasure occurring in the soul, and pain, are both a kind of motion. Not so?

Yes.

But didn't it appear just now that what is neither painful nor pleasant is   584a
a kind of quietness, and a mean between the two?

Yes.

How then is it right to believe that not suffering pain is pleasant, or not feeling pleasure painful?

It is not.

Then there is no reality, but only appearance, I replied, when quietness appears pleasant compared to pain, and painful compared to pleasure. Nothing is sound among these appearances relative to the truth and reality of pleasure; they are a kind of bewitchment.

So at any rate the argument signifies, he said.

Look then, I said, at pleasures which are not derived from pains, so that   b you may not suppose, as you on occasion at present might do, that pleasure is surcease from pain, pain surcease from pleasure.

Look where? he said. What do you mean?

There are many other examples, I said, but especially consider, if you will, the pleasures of smell. For they suddenly become surprisingly great in magnitude without previous pain, and when they cease they leave behind no pain at all.

Very true, he said.

c   So let us not be persuaded that cessation of pain is pure pleasure, nor cessation of pleasure pure pain.

No.

On the other hand, I said, the so-called pleasures which reach the soul through the body are pretty nearly the most numerous and greatest, and they are of this form: a kind of relief from pains.

Yes.

So too the pleasures and pains of anticipation which precede them?

Yes.

d   Do you know what they are, I said, and what they're like?

What? he said.

You acknowledge, I said, that there is in nature such a thing as up, down, and in the middle?

I do.

Do you think that if someone were carried from below to the middle, he would think he was being carried anywhere but up? And if he stood in the middle and looked back to the place from which he had been carried, that he'd believe he was anywhere except on top—not having seen what is truly above?

I doubt he'd think otherwise, he said.

e   If he were carried back again, I said, he'd think he was being carried downward, and he'd think truly?

Of course.

All this then would happen because he was not experienced in what is genuinely above and in the middle and below.

Clearly.

Would you be surprised, then, if people without experience of truth have unsound opinions about many other things? If they are so disposed toward pleasure and pain and what is intermediate that when they are carried toward pain, they are really in pain and truly suppose so, but when carried from pain toward what is intermediate, they firmly suppose they are arriving at fulfillment and pleasure? It's as if they were to compare gray to black without experience of white. In the same way, they compare pain to the absence of pain without experience of pleasure, and are deceived.

585a

I shouldn't be at all surprised, he replied, but much more surprised if it were otherwise.

Then consider this, I said: are not hunger and thirst and such things kinds of emptiness in the disposition of the body?

Certainly.

b

And are not ignorance and foolishness, again, emptiness in the disposition of the soul?

Of course.

Now, someone who comes to partake of food and someone who gets reason would both be filled?

Of course.

Does a truer fulfillment come from the less or the more real?

Clearly, from the more real.

Then which kind do you believe has a greater share of pure reality: things such as bread, meat, and drink and all the various kinds of nourishment, or the form of true belief and knowledge and thought and in a word all virtue? Decide on this basis: Does what is always alike and immortal and true and, since it is itself of that sort, comes to be in what is of that sort, seem to you more real? Or what is mortal and never alike, and itself of the sort of that in which it comes to be?

c

What is always alike is much superior, he said.

Then does the reality of what is always alike have a greater share of reality than of knowability?

Not at all.

What about truth?

Nor of that.

If less of truth, then less also of reality?

Necessarily.

d   In general, then, the kinds concerned with service to the body have less share of truth and reality than kinds concerned with service to the soul?

Far less.

Do you think it so of body by itself, compared to soul?

I do.

Now, what is filled with more real things and is itself more real is really more filled, compared to what is filled with less real things and is itself less real?

Of course.

e   So if being filled with things which are by nature befitting is pleasant, then what is really more filled and filled with things more real would more really and truly cause enjoyment of true pleasure; but what comes to have a share of less real things would be less truly and abidingly filled, and would come to have a share of a pleasure less trustworthy and less true.

Quite necessarily, he said.

586a   So those who have no experience of wisdom and virtue, who spend their time in constant banqueting and such, are carried downward, it seems, and back up again only so far as what is intermediate; and in this way they wander throughout life. They never step outside, never look up, nor are carried to what is truly above. They are never really filled with what is real, never taste a pleasure abiding and pure, but like cattle ever gazing downward, with heads bowed to earth, they graze at table and eat their fill and copulate, and because of overreaching to have more of these things, they butt and kick each other with horns and hooves of iron, killing through insatiable greed because they cannot fill what is neither real nor continent in themselves with what is not real.

b   Socrates, your description of the life of most men is that of an oracle, said Glaucon.

So also they necessarily dwell with pleasures mixed with pains, with false images of true pleasure—shadow paintings which gain their color by juxtaposition with one another, so that they each appear intense and engender frenzied love in foolish men. They are fought over as Stesichorus claims the false image of Helen was fought over by those at Troy, through ignorance of the truth.

It must be something like this, he said.   c

But then, doesn't something else of this sort necessarily also occur concerning the spirited element? Whoever tries to satisfy it by itself—ambition by envy, contentiousness by force, discontent by anger—pursues a surfeit of honor and victory and anger without reflection and thought.

That too is necessary, he said.   d

Very well then, I replied. We may confidently claim that all desires concerned with the love of gain and the love of victory, when they follow upon knowledge and reason, and pursue the pleasures which intelligence prescribes in company with those, admit and will receive the truest pleasures truly possible for them, because they follow on truth and what is properly and peculiarly their own—if indeed that which is best for each is also most properly and peculiarly its own.

But surely it is, he said.   e

So when the whole soul follows the wisdom-loving part, and each part without internal strife does what is its own in respect to the others and is just, then each part also enjoys its own pleasure, the best and truest possible to it.

Yes.   587a

And so, when some other part gains the upper hand, it does not find its own pleasure, and compels the others to pursue an alien and untrue pleasure.

Yes, he said.

Now, what stands farthest from philosophy and reason would most especially accomplish this?

Of course.

And isn't what stands farthest from reason also farthest from law and order?

Clearly so.

But didn't lustful and tyrannical desire appear to stand farthest away?

b   Of course.

And the royal and orderly desires least far?

Yes.

Then the tyrant, I suppose, will stand farthest from true pleasure and his own pleasure, the king closest.

Necessarily.

So the tyrant will live most unpleasantly, I said, the king most pleasantly?

Necessarily.

THE MEASURE OF TYRANNY (587B–588A)

Do you know then, I replied, by how much a tyrant lives less pleasantly than a king?

Tell me, he said.

c   There are three kinds of pleasure, it seems, one genuine, two spurious. The tyrant steps beyond the bounds even of the spurious: he flees law and reason and dwells with a slavish bodyguard of pleasures, and it is not very easy to say by how much he is inferior, except perhaps as follows:

How? he said.

The tyrant, no doubt, stood at a third remove from the oligarch; for the democrat was between them.

Yes.

Then he would also dwell with an image of pleasure at a third remove relative to truth from that other, if what was formerly said is true?

That's so.

Yes, but the oligarch, again, is at a third remove from the king, if we assume that aristocratic and kingly rule are the same.

d   Yes.

So a tyrant stands distant from true pleasure thrice three times in number, I replied.

Apparently.

It seems then, I said, that the image of tyrannical pleasure with respect to the number of its length would be a plane number.

Quite so.

But it is clear then by how great an interval they are separated, in respect to a power and a third increase.

Yes, he said, at least to a calculator.

Conversely, if one states the distance at which the king stands from the tyrant in truth and reality of pleasure, he will find, when the multiplication is completed, that he lives seven hundred and twenty-nine times more pleasantly, and the tyrant more painfully by this same interval.

e

What an astonishing calculation you've brought to bear on the difference between the two men, he said, just and unjust, relative to pleasure and pain.

588a

And yet it is both true, and applicable to their lives, I replied, if days and nights and months and years are applicable to them.

As surely they are, he said.

Then if the good and just man wins in pleasure over the evil and unjust man in such degree as this, how much more astonishingly will he win in gracefulness of life and in beauty and virtue?

An astonishing amount indeed, he said.

JUSTICE AS PROFITABLE (588B–592B)

Very well then, I said. Since we have arrived at this stage of argument, let us take up again what was said at first, through which we came here. It was said, surely, that doing injustice is profitable for one who is perfectly unjust, but seems just. Wasn't it so stated?

b

Yes, it was.

Now then, I said, since we have reached agreement about what power doing injustice and acting justly each have, let us discuss it.

How? he said.

By fashioning an image of the soul in speech, so that he who says this may know the kind of thing he was saying.

c   An image of what kind? he replied.

One of those ancient natures of the sort described in myth, I replied—the Chimaera, or Scylla, or Cerberus, and a pack of others said to consist of many forms grown together into one.

Yes, he said.

Imagine then one form of a manifold and many-headed beast, with a circle of bestial heads both tame and wild, and able to change and grow them all from within itself.

d   Work of a clever artist! he said. Still, since speech is even more easily shaped than wax and the like, let it be so imagined.

Then let one distinct form be a lion, and one a man. Let the first be much the largest, and the second, second in size.

That's easier, he said, and it has been done.

Fasten them together then as three into one, so that they are somehow grown together with each other.

They're together, he said.

Then shape them round from without in an image only to see the outward shell, it appears to be one animal, a man.

e   They are so shaped, he said.

Then we may say to him who says that to do injustice is profitable for a man and it is not of advantage to act justly, that he is claiming nothing other than that it pays to feed up the manifold beast and make it strong,

589a   and the lion and what belongs to the lion, but to starve the man and make him weak, so that he is dragged in whatever direction the other two may take. That it pays, not to accustom one to the other, not to make them friends, but to allow them to devour each other, biting and battling among themselves.

That's exactly what he who praises the doing of injustice would say, he replied.

b   Then again, he who says that just things are profitable would claim it necessary to do and say those things from which the man within will most completely master the man. He will care for the many-headed creature like a farmer, nurturing and nursing plants while preventing the growth of weeds. He will make an ally of the lion's nature, and care for all in common and make them friendly to each other and to himself. In this way will he nurture them.

Again, that's precisely what anyone who commends the just is saying.

In every way, then, he who praises just things would speak truly, he who praises unjust things falsely. For in examining pleasure, and good repute, and benefit, he who commends the just tells the truth; but there is nothing sound in him who disparages it, nor does he know in condemning it what it is he condemns.

c

No, I don't think he knows at all, he replied.

Then let us try to persuade him gently—for he does not err voluntarily— by asking, "My friend, may we not claim that beautiful and ugly laws and customs arise through this: beautiful things put the beastlike elements of our nature under the man, or perhaps rather under what is divine, but ugly things enslave the tame and put it under the wild?" Will he agree?

d

Yes, he said, if he is persuaded by me.

Then from this argument, what would it profit a man to steal gold, take it unjustly, if indeed as a result of taking the gold he at the same time enslaved the best of himself to the worst? If he were to enslave a son or daughter, and this among wild and evil men, it would not profit him to take the most enormous amount of gold for such a purpose. But if he enslaves without pity what is most divine of himself and puts it under what is most ungodly and polluted, is he not therefore made miserable? He takes a bribe of gold for a more terrible destruction than Eriphyle, who accepted a necklace for her husband's life.

e

Much more terrible destruction, Glaucon replied: I'll answer in his behalf.

590a

Do you then also suppose that being intemperate has long been condemned for this reason, that what is terrible in such a man, that great and multiform beast, is released beyond what is necessary?

Clearly, he said.

And are not self-will and bad temper to be condemned, when what is lionlike and serpentlike grows and stretches itself disproportionately?

b   Of course.

And are not effeminacy and softness condemned for relaxing and loosening this same part, when they implant cowardice in it?

Of course.

Is it not flattery and baseness when one puts this same element, the spirited element, under the moblike beast, and for the sake of money and the insatiability which attaches to it, accustoms it from youth up to endure insult and abuse, to become an ape instead of a lion?

c   Yes.

Why is it then, do you suppose, that coarse vulgarity bears reproach? Shall we say it is through anything else than when the form of what is best has some weakness in nature, so that it cannot rule the creatures within, but serves them and learns only how to flatter them?

It seems so, he said.

d   Then in order that such a man may be ruled by what also rules the best man, we claim he must be a slave of him who is best and contains within himself the divine ruler. We do not suppose the slave should be ruled to his own harm, as Thrasymachus supposed of those ruled, but that it is better for all to be ruled by divine intelligence. It is best that he have what is properly his own within himself, but if not, let it be set over him from without, in order that so far as possible we may all be alike and friends, guided by what is the same.

Yes, and rightly, he said.

e   Yes, I replied. It is clear that the law intends this, since it is an ally of everyone in the city; and that the rule of children intends it, by not allowing them to be free until we have established a constitution within them as within a city. Serving what is best in them with what is best in ourselves, we establish as counterpart a like guardian and ruler within the child, and only then release him as free.

591a   Yes, he replied.

How then, and by what argument, Glaucon, shall we claim that it pays to do injustice or to be intemperate or to do anything shameful, as a consequence of which one will be more vicious, but possessed of more money or any other kind of power?

In no way, he replied.

Then how can it pay to escape detection in doing injustice and not render penalty? Doesn't one who escapes detection become still more vicious? In him who does not escape detection and is punished, the beastlike part is quelled and tamed, the tame part set free, and the whole soul established in its best condition. Since it is possessed of temperance and justice in company with wisdom, it receives an even more valuable disposition than a body receiving strength and beauty in company with health, just in so far as soul is more valuable than body.

Certainly, he said.

Then the reasonable man will direct all that is his own to this throughout his life, valuing first and primarily the studies which make his soul of this sort, despising the rest.

Clearly, he said.

And next, as to the disposition and nurture of the body, I said. So far from betraying it to beastlike and irrational pleasure, he will turn from that and live. He will not even look to health, or consider it of importance that he be strong or healthy or handsome, if he does not also become temperate from them, but he will appear always to attune his body for the sake of the concord in his soul.

Exactly so, he said, if he is to be musical in very truth.

Now, there is also an order and concord in his possession of property, I said. He will not allow himself to be thrown off balance by the applause of the multitude, and increase the mass of his wealth without limit, and have evils without end.

I think not, he said.

But he will look to the constitution within himself, I said, and guard against any disturbance there, through too much wealth or too little. He will steer his course thus, so far as he can, in adding to and spending down his estate.

Quite so, he said.

592a   And again in respect to honors, he will look to the same thing. He will voluntarily partake of and taste those he may believe will make him better, but those which might loosen his established disposition he will flee both in public and private.

Then since he is concerned about that, he will refuse to take part in political affairs, he said.

Yes, by the Dog, I replied. At least, he will take part in his own city, very much so, though perhaps not in the land of his origin, unless some divine fortune occurs.

I understand, he said. You mean in the city established in reasoning which we are founding and have now described, though I think it does not exist anywhere on earth.

b   But perhaps it is laid up as a standard or pattern in heaven, I replied, for him who wishes to see and, seeing, to found a colony of it within himself. It makes no difference whether it exists somewhere, or ever will: he acts for this city alone, and for no other.

Yes, he said.

Book X

WHAT IS IMITATION? (595A–596A)

Why really, I said, I think we were perhaps quite right about many other things in founding the city,[1] and not least in our reflections about poetry.

In what respect? he said.

I am thinking of our refusal to admit it in so far as it is merely imitative.[2] I think it now appears clearer than ever that it is inadmissible, since the forms of the soul have each been distinguished as separate.

How do you mean?

To speak among ourselves—for you surely won't denounce me to the tragic poets and all those other imitators—everything of this sort seems to be a corruption of understanding for hearers who do not have, as an antidote, knowledge of what things happen to be in themselves.

595a
b

---

1. That is, about the city founded in discourse, an ideal which perhaps exists nowhere on earth: IX 592a.
2. Not "so much of it as is imitative," a mistranslation. This is not a rejection of all imitative art: in Book III (394b–398b, 401b–402c; cf. X 595c, 607a, 698a) poetry which imitates what is good is accepted as important for education. But imitative art is rejected in so far as it is *merely* imitative, in abstraction from what is imitated: art, if imitative, must be more than imitative if it is to be accepted. Art can also imitate the ideal: V 472d; cf. III 402c. See below, 597e.

What do you have in mind by saying that? he said.

It must be told, I replied. And yet, a certain love and reverence I have had for Homer since childhood prevents my speaking. For he seems first teacher and guide in all that is beautiful pertaining to tragedy. But a man is not to be honored before the truth; as I say, it must be told.

Of course, he said.

Listen then. Or rather, answer me.

Go on.

Can you tell me what imitation in general is? For I don't myself quite understand what it means to be.

I suppose then I'll understand it? he said.

It wouldn't be at all surprising, I replied—though of course those of sharper sight often see after the dull in vision.[3]

That's so, he said. But with you present, I couldn't speak with confidence even if something appeared clear to me. Please consider it yourself.

Would you have us then here begin our inquiry in the accustomed way? For we are accustomed, surely, to assume some one single form for each plurality to which we apply the same name. Do you follow?

I do.

Then let us also now assume whatever plurality you please. For example, if you will, there are surely many beds and tables.

Of course.

But surely only two ideas of these artifacts: one of bed, one of table.

Yes.

Again, we are also accustomed to say that the craftsman of each artifact looks to the idea, and thus one makes the beds and the other the tables which we use; and the same with other things? For surely no craftsman makes the idea itself. How could he?

3. Dullness of vision is associated with age, sharpness with youth; self-deprecation combined with a delicate compliment to Glaucon.

He couldn't at all.

But see then what you would call the following craftsman:

Of what sort?

c

Who makes everything made by each single one of the craftsmen.

You describe a clever and marvelous fellow!

Not yet, but you'll soon have more reason to say so. For this same crafts-man is able to make not only all artifacts but also everything that grows from the earth, and he produces all animals, both others and himself, and in addition, he produces earth and heaven and gods and everything in heaven and in the place of the dead beneath earth.

You describe a marvelous skill![4] he said.

d

Are you in doubt? I replied. Tell me then, does such a craftsman seem impossible to you? Or might there be a maker of all these things in one way but not in another? Don't you perceive that even you yourself could make all these things, at least in a sense?

And what way is that? he said.

It's not difficult, I replied. Why, you can do it in many places and quickly. The quickest is if you're willing to take a mirror and carry it around everywhere. You'll quickly make a sun and the things in heaven, and an earth, and yourself and the other animals and artifacts and plants, and everything else just now mentioned.

e

Yes, he said, in appearance, but surely not in truth.

Fine, I replied. You've come to the nub of the argument. I suppose the painter is also a craftsman of this sort, isn't he?

Of course.

But you'll say that he does not make what he makes really and truly, I suppose. And yet, in some way, the painter surely does make a bed, doesn't he?

Yes, he said. At least he makes an apparent bed.

What about the bed maker? Didn't you just now say that he does not make the form, which indeed we say is what it is to be a bed, but a kind of bed?

597a

4. *sophisten:* a man of exceptional skill, or sophist.

Yes, I did.

Then if he does not make what it is, he would make not what is real but only something of such sort as what is real but not real.[5] If someone should say the work of the bed maker or of any other artisan is completely real, it very likely would not be true?

No, he said. At least, it would not seem so to people schooled in such arguments as these.

Then let us not be surprised if it also happens to be somewhat dull and indistinct relative to truth.

b No.

Would you have us then, I said, inquire from these same considerations what this imitator is?

If you wish, he said.

Then there are these three kinds of bed. One exists in the nature of things, which we might I suppose say that god would make. Or does someone else make it?

No one else, I think.

Yes, and one which the carpenter makes?

Yes, he said.

And one which the painter makes. Not so?

Let it be so.

Then these three—painter, bed maker, god—preside over three forms of bed.

Yes, three.

c But the god, either because he didn't wish it or because some necessity was present not to produce more than one bed in nature, made only that one by itself, what a bed is. Two of this sort or more were not produced by the god, nor could they come into being.[6]

How so? he said.

Because, I replied, if he should make no more than two, another one

---

5. See above, 477a. In the *Sophist* (248e), images are not fully real but really are images.

6. There is a jocular tone here: the Greek can also mean "were not planted by god, nor do they grow and put forth shoots."

would again make its appearance, of which both those in turn would have the form, and that, but not the two, would be what a bed is.

Right, he said.

But I suppose the god knew this, and wishing to be a real maker of a bed   d
which really is, not some particular bed maker of some particular bed, he created it one in nature.

It seems so.

Would you have us then call him the natural craftsman of it, or something like that?

It would be just, at any rate, he said, since he has made this and all else in nature.

What about the carpenter? Isn't he craftsman of a bed?

Yes.

And is the painter also a craftsman and maker of this sort of thing?

Not at all.

What will you say he is of a bed?

I think he'd most fitly be called an imitator of that of which those others   e
are craftsmen, he replied.[7]

Very well, I replied. You call an imitator, then, one who is at three removes[8] from the nature?

Certainly, he said.

So also then the tragic poet, since he is an imitator, and all the other imitators, will naturally be at a third remove from the king[9] and the truth.

Very likely.

So we're agreed about the imitator. But tell me this about the painter: Do   598a

7. This suggests that the imitator may imitate not only the physical bed but the ideal bed. The text was important for the Neoplatonic and Renaissance interpretation that though the artist sometimes offers an imitation of an imitation three removes from reality, he may also offer an imitation of essence which is perhaps closer to reality than physical objects themselves. The artist then becomes equal to the philosopher or theologian, offering direct insight into the mind of God. Thus Ficino, for example, by way of the *Enneads*.

8. At three removes because Greek, unlike English, counts the first in the series: a grandchild is at three removes from his grandfather, an imitation of something which has a nature at three removes from the nature. See above IX 587c–d.

9. That is, god; cf. VI 509d, *Philebus* 22c.

you think he in each case tries to imitate what is by itself in the nature of things, or the works of the craftsmen?

The works of the craftsmen, he said.

As they are, or as they appear? Please distinguish this still further.

What do you mean? he said.

This: whether you look at a bed from the side or straight on, or any other way, does it at all differ from itself, or does it not differ at all, though it appears differently? And so for other things?

Thus, he said. It appears so, but doesn't differ at all.

b   Then consider just this point: To what is the art of painting directed in each case? To imitate what is, as it is, or to imitate what appears, as it appears? Is it imitation of appearance, or of truth?

Of appearance, he said.

So the art of imitation is surely far removed from the truth, it seems, and that is why it produces everything, because it only touches some small element of each thing, and that an image. For example, the painter, we say, will

c   paint us a cobbler or a carpenter or some other craftsmen, while understanding nothing whatever about those arts. Nevertheless, a good painter might draw a carpenter and show it at a distance, and deceive children and unwary adults into thinking it is truly a carpenter.

Of course.

But my friend, I think in all such cases one must bear in mind the fol-

d   lowing: when someone reports to us that he has met a man who has knowledge of all the arts and everything else, that he knows as much as each single craftsman knows, that there is nothing whatever he himself does not know more accurately than anyone else, one must understand that here is a simple-minded fellow, and it seems he's met a magician and been deceived by an imitator, so that he thought him all-wise because of his own inability to discriminate between knowledge, ignorance, and imitation.

Very true, he said.

e   Then we must next consider tragedy, I replied, and Homer as the leader of it. We hear from some people that tragic poets know all arts, all things human relative to virtue and vice, and divine things too; because the good poet necessarily, if he is going to deal well with the subjects with which he deals, must therefore have knowledge or he couldn't do it. So we must inquire whether they have met these imitators and been deceived by them, and whether they do not perceive, in viewing their works, that those works are at three removes from what is, and easy to make without knowing the truth—for they make appearances, not realities—or whether there is actually something in what they say, and our good poets really do have knowledge about those things concerning which the multitude think they speak well.

599a

It must certainly be investigated, he said.

Do you suppose that if someone could make both what is being imitated and its image, he would allow himself to take the production of images seriously and set this in the forefront of his own life, supposing it his noblest possession?

No, I don't.

Rather, I think, if he had knowledge in very truth about those things he also imitates, he would devote himself much more earnestly to real things than to their imitations, and undertake to leave behind a noble multitude of his own works as a memorial, more eager to be praised than to praise.

b

I think so, he said. The honor and the benefit are scarcely commensurate.

Then let's not demand an account of other matters from Homer or any other of the poets, asking whether any of them was a physician, as distinct from a mere imitator of medical talk, or what persons, ancient or modern, any poet is said to have made healthy, as Asclepius did, or what students of medicine he left behind, as Asclepius left his offspring. Nor will we ask them about the other arts, but dismiss it. Yet surely it is fair to inquire about the most important and noblest things of which Homer undertakes to tell concerning war and generalship and the governance of cities and the education of men, and to ask: "My dear Homer, if indeed you are not at three removes from truth about virtue, a craftsman of images whom we therefore defined as an imitator, if you are even second, and able to know what sorts of pursuits make men better or worse in private and public, tell us what city

c

d

e is better governed because of you. Sparta had Lycurgus. Many other cities, great and small, have had many others. What city holds you responsible for having been a good lawgiver and for benefiting them? Italy and Sicily claim Charondas, and we in Athens Solon. What city claims you?" Will he be able to mention any?

I think not, said Glaucon. Not even his own Homeridae[10] claim it.

600a But then, what war is remembered as having been well waged in Homer's time because of his leadership or advice?

None.

But are there then many ingenious inventions of the sort a wise man makes, in respect to arts or any other practical affairs, attributed to Homer as they are to Thales the Milesian and Anacharsis of Scythia?

Nothing at all of the sort.

But then, is it told that Homer himself while alive was privately, if not b publicly, a guide in the education of people who loved him for his company and handed down to posterity a Homeric way of life? Pythagoras was himself surpassingly loved for this, and his successors continue to call their way of life Pythagorean even to this day, and are thought to be in some sense exceptional among the rest of mankind.

Once again, nothing of the sort is told, he said. Homer's friend Creophylus, Socrates, would perhaps appear even more ridiculous than his name in the matter of culture and education[11] if the things told about Homer are true. For it is said that Creophylus was quite neglectful of him while Homer was still alive.

c Yes, I replied. But Glaucon, do you think that if Homer really could educate men and make them better because he did not imitate in these matters but was capable of knowing them, he would not have had many companions who valued and loved him? Protagoras of Abdera and Prodicus of Ceos, and a host of others, are able in private intercourse to convince their

---

10. A family or guild of poets whose members claimed to be descended from Homer and handed on from father to son the tradition of reciting his poems. Cf. *Ion* 530d, *Phaedrus* 252b. Adam suggests as a translation "votaries of Homer."

11. *Creophylus* = "of the flesh tribe."

contemporaries that they won't be able to manage their own house or city   d
unless these masters superintend their education, and they are so passion-
ately admired for their wisdom that their companions all but carry them
around on their shoulders. If Homer was able to benefit men in the matter
of virtue, would his contemporaries have allowed him or Hesiod to wander
around reciting poems? Wouldn't they instead have clutched them tighter
than their gold and compelled them to stay at home with them, or if they
failed to persuade them, themselves have attended them wherever they
went until they got a sufficient share of culture and education?

I think you're quite right, Socrates, he said.   e

Let us then assume that the poets, beginning with Homer, are all imitators of images of virtue and the other things they deal with, but do not
touch the truth. On the contrary, the painter, as we were just now saying,
will make what seems to be a cobbler to those who understand as little
about shoemaking as he does, but judge from colors and shapes.

Certainly.   601a

Thus then, I suppose, we'll say that the poet also applies certain colors,
rendering color with certain words and phrases which belong to each of the
arts, without understanding anything except how to imitate, so that he
seems to speak very well to others of the same sort, who judge only from his
words, whether he is talking about shoemaking or generalship or anything
else whatever. So great is the charm that meter, mode, and rhythm naturally   b
possess. Though when the works of the poets are stripped of their musical
colors and stated by themselves in plain prose, I think you know how they
appear. You've no doubt seen them.

Yes, he said.

They're like faces which are young but not handsome, I replied, after
they have lost the bloom of youth.

Quite so, he replied.

Come then, consider: we say that the maker of the image, the imitator,
understands nothing of what is, but only what appears. Not so?

Yes.   c

But that's only half the story.

Go on, he said.

A painter, we say, will draw reins and a bit?

Yes.

But a cobbler and smith will make them?

Of course.

Does the painter understand of what sort reins and a bit must be? Or does not even the maker, the smith and the cobbler, understand, but only the horseman who knows how to use them?

Quite true.

Shall we say it is so of everything?

What?

d   That in each case there are these three arts, of using, making, and imitating?

Yes.

Now, the virtue and excellence and rightness of each artifact and every living thing and action does not depend on anything except the use for which it is made or naturally adapted?

True.

So the user of each thing must be thoroughly experienced in it, and report to the maker what is well or badly made in the use to which it is put. The flutist, for example, pronounces to the flute maker about flutes serviceable for fluting, and will order the kind to make; and the other will serve him.

e   Of course.

Then he who knows pronounces about good and bad flutes, and the other obeys and will make them?

Yes.

So the maker will have right belief about excellence and defect of the same artifact, because he associates with him who knows, and is compelled to listen to him who knows. It is the user who has knowledge.

602a   Of course.

Will the imitator have knowledge derived from use about whether the things he draws are excellent and right? Or does he have right opinion because of necessary association with him who knows and from being ordered how to draw it?

Neither of the two.

So the imitator will neither know nor have right opinion about what he imitates relative to its excellence or vice.

It seems not.

Charming indeed is the imitator in his making, relative to wisdom about what he makes.

Not very.

Nevertheless he will imitate, without knowing of each thing in what way   b it is bad or good. Instead, it seems, he will imitate the sort of thing that appears good to the ignorant multitude.

What else?

It appears then we may properly agree that the imitator knows nothing worth mentioning about what he imitates. On the contrary, imitation is a kind of play, and not serious. And those who touch tragic poetry, dramatic and epic, are all most especially imitators.

Of course.

THE PSYCHOLOGY OF IMITATION (602C–607A)

This kind of imitation surely concerns what is at a third remove from the   c truth? I replied.[12]

Yes.

Relative then to what possession among those belonging to a man does it have the power it has?

What exactly do you mean?

This: the same magnitude surely does not appear equal to sight when near and far off.

---

12. Given the distinction between the worlds of knowledge and belief, imitative art is three times removed from knowledge of reality; given the tripartite division of the soul, and the distinction between necessary and unnecessary pleasures, imitative art is psychologically injurious, since it rouses emotion and weakens self-control.

No.

d   And the same things appear bent and straight when viewed in water and out of it, and again, both concave and convex through wandering of vision about colors. Indeed, scene painting is nothing short of witchcraft in exploiting this affection of our nature, and so is conjuring and many other devices of the sort.

True.

Now, measuring and counting and weighing have proved a welcome help in these matters, so that the apparent greater or less or more or heavier does not rule in us, but what has calculated and measured or weighed?

Of course.

e   But surely this would be a work of the rational part in the soul?

Yes.

But often when this has measured, and signifies that some things are larger or smaller than others, or equal, the opposite appears at the same time about the same things.

Yes.

Now, we were saying that it is impossible for the same thing to judge oppositely at the same time about the same things?

Yes, and we were right.

603a   So that of the soul which judges contrary to measure would not be the same as what judges according to measure.

No.

But surely, what relies on measurement and calculation would be what is best in the soul.

Yes.

So what is in opposition to it would be something inferior in us.

Necessarily.

This then is what I wished for us to agree upon when I said that painting, and imitative art generally, produces its own work at a far remove from the truth, and has intercourse with that in us which again is far removed from wisdom, a mistress and lover for a purpose neither healthy nor true.

b   Quite so, he replied.

So the imitative art is inferior, and having intercourse with an inferior begets inferiors.

It seems so.

Only with respect to vision? I replied. Or hearing too, which we in that case call poetry?

Very likely that too, he said.

Then let us not rely only on the comparison to painting, I replied. Let us also proceed to that element of the understanding with which imitative poetry has intercourse, and see if it is inferior or serious.

We must do so.   c

Then let us put it this way: Imitative poetry, we say, imitates people acting voluntarily or under constraint, and supposing themselves to have done and fared well or badly from the action, and in all this then feeling grief or joy. It is nothing else besides this, is it?

No.

Now, is a man of undivided mind in all this? Or even as he was self-   d
divided with respect to vision and held within himself opposite opinions at the same time about the same things, is he thus also self-divided in his actions and at war with himself? I recollect that there is no need for us to agree on this now, for we already sufficiently agreed to all this in previous discussions: that our soul teems with countless results of opposition of this sort, occurring at the same time.

And we agreed rightly, he said.

No doubt, I replied. But I think we must now explain what we then left   e
out.

What's that? he said.

Suppose a man of good character, I replied, meets with such misfortune as loss of a son, or something else he counts of utmost importance. We surely also then said that he will bear it much more easily than others.

Of course.

Let us now consider whether he will not be troubled at all, or whether since this is impossible, he will somehow be measured in his grief.

The truth is rather the latter, he said.

604a   Now tell me this about him: Do you think he will fight the pain and resist it better when observed by his peers, or alone and by himself in solitude?

It will surely make a big difference, he said, when he is observed.

When alone, I suppose, he will venture to utter many things he would be
ashamed to have anyone hear, and do many things he would refuse to have
anyone see him doing.

That's so, he said.

b   Now, what bids him resist is reason and law, but what draws him to give
way to grief is the affliction itself?

True.

When opposite leadings occur in a person about the same thing at the
same time, we say there necessarily are two things in him.

Of course.

One of them is ready to follow the law in what the law prescribes.

How so?

The law[13] surely says that it is best to keep as quiet as possible in these
misfortunes and not complain, supposing that what is really good and bad
in such matters is unclear, that taking it hard makes the future no better,
that nothing human is worthy of great concern, and that grieving is an im-
pediment to what we require for quickest aid in our misfortune.

c   To what do you refer? he asked.

What we require is reflection about what has happened, I replied, and as
though it were a fall of the dice, to put one's own affairs in order in whatever
way reason may decide is best. Instead of holding the place that's been hurt,
like children when they stumble, and spending time bawling, we must ever
accustom the soul to heal the hurt as quickly as possible, to raise up what is
fallen and unsound and to make lamentation disappear by healing art.

d   That's surely the most correct way to bear misfortunes, he said.

Then, we say, what is best will follow this reflection.

Clearly so.

13. It is helpful in what follows to recall that *nomos* means not only law but custom, and is cognate
with a verb which means to dispense, distribute, or allot—what is obligated or required.

Shall we not also say that what leads toward recollection of suffering and grief, and is insatiable for them, is irrational and idle and a friend to cowardice?

Yes.

Now, what complains admits of much and varied imitation. But the wise and quiet character, since it is ever very like itself, is neither easily imitated nor, when imitated, understood without trouble—especially by a festive mob of diverse people gathered in a theater. For it is imitation of an experience alien to them.

Certainly it is.

Then clearly, it is not toward this element in the soul that the imitative poet is naturally directed, nor is his wisdom fixed on pleasing it, if he intends to be thought well of among the multitude. It is directed toward the complaining and variable character because it is easily imitated.

Clearly.

At this point, we might justly catch hold of the imitative poet and put him as counterpart to the painter; for, in fact, he resembles him in that what he makes is inferior relative to truth, and he has intercourse with an inferior part of the soul, not the best. And thus at this point it would be wrong to admit him to a city which is to be well governed, because he rouses this in the soul and nourishes it and makes it strong, but destroys the rational part; it is as in a city, when someone betrays the city by making rascals powerful, but ruins the better sort. In the same way we'll also say that the imitative poet sets up an evil constitution in the soul of each individual and gratifies what is irrational in it; he distinguishes neither larger nor smaller, but believes the same things sometimes large, sometimes small, an image maker whose images are far removed from the truth.

Of course.

But we have yet to bring the most serious charge against imitation. For what is surely terrible is that it is sufficient to corrupt even decent men, apart from a very few.

Terrible indeed, at least if it really does it.

Hear and decide. For surely even the best of us, when we hear Homer or

e

605a

b

c

d   some other tragic poet imitating one of the heroes in mourning, drawing out a protracted speech of lamentation or chanting and beating his breast —you know that we enjoy it and give ourselves up to it. We follow it with eager sympathy, and praise as a good poet whoever most especially so affects us.

I do know. Of course.

But when one of us has a loss of our own, you realize, again, that we pride ourselves on just the opposite. If we are able to keep quiet and bear up, we think this is a man's part, while what we were praising before belongs to a woman.

e   Yes, he said.

Is this praise proper? I replied. To watch such a man as one would scorn to be oneself, yet not disgusted, but enjoying and praising it?

Surely not, he said. It doesn't seem reasonable.

606a   It does, I replied, if you consider it this way.

How?

If you reflect that what is contained by force in our own misfortunes, hungry for tears and the satisfaction of sufficient lamentation since it is by nature such as to desire them—that is what the poets satisfy and please. What is by nature best in us, because it has not been sufficiently educated by reason nor even by habit, relaxes its guard over this element, which is

b   suited for dirges because it contemplates the sufferings of others. There is no shame to itself in praising and pitying another, if he claims to be a good man but expresses excessive and unseasonable grief. On the contrary, it believes that the pleasure is steady gain, and refuses to be deprived of it by disdaining the whole poem. It occurs only to a few, I think, to reckon that to gain the benefit of what belongs to another is necessarily to gain it for one's own. Nurturing strong pity elsewhere, it is not easy to restrain it in one's own sufferings.

c   Very true, he said.

Doesn't the same account also apply to humor? You'd be ashamed to act the fool yourself. But if you delight in hearing it in comedic imitation or in private life and do not despise it as base, you're doing the same thing which you did in matters of pity. The wish to act the fool, which you restrain in yourself for fear of being regarded as a buffoon, you release at the theater and there make it brash and lively, unaware that you often get so carried away that you become a comedian in your own affairs.

Indeed, he said.

As for sex and anger, and all the desires and pains and pleasures in the soul which we say follow us in every action, poetic imitation produces effects on us of the same sort. It waters and nurtures them when they ought to be dried up, and establishes them as rulers in us when they ought to be ruled so that we may become better and more happy instead of worse and more miserable.

I cannot deny it, he replied.

Then Glaucon, I said, when you meet people who praise Homer and claim that this poet has educated Greece, and deserves to be taken up and studied both for the conduct of human affairs and for education and culture, and that the whole of one's own life should be ordered according to this poet, one should welcome them as friends in the belief that they're doing the best they can, and concede that Homer is most poetical and first among tragedians. Be assured that hymns to gods and encomia to good men are the only poetry to be admitted into the city. If you once admit the pleasurable muse in lyric or epic, pleasure and pain will be sovereign in your city, instead of law and reason, which is ever in common judged to be best.

Very true, he said.

THE QUARREL BETWEEN POETRY AND PHILOSOPHY (607B-608B)

Let this then be our defense, I said, for recollecting that we perhaps reasonably dismissed poetry from the city because of what she is. For the argument constrained us. And lest she accuse us of any harsh rudeness, let us further tell her that there is an ancient quarrel between philosophy and poetry. In fact, such lines as "a dog yelping at its master and barking," and "great in the empty talk of fools," and "the crowd mastering those who are c too wise," and "subtle thinkers even though they're poor,"[14] and countless other remarks, are signs of their ancient opposition. Nevertheless, let it be said that if imitative poetry directed toward pleasure can offer any reason to exist in a well-governed city, we would be delighted to welcome her back, for we are ourselves conscious of her charm. Still, it is impious to betray what seems true. Aren't you charmed by her too, my friend? Especially when you contemplate her through Homer?

d Yes, very much so.

Then it is right that she thus return, after making her defense in lyric or some other meter?

Of course.

Yes, and we'd surely also allow those of her champions who are not poets but lovers of poetry to plead in her behalf, without meter and in prose, that she is not only pleasant but beneficial to constitutions and to human life. And we shall listen kindly. For we shall surely profit, if she should prove not only pleasant but beneficial as well.

e Certainly, he said.

But otherwise, dear friend, we shall be like former lovers, who, hard as it may be, force themselves to stay away if they come to believe their love is not beneficial. So also we, because love of this sort of poetry has been bred into us by the nurture of noble constitutions, will be glad if she appears as

608a good and true as possible. But as long as she is unable to offer a defense, we shall hear her while chanting this account, which we put to ourselves like an incantation, taking care not to fall back into the childish love which belongs to the multitude. We are aware, then, that this sort of poetry is not to be taken seriously, as though it laid hold of truth in all seriousness. On the contrary, the hearer must be on guard against it, afraid for the constitution within himself, and acknowledge as true what we have said about poetry.

b I completely agree, he replied.

Yes, I said. For great is the contest in respect to becoming good or evil,

14. These are apparently quotations from works now lost attacking philosophy. See *Laws* XII 967c–d.

my dear Glaucon—great, and not small, as people think. So it is of no advantage to be led astray by honor or money or office, nor poetry either, to the neglect of justice and the rest of virtue.

I agree with you, he said, from what we have discussed, and I think everyone else would too.

THE IMMORTALITY OF THE SOUL (608C–611A)

And yet, I replied, we have not discussed the most important wages of c virtue, and the prizes ordained for it.

You mean an extraordinary importance indeed, he said, if there are others greater than those we have mentioned.

What would be great, I replied, at least in so brief a time? For surely, all this our time from childhood to old age would be brief compared to all time.

It is as nothing, he said.

Then do you think that an immortal thing should seriously be concerned for this much time, but not for all time?

Yes, he replied. But why do you say this?

Are you not aware, I replied, that our soul is immortal and never perishes? d

He looked at me in wonder and said, No, I most certainly am not. But can you say this?

Yes, if I am not mistaken, I said, and I think you can too. For it is nothing difficult.

It is to me, he said. I would gladly hear from you about this thing that is "not difficult."

Then listen, I replied.

Go on, he said.

You call something good, I said, and something evil?

I do.

Then do you conceive of them as I do? e

How?

All that is evil corrupts and destroys, but the good preserves and benefits.
I agree, he said.

Next then, do you say there is something evil and something good for each thing? For example, ophthalmia for eyes and disease for the whole body, mildew for grain, rot for timber, rust for bronze and iron, and, as I claim, a cognate evil and disease for pretty nearly everything?

I agree, he said.

Now, when some one of them comes to be present to something, it makes that to which it has come to be present worse, and in the end dissolves and destroys it as a whole?

Of course.

So the cognate evil of each thing, its vice, destroys each thing; or, if this will not destroy it, it would not otherwise be corrupted. For surely the good will never destroy anything, nor again, what is neither evil nor good.

How could it? he said.

So if we discover among things which are something which has an evil which makes it bad but which cannot dissolve and destroy it, will we not at that point know that there is no destruction for what is so constituted?

That is reasonable, he said.

Well then, I replied, does not soul have what makes it evil?

Yes indeed, he said. All the things we just now discussed: injustice and intemperance and cowardice and unwisdom.

Then does any among them dissolve and destroy it? Be careful that we are not misled by assuming that the unjust and irrational man, when caught doing injustice, is then destroyed by the injustice, which is vice of soul. Instead, conceive of it this way: even as vice of body, which is disease, wastes and destroys a body and leads it not even to be a body, so also everything we were just now mentioning will be brought to not being by its own special evil, which destroys it by being seated and present in it—not so?

Yes.

Come then, and consider soul in the same way. Does injustice and other such evil, as present in it, destroy it by being seated and present in it, and cause it to waste away, until it separates it from the body and leads to death?[15]

Not at all, he said.

Yet surely it would be absurd, I replied, for something to be destroyed by the vice of another, but not its own.

Yes.

For observe, Glaucon, I replied: we do not think it necessary to say that a body is destroyed by the badness of its foods, which belongs only to the foods themselves—staleness or rottenness or whatever. But if badness of foods introduces vice of body to the body, we will say that it is destroyed through them by its own evil, which is disease. But since the body is one thing and its foods another, we will never infer that it is destroyed by badness of its foods—that is, by an alien evil which does not introduce the evil native to it.

You are quite right, he said.

Then by the same account, I replied, if badness of body does not introduce badness of soul to soul, let us never infer that soul is destroyed by an alien evil without its own peculiar badness, one by the evil of another.

That makes sense, he said.

Then let us either refute this as mistaken, or while it is unrefuted, let us never claim that soul is destroyed by fever or other disease, or even by butchery—not even if the whole body is chopped up into little bits—unless one proves that soul herself becomes more unjust and unholy through these affections of the body. When an alien evil comes to be present in another, and its own peculiar evil is not present, let us not allow anyone to claim that soul or anything else is destroyed.

But surely, he said, no one will ever show that the souls of the dying become more unjust through their death.

Yes, I said, but if someone ventures to attack the argument, and claims

e

610a

b

c

15. Adam remarks, "Soul is always soul, and no soul is more a soul than any other (*Phaedo* 93b); hence the soul which is made evil by vice retains its vitality unimpaired. . . . It is on the essential connection between 'soul' and 'life' that Plato builds his crowning argument for the immortality of the soul in the *Phaedo* (100b ff., especially 105c–d)."

that someone who is dying becomes less virtuous and more unjust, in order not to be compelled to agree that souls are immortal, we will surely infer, if he is telling the truth, that injustice is as deadly as disease to its possessor, and that those who catch it die of it, since it kills by its own nature: those especially unjust die quicker, those less unjust at a slower pace, not as the unjust die now, through being punished by the agency of others.

Why really, he replied, injustice will not perhaps appear wholly terrible, if it proves deadly to him who catches it, for it would then be a release from evils. But I think it will appear utterly opposite, killing others if it can, but making one who has it quite lively—and watchful and wakeful in addition to being lively. So remote does it dwell, it seems, from deadliness.

Excellently put, I replied. For when its own peculiar vice and its own peculiar evil are not sufficient to kill and destroy soul, what is ordered as an evil to something else will scarcely destroy soul or anything, except that to which it is ordered.

Yes, that's likely, he said.

Then if it is never destroyed by any one evil, neither its own peculiar evil nor another's, it is clear that it necessarily always is. But if it always is, it is immortal.

Necessarily, he said.

Then let it be so, I replied. But if it is so, you realize that the same souls would always exist. For they surely could not become fewer, since none is destroyed, nor again more numerous: for if anything whatever among things immortal became more numerous, you know that it would become so from the mortal, and all would be immortal in the end.[16]

True.

16. In the *Phaedo* (70c–72d) Socrates argues that opposites come to be from opposites, and that the living have come to be from the dead as the dead have come to be from the living. If this were not so, all things would cease to come to be, and sleeping Endymion would be a mere trifler, since everything would be affected as he is, and be asleep. And if everything were mixed together and not separated, the saying of Anaxagoras (DK Fr. 1) would be true, "All things the same," the chaos in which things are identified before the intervention of mind. If every living thing dies, and doesn't come back to life again, everything would end up dead. The present argument posits an analogous converse.

THE MYTH OF GLAUCUS (611A-612A)

But let us not suppose this, I replied—for the argument will not allow it—   b
nor suppose again that soul in its truest nature is of such sort that in itself it
teems with manifold diversity and unlikeness and disagreement relative to
itself.[17]

How do you mean? he said.

It is not easy, I replied, for a compound derived from many things and
not put together in the best way, as the soul now appeared to us,[18] to be
everlasting.

No, probably not.

That soul is immortal, both the present argument and other arguments   c
would require. But as to what it is in very truth, one must contemplate it,
not mutilated by its intercourse with the body and other evils, as we view it
now, but as it is when it is become pure, such that it must be sufficiently discerned only by reason and reflection. One will then find it more beautiful
by far, and distinguish more clearly justices and injustices and everything
which we now discussed. We have now stated the truth about it as it appears   d
at present. However, we have contemplated its condition even as those
who, in seeing the sea-god Glaucus, could not still easily discern his ancient
nature, because some of the original parts of his body had been broken off
or crushed and mutilated by the waves, and because other accretions of
shells and seaweed and rocks made him more closely resemble a wild beast
than the god he is by nature. So do we also contemplate the soul, marred by
countless evils. But Glaucon, it is necessary to look beyond.

Where? he replied.

To her love of wisdom. And to realize what it is she touches and what   e
sort of intercourse she longs for, since she is akin to the divine and immor-

---

17. The *Phaedo* (78b–81a) suggests that the soul in its essential nature is akin to what is simple and
incomposite. The *Republic* has much to teach about justice, but does not define it. The same is
true of the soul. Perhaps in its inner nature it is simple, not manifold or multiform, but we
here view it under the circumstances of mortal life. Hence the Myth of Glaucus.

18. See IV 435aff., VI 504a–d. There is presumably a bodily foundation for appetite and spirit. Cf.
Phaedo 66c–67b, 79c–e.

tal and to what always is, and what she would become if she completely pursued what is like that, and by this impulse was lifted from the sea in which she now is, and stripped of the stones and shells which now attach to her because she feasts on earth, overgrown with earthy, stony things, many and savage, due to feasts said to be happy. Then one might see her true nature, whatever it may be, whether manifold in form or single in form. But as it is, we have, I think, sufficiently described her affections and forms in human life.

Most certainly, he said.

THE WAGES OF JUSTICE AND INJUSTICE IN THIS LIFE (612B–613E)

Now, I replied, we have cleared away the other difficulties in the argument, and we did not introduce the wages or reputation of justice, as you said Homer and Hesiod do. But we found that justice by itself is best for the soul by itself, and just things must be done by her, whether or not she has the ring of Gyges and the cap of invisiblity[19] to boot.

Very true, he said.

Then at this point, Glaucon, I replied, there can be no objection if we now restore to justice and the rest of virtue the rewards and wages,[20] such and so many, that it provides to the soul from men and gods, both while still man alive and after death?

Most certainly, he replied.

Then will you return to me what you borrowed in the argument?

What, especially?

I gave you that the just man should seem to be unjust and the unjust just. For you believed that even if it could not possibly escape the notice of gods and men, this nevertheless had to be granted for the sake of the argument, so that justice itself might be judged against injustice itself. Don't you recall?

19. Literally, "the Cap of Hades," which Athena dons so that Ares cannot see her. *Iliad* V 845.

20. See 614a. The argument of the *Republic* is now brought to a conclusion with an affirmation of divine providence. It is Socrates' claim in the *Apology*, that there is no evil for a good man in living or dying, and the gods do not neglect his affairs.

Why, it would be unjust in me if I didn't, he said.   d

Then since they have been judged, I replied, I demand back again in behalf of justice the reputation she in fact enjoys among gods and men, and
that we agree also of her that she should seem so, so that she may also carry
off the prizes which derive from seeming and give them to those who possess her, since she has already proved to give the goods derived from being,
and does not deceive those who really accept her.

A just request, he said.   e

Then first, I replied, you will grant this, that what each of them is does
not escape the gods?

Yes, he said.

But if it does not escape them, then the one man would be dear to the
gods, the other hated by the gods, even as we agreed to begin with.

That's so.

Shall we not agree that for someone who is dear to god, all that comes   613a
from the gods is as good as possible, unless it were some necessary evil due
him from former sin?

Of course.

So it must thus be understood of the just man, whether he is in poverty
or disease or some other apparent evil, that these things will end in something good for him, in life or at any rate after death. For he surely will never
be neglected by gods, if he is sincere in his willingness to become just, and
by practicing virtue to become like god so far as it is possible for man.[21]

It is probable, he said, that such a man is not neglected by what is like   b
him.

Now, one must think the opposite of this true of the unjust?

Yes, very much so.

Such then would be the prizes of victory for the just man from gods.

In my opinion, at any rate, he said.

What about prizes from men? I replied. If one must assume what is, isn't

21. Becoming like god is the ethical end for man: II 383c, VI 500c–d, 501b–c; cf. *Theaetetus* 176b–
177a, *Laws* 716b–d, and the doctrine that philosophy is the practice of death in the *Phaedo*.

it this way? Clever and unjust men are like runners who run well at the start

c of a race but flag at the finish; quick off the mark, at the end they become laughingstocks, trotting off uncrowned with their ears on their shoulders; but those who are runners in very truth reach the end, take the prizes, and win the crown. Isn't this also true of just men, for the most part? That toward the end of every action and association, and their life, they are held in honor and carry away prizes from men?

Indeed.

d Will you bear with me then if I say of them what you said of the unjust? For I say that the just, when become older, rule in their own city if they wish offices, marry where they please, give in marriage to whom they will; and everything you said of the one I now say of the other. Again, I say of the unjust that most of them, even if they escape detection while young, are laugh-

e ingstocks when they are caught at the end of the race, and when they are old, they are insulted in their misery by strangers and citizens alike. They are beaten and suffer what you truly described as savage—they are afterward racked and branded. Assume you have heard also from me all those things they suffer. See if you will bear with what I say.

Yes indeed, he said. For what you say is just.

THE MYTH OF ER (613E–621D)

Such then, I replied, are the rewards and wages and gifts from gods and men

614a to the just man while he lives, in addition to those goods which justice herself provided.

Yes, he said, and they are abidingly beautiful.

Well, they are as nothing, I replied, either in multitude or magnitude, compared with what awaits each of the two men after death. It is necessary to hear it, so that each may receive what is due at the hands of the argument.

b Please speak, he said, for there are few things I would more gladly hear.

I will not tell you a tale like the tale Odysseus told Alcinous,[22] I said, but

---

22. The lengthy narration by Odysseus to Alcinous in the *Odyssey* (Books IX–XII) became the archetype of the long story. It includes Odysseus's account of his visit to the place of the dead.

still, it is about a valiant man, Er, son of Armenius of the Pamphylian race. He was killed in battle, and when the corpses were taken up on the tenth day already in a state of decay, his was taken up sound. He was brought home, and preparations were made on the twelfth day for his funeral, but when laid on the pyre, he came back to life, and then told what he saw there.

Er said that when his soul went forth from his body, it journeyed along with many others until they arrived at a marvelous place, where there were two openings in the earth next to one another, and opposite again two others above them in the heaven. Judges were seated between them,[23] and after they rendered judgment, they ordered the just to journey up through the heaven to the right, and fastened tokens on their front signifying the judgment rendered. The unjust they ordered downward and to the left, with tokens on their back signifying all that they had done.

When Er himself approached, they told him he must become a messenger to men of things Yonder, and he said he was ordered to hear and observe all things in that place.

He said he saw souls depart by each of two openings of heaven and earth after judgment, while from the other openings, some souls came up travel-stained and dusty from out of the earth, while from the other opening others came down from heaven clean and pure. Those who kept arriving appeared to come as from a long journey, and departed rejoicing into the meadow and camped as if at a festival; those acquainted with each other greeted each other: those who came up from the earth inquired of the others about things yonder, and those from heaven about things beneath earth. They described their worlds to each other, one group weeping and wailing as they remembered how much they had suffered and seen in their journey beneath earth—it was a journey of a thousand years—while those from heaven described delights, and visions unsurpassed in beauty.

It would be a long time in the telling, Glaucon, but the sum of it is this: for every injustice they had ever done to anyone, for every person they had

c

d

e

615a

23. At *Gorgias* 523e, Minos, Rhadamanthus, and Aeacus.

wronged, they paid penalty for each in turn tenfold—that is, once every
hundred years, because this is the span of human life—in order that the
punishment imposed might be ten times the crime. For example, if they
caused many deaths or betrayed cities or armies and reduced them to slavery, or were accessories to any other wickedness, they would reap from all
this ten times the suffering for each crime; and again, if they had worked
any benefit and become just and holy, they reaped their due in the same
measure.

Er told other things not worth remembering, about those who had
lived only a little time after birth.[24] But he described still greater wages for
piety and impiety in respect to gods and parents, and murder by one's own
hand.

He said he was present when one was asked by another where Ardiaeus
the Great might be. This Ardiaeus had been tyrant in a certain city in Pam-
phylia just a thousand years before that time, and had killed his old father
and an elder brother and done many other unholy deeds, as is told. Well, he
said the person questioned replied, "He has not come, nor will he come
hither. For we saw him among the terrible sights near the mouth, when we
were about to come forth and all else had been suffered. Then, suddenly, we
saw him and others—nearly all of them were tyrants, but there were also
some private persons who had greatly sinned—who thought they might at
that point ascend. But the mouth refused them. It roared whenever someone incurable in respect to vice or insufficiently punished tried to ascend,
and at that point," he said, "savage men, hot and fiery to look at, stood
nearby and recognized the roar, and took some of them and led them away;
but Ardiaeus and others they bound hand, foot, and head, and threw them
down and flayed them, and then dragged them along the way outside, card-
ing their flesh like wool with thorns. They told those who were passing by
the reason for it, and that they would be led away and cast into Tartarus. Of
the many and varied fears which befell them there, this," he said, "was the
greatest: that the roar might come when one of them tried to ascend. When

b

c

d

e

616a

24. Cornford remarks that this suggests a limbo for infants.

it did not, most gladly did they each ascend." Judgments and punishments were of this sort, Er said, and again, the benefits corresponding to them.

After each company was there in the Meadow seven days, they had to arise on the eighth day and begin a journey. In four days they arrived at a place where they saw, from above, a straight light stretched like a pillar through the whole heaven and earth, very like the rainbow but brighter and purer. They reached it after going forward a day's journey, and there, at the middle of the light, they saw the extremities of its bonds stretching from the heaven; for this light binds the heaven together, holding the whole revolving firmament like the undergirths of a warship. From its extremities is stretched the spindle of necessity, by means of which all the circles revolve. The shaft and hook are of adamant, but the whorl is a mixture of this and other substances. The nature of the whorl is as follows:

In shape it is like an ordinary whorl, but one must conceive, from what Er said, that it is as if, within one large whorl, scooped and hollowed out, there lay closely fitted another smaller whorl of the same kind, as boxes fit into each other; and so too a third, a fourth, and four others. For there are eight whorls in all, lying within each other, showing from above their rims as circles, and forming the continuous surface of a single whorl around the shaft, which is driven through the center of the eighth.[25]

The first and outside whorl [of the Fixed Stars] has the broadest circular rim; that of the sixth [Aphrodite, Venus][26] is second in breadth; third is that of the fourth [Ares, Mars]; that of the eighth [Moon] is fourth; that of the seventh [Sun] is fifth; that of the fifth [Hermes, Mercury] is sixth; that of the third [Zeus, Jupiter] is seventh; that of the second [Kronos, Saturn] is eighth.

The rim of the largest whorl [the Fixed Stars] is spangled; that of the seventh [the Sun] is brightest; that of the eighth [the Moon] has its color from the seventh, which shines on it; that of the second and fifth [Saturn, Mercury] are like each other in being yellower than the others; the third

b

c

d

e

617a

25. As a model of the universe, this must be understood as abstract and incomplete, for it fails to distinguish ecliptic from celestial equator.
26. The names of the planets are not here given; they occur first at *Epinomis* 987b–c.

[Jupiter] has a very white color, the fourth [Mars] is rather red, and the sixth [Venus] is second in whiteness.

The spindle rotates as a whole with the same motion, but within the whole, as it revolves, the seven circles revolve slowly in a sense contrary to the whole; of these, the eighth goes most swiftly; second in speed and to-
b   gether, the seventh, sixth, and fifth; third in speed as it revolves, it appeared to them, is the fourth; fourth in speed is the third, and the second fifth. The Spindle turns on the Knees of Necessity.

Up above, on each circle, stands a Siren carried with it in its revolution, uttering one tone, one note; and from all eight notes is formed the concord of a single scale or mode.

c   Three others were seated round about at equal intervals, each on a throne: the Fates, Daughters of Necessity, all clothed in white with garlands on their heads, Lachesis and Clotho and Atropos, chanting to the scale or mode of the Sirens, Lachesis of what has been, Clotho of what is, Atropos of what is to come. And Clotho touches with her right hand the outer rim of the spindle and helps turn it, pausing from time to time; Atropos in like manner in turn touches the inner circles with her left hand; Lachesis touches each with each hand alternately.

d   Well, those souls who arrived had to go straight before Lachesis. An In-terpreter first marshaled them in ranks, then took from the lap of Lachesis both lots and patterns of lives. He mounted a high platform, and spoke:

"The Word of Lachesis, maiden daughter of Necessity. Souls! Creatures of a day! So begins another period of membership in the race of mortals, whose birth brings death. No fate shall fall to you by lot: you shall chose a
e   fate.[27] Let him to whom the lot first falls first choose a life which shall of ne-cessity be his. Virtue is without master: each shall have more and less of her according as he honors or dishonors her. The responsibility is his who chooses. God is not responsible."

So saying, the Interpreter flung the lots among them all, and each picked up the lot which fell beside him, except for Er, who was not allowed, but he

27. Plato's first readers would have recalled the saying of Heraclitus, that character is fate.

who picked a lot saw clearly what number he had drawn. After this again, the Interpreter laid the patterns of lives on the ground in front of them, more numerous by far than those who were present, and very various, for there were lives of all kinds of animals, and especially all kinds of human lives. There were tyrannies among them, some permanent, others destroyed in midcourse and ending at last in poverty and exile and beggary. There were also lives of men distinguished for beauty in respect to their form, others for bodily strength and athletic prowess, or for birth and the virtues of their parents; and there were lives undistinguished in these same respects, and so similarly for women. But no order of soul was present in them, because to choose a different kind of life is necessarily to become different in character. As for other things, they were mixed with one another; with wealth and poverty, disease and health, and things intermediate between these.

Here then, as it seems, dear Glaucon, is the supreme risk for a man, and for this reason it is specifically necessary to take care that each of us seek and study this to the neglect of other studies—that he somehow learn and discover who can enable him to tell the difference between good life and bad, and always and everywhere choose the better from among those possible. Reflecting on all that has now been said, separately and in combination, about how things stand relative to excellence of life, he should know what beauty when mixed with poverty or wealth, and accompanied by what dispositions of soul, effects for good or ill. And good birth and the lack of it, private citizenship and public office, physical strength and weakness, intelligence and slowness of wit, and all such things acquired and belonging to soul by nature, what they effect when mixed together, so that, from reflecting on all this, he can look to the nature of the soul and choose the worse and better life. He will call worse that life which leads it to become more unjust, better whatever leads it to become more just, and dismiss all else. For we have seen that this is the sovereign choice in living and dying. One must therefore, in going to the place of the dead, hold this opinion as in bonds of adamant, so that one may not there be dazzled by wealth and such evils as that, nor be thrown into tyranny and other such actions as that,

618a

b

c

d

e

619a

working many incurable evils and suffering still worse himself. Rather, he will be able to choose a life which is ever a mean between such things, to shun excess in either direction, both in this life, so far as possible, and in all of the life to come. For in this way does man become most happy.

b   Then Er, the messenger from beyond, further reported that the Interpreter spoke thus: "Even for him who comes last, if he chooses with intelligence and lives strenuously, a welcome life, not a bad one, is left. He who begins should not be careless in choosing, nor he who goes last discouraged."

When the Interpreter had spoken, Er said that the first to choose at once came forward and chose the greatest tyranny; due to folly and greed, he

c   chose without sufficiently examining it all, and it escaped his notice that he was destined to eat his own children, along with other evils; when he examined it at leisure, he beat his breast and bewailed his choice. But he disregarded the admonitions of the Interpreter: for he did not blame himself for these evils, but blamed fortune and fate and everything except himself. He had come down from heaven, having lived his previous life under a settled constitution, and had gotten a share of virtue by habit without philosophy.

d   Indeed, it could be said that quite a few of those coming from heaven were caught this way, because they were unexercised by troubles. But the majority of those coming from the earth, because they had themselves suffered and seen others suffer, did not make their choices precipitously. So among the majority of the souls there was an exchange of evils and goods as well as

e   through the fortune of the lot. Though if anyone, when he returns to life here, soundly loves wisdom, and the lot which falls to his choice is not among the last, it is likely, to judge from what Er has reported, that not only will he be happy here, but also that the journey from here to Yonder and back will not be under the earth and rough, but easy and through Heaven.

For indeed, Er said, it was a sight to see how the souls each chose their

620a   lives; it was pitiful to see, and ridiculous, and surprising. They for the most part chose according to the character of their preceding life. Er said he saw the soul which had once been Orpheus choose the life of a swan; he hated womankind because of his death at their hands, and refused to be conceived and born of woman. He saw the soul of Thamyris choose a nightingale, but he also saw a swan choose to change to human life, and other musical animals in like manner. A soul drew the twentieth lot and chose the life of a lion; it was the soul of Ajax son of Telamon, who shunned becoming a man because he remembered the decision over the armor of Achilles. The next soul was Agamemnon, who hated the human race because of his sufferings and changed to the life of an eagle. The soul of Atalanta drew a middle lot; seeing the great honors of an athletic man, she could not pass them by but took them. After her, he saw the soul of Epeius son of Panopeus assume the nature of a craftswoman, and way at the end, he saw the soul of the buffoon Thersites clothing itself as an ape. By chance, the soul of Odysseus drew the very last lot of all and came to make its choice; relieved of ambition by memory of previous troubles, he went around for a long time looking for the quiet life of an ordinary citizen, and with difficulty found it lying somewhere neglected by others; when he saw it he took it gladly, and said he would have done the same even if he had had the first lot. In like manner some of the other beasts went into men and into each other, the unjust changing into the wild animals, the just into tame animals, mixed in every kind of mixture.

When then every soul had chosen its life as allotted, they all went in order before Lachesis. She sent with each his chosen fate as guardian of his life and fulfillment of what had been chosen. This fate led the soul first before Clotho, under her hand and beneath the turning of her whirling spindle, ratifying the destiny chosen by lot. After touching her, the fate next led the soul to the web of Atropos, who made the thread of destiny irreversible. From there, without turning back, the souls went beneath the Throne of Necessity, and after the others passed beyond it, they all journeyed into the Plain of Lethe, Forgetfulness, through terrible stifling heat. In fact, it was barren of trees and everything that grows in the earth. When evening came, they camped beside the River of Oblivion, whose water no vessel can hold. It was required of all to drink a certain measure of the water, and those not preserved by wisdom drank more than due measure. One who drinks always forgets everything. After they had fallen asleep, there was a thunderclap, and an earthquake in the middle of the night, and they were suddenly carried up from there like shooting stars in different directions to their births. Er himself was forbidden to drink the water. How and in what way he returned into his body he did not know, but he suddenly looked up to see himself at dawn, lying on the pyre.

c   And thus, Glaucon, the story was preserved and not lost, and it would preserve us, should we be persuaded by it, and we shall safely cross Lethe, the River of Oblivion, and not be stained in soul. But if we are persuaded, and acknowledge that soul is immortal and capable of bearing all good things and all evils, we shall always hold to the upward path, and in every way pursue justice in company with wisdom, so that we may also be friends

d   to ourselves and to the gods, both while we abide here and afterward, when we receive the rewards of justice, like victors at the Games who collect their prize.

And both here and in the journey of a thousand years which we have described,

Let us do and fare well.

Index

Achaeans, 75, 76, 79, 80–81

Achilles, 73, 76, 77, 230n2, 357

Adeimantus, 148, 263; on division of labor, 51, 52; introduction to, 1; support for Glaucon (on justice), 43–49; on uselessness of philosophers, 194–195

Aeschylus, 42, 65, 69, 270, 287

Agamemnon, 69, 76, 79, 80, 237, 357

age, authority and, 168

Aglaion, 139

Ajax, 173, 357

Alcibiades, 203n7

Alcinous, 350

Anacharsis of Scythia, 332

anarchy, 280, 284, 286, 301

animals, domestic, 287

animals, wild, 140

Aphrodite [Venus] (goddess), 76, 196n2, 353, 354

Apollo (god), 69, 77, 81, 88, 222; As-

clepius as son of, 99; Delphic oracle and, 120n4, 174n9

appetite, reason and, 138

Arcadia, 290

Archilocus, 46

architecture, 90

Ardiaeus the Great, 352

Ares [Mars] (god), 76, 353, 354

Arion, 154n4

aristocracy, x, 15, 147, 264

Ariston, 49, 121

Aristonymus, 2

Aristotle, xviii, xx, xxi, xxvi

arithmetic, 240–242

Asclepius, 96–99, 331

assent, inward, 134–135

astronomy, 244, 246–248

Atalanta, 357

Athena (goddess), 65

Athens, x, xvii, xix, 332

athletes, 94, 101, 114, 236

Atreus, 79

Atropos, 354
Autolycus, 9

bad men, 11, 12, 83, 100
barbarians, 174, 175, 203, 209, 263
beauty, 152, 158, 182, 210; desire and,
    xxvii; opinion and, 187, 188
beggars, 273
Bentham, Jeremy, xxiv, xxv–xxvi
bewitchment, 105–106
Bias, 12
Blackstone, William, xxiii
body, soul and, 93, 165, 208, 316; im-
    mortality of soul and, 345; physi-
    cians' art and, 99; value of soul over
    body, 323. *See also* soul
boulesis (rational wish), xv
Bradley, F. H., xix

Cadmus, 106n18
Categorical Imperative, xxi
Cave metaphor, xxvii, 227–230, 230–
    232, 234n5, 250, 259
Cephalus, x, xix, xxi, xxiv, 2–6
Chambry, Emile, xvi
character, good or beautiful, 90, 92,
    100, 198, 337
Charmantides of Paeania, 2
Charondas, 332
Cheiron, 77
children, xii, 117, 129; begetting and
    bearing of, 116, 162–164, 213; com-
    munity of, 149–150, 159, 262; con-
    stitution within, 322; illegitimate,
    254; program of studies and, 260–
    261; raising of, 153; temperance
    and, 126; war and, 170–171, 256
Chryses, 79, 80–81
cities, 15, 339; class division within,
    113–116, 272; constitutions of, 262–
    264, 322; founding of, 50–51, 63,

207; government of, 234–235;
    guardianship of, 58, 104, 106, 122;
    happiness of, 111–113; justice and,
    50, 60; luxurious, 55–56; rulers of,
    21, 28. *See also* state, the
citizens, 141, 166, 350; constitutions
    and, 264; democracy and, 286;
    temperance and, 142; virtue and,
    277–278
Civilisation and Its Discontents
    (Freud), xxvi
classes, political and social, xii, xiv,
    115, 169, 234; in cities, 113–116, 272;
    oligarchy and, 272
Cleitophon, 2, 17
Clotho, 354, 357
comedy, 81, 82, 340–341
constitutions, x, 148–149, 179; com-
    munity of women and children
    and, 164; democratic, 279–280;
    guardian class and, xii, 103–106,
    108–110; kinds of, 262–264; music
    and, 116–118; myth of metals, 106–
    108; oligarchic, 271–273; patterns
    of, 147; philosopher-kings and,
    207, 209, 211; program of studies
    and, 260, 261; of United States, xiii
Corinth and Corinthians, 95, 154n4
corruption, 197–200, 204
courage, 91, 119, 194, 203, 254; corrup-
    tion and, 199; education and, 70–
    74; political, 123–125, 129; spirit
    and, 101
craftsmen, 25, 42, 53, 129, 169; chil-
    dren of, 170–171; division of labor
    and, 57; guardians as, 113; imitation
    and, 83, 326–330; medicine and,
    97; supervision of, 90; wealth and
    poverty and, 113–114
Creophylus, 332
Crete and Cretans, 152, 263, 302

and, 243; guardians and, 56–57;
gymnastic training and, 94; mathe-
matics and, 237; oligarchy and,
272; usages of, 170–176; wealth
and, 114, 115; women and, 152, 177
wealth, 4, 56, 146, 204, 355; artists
and, 113–114; oligarchy and, 271;
war and, 114, 115
wisdom, 30–31, 144, 323; gender and,
156; guardians and, 60; imitation
and, 336; injustice and, 28; justice
and, 358; opinions of multitude
and, 201–202; political, 122–123,
129; sophistry and, 201–202, 205;
truth and, 192, 310

women, xii, 73, 83, 87, 129, 356–357;
community of, 149–150, 159–170,
262; equality of men and women,
151–158, 260, 287; temperance and,
126; war and, 152, 177

youth (young men), 3, 207–208; democracy and, 283; oligarchy and,
277, 278; timocracy and, 269–
270

Zeus [Jupiter] (god), 64–65, 69, 78;
lusts of, 76; Olympian, 312; shrine
of Lycaean Zeus, 290; Spindle of
Necessity and, 353, 354